HARD NIGHTS

My Life In Liverpool Clubland

by

Roy Adams

Acknowledgments

Special thanks to Rikki Allen for her substantial time and effort in transferring the bulk of my not so legible longhand to computer.

To Mr. Universe contestant Cyril Aspinall for his time and patience continuing the task.

To Phil Thomson, Author of 'The Best Of Cellars' for the extract from his book.

To the 'Liverpool Daily Post and Echo'; 'Rolling Stone' music paper; 'The Sun' Newspaper; 'Daily Mirror' Newspaper; 'Nite Out' Newspaper; and 'Combat' Magazine for their extracts, and to 'Fighting Arts International' for their contribution.

Thanks also to the many friends and characters featured - for their time and co-operation.

Dedication

I dedicate this book to my parents
Jack and Molly
who gave us a good upbringing in difficult times;
and also to my dear sister
Freda
who shared so many of the experiences I've written about.

ISBN – 0-9547197-0-0

Published by Cavernman Publications

To obtain further copies of HARD NIGHTS by Roy Adams
Visit our website http://www.cavernman.com
Telephone: 01704 577111
or write to:
Cavernman Publications
1-2 The Promenade,
Ainsdale
Southport
PR8 2QB

Printed in the UK by T. Snape & Co. Ltd., Preston. Tel: 01772 254553

Contents

Preface 1

Chapter 1
Cavern etc 5

Chapter 2
Wartime 39

Chapter 3
Moving South 53

Chapter 4
I Get Called Up ~ (Germany and the Tower of London) 63

Chapter 5
Gyms and Gym Heroes 79

Chapter 6
Labouring Days 95

Chapter 7
Out and About ~ ("Teds" ~ Back to the Circus and on to The Door) 105

Chapter 8
First Club 131

Chapter 9
Jokers & Tricksters 145

Chapter 10
Singers 159

Chapter 11
Running the Gauntlet 175

Chapter 12
A Day Out 183

Chapter 13
Martial Men 191

Chapter 14
Personalities 205

Chapter 15
Chelsea Times 213

Chapter 16
Gatsby Girls and Punk 229

And finally … 241

Foreword

by Terry O'Neill
(Fighting Arts International)

PROVIDING a foreword to the autobiography of a person I have held in the highest regard for a great many years is not only a pleasure – but I consider it an honour.

Which is quite ironic considering how disappointed I was with him at our first meeting. You see, he wasn't who I thought he was. As I approached the door of the Chequers Club I couldn't believe my eyes, there filling the doorway with his impressive build was my all time hero Tarzan, dressed in a tuxedo! (Well actually the eleventh and the best screen version of the apeman movies Gordon Scott!)

I was fumbling in my pocket for a pencil to obtain his autograph when he stepped forward saying

"Hi, I'm Roy Adams".

He knew nothing about my thoughts, I was a 16 year old kid, later when I worked on the doors I always referred to him in conversation with my colleagues as Gordon.

He had a good attitude on the door which coupled with his appearance and air of confidence made him popular. He'd weight trained for years and done some wrestling which all helped. 'Good guys and bad guys alike' agreed that Big Roy was a gentleman.

In my opinion in his book Hard Nights, Roy is guilty of understatement, I've known him to face tough situations not even mentioned but he always plays them down. I'm pleased that he's painted a picture of how things were – if brings back so many memories.

I'm proud to call him my friend.

Terry O'Neill

Preface

THE PEOPLE OF Liverpool have always had a big appetite for a night out, and I have been serving them up for more than four decades.

My Name is Rowland John Adams – Rowland being a family name. My mother called me Rowie which eventually led to me being called Roy. Its certainly one of the more respectable names I've been called over the years. My life's work has been keeping doors and running nightclubs – from 1957 until 1999, which is 42 years in total. To say that I have come from the school of hard knocks is an understatement.

From bouncing difficult customers and knocking together terraced houses to build my first place, to owning and running some of the most famous named clubs that there have ever been, I have done the lot. Occasionally I even had time to enjoy myself in them too. I have been involved in more than twenty different entertainment venues over the years, most of them in and around Liverpool.

Among them was Liverpool's legendary Cavern Club in Matthew Street of which I was the last owner.

In the 50s and 60s, there was no better place for a night out than in the smoky redbrick and stone city by the Mersey that I call home. Back then it was the centre of the world for popular music and entertainment.

Liverpool was a tough town too in all senses. Life was hard and work (if you could find any) was also hard. Because of that, the night was when people let off steam and Clubland was where they did it.

And if Liverpool was tough, then it should come as no surprise that making a living in the clubs there was just as tough. It was a matter of survival. Looking back, it seems that everyone was a hard case, not just the gangsters and villains and some club owners, but the customers and the police too.

Perhaps it was the other side of my life that helped me to get through all of that. My obsession with physical training – developing the body and trying to obtain that elusive perfection of physique has shaped my life – perhaps just as much as the clubs did.

Training can be addictive. Maybe it's because of the feeling of body tone; the muscles in a slightly tensed condition making the skin tighter and smoother, which depletes when not training. I have never felt quite right unless I can do some exercise and even as I write this I train most days. I have known some of the greatest names in the sport. Many of the trainers joined me in the club scene either to do the doors or start their own clubs. This is as much their story as it is mine – in fact you can't talk about night clubs without featuring the most important personnel in clubs – the doormen.

They dictate the success or failure more than anyone else. After all the customers are the club and the standard of the customers is decided by who the doormen let in – that's why I think it's interesting to look at their capabilities, which is something I've tried to feature.

I can understand that some of the expressions I use may cause offence; this is because I talk in the language of the period I'm writing about. If I didn't, it wouldn't sound right – not to me, anyway.

I'm only covering the first twenty years of the nightlife – just giving a flavour I hope, of how things were.

* * *

As Liverpool's most famous band The Beatles sang in 1964 *'It's been a hard day's night, and I've been working like a dog'*. Well, that just about sums up what it was like for me during all my working life. But as I cast my mind back over the years, I realise now that I was living through a golden age when Liverpool was the place to be.

It was a time of hard work yes, but also of opportunity. It was a time when a lad could start his own club and strike it lucky. A time when coat-check girls could get a number one hit; when kids with a bit of Scouse wit could become the variety stars of national TV; where scruffy beat bands thumped their way to become the biggest pop stars in the world.

I have seen them all come through the doors of my clubs.

When my father was courting my mother, he noticed that her dad always had his nose in a cowboy novel. He said: "Pop, I see you like to read (Pop didn't go down too well). I'm writing a book and next trip I'll bring it for you to look at". He was a merchant sailor and gave the manuscript to my grandfather to read. On his next visit some months later, granddad handed the manuscript back to him saying: "Ah, you copied it out of a book!" whereupon my father threw it into the back of the fire. Now that was a serious put down.

It's an incident I've thought about from time to time and now I've decided to have a go, I hope it won't have to face the flames!

A Taste ... ?

ONE NIGHT myself and another doorman had been getting grief from a bunch of yobs we'd knocked back on the door.

Eventually it all calmed down and we stepped back out onto the front step.

I stooped down to fasten my shoelace hearing a thud as I started to bend forward. I looked behind me and there was a large triangle of glass with the point buried in the door just where my head had been.

As I realised it another shard of glass just missed my face. Next thing pieces of glass were flying at us.

Two of the crowd we'd knocked back had dragged a large cardboard box full of broken panes of glass from a rubbish skip down the street. They'd hidden behind a parked car. We managed to scramble inside but not before I'd been caught on the leg and my colleague had a gash on his hand.

This was my first experience of the Liverpool determination for revenge when they feel rebuffed.

Future missiles in similar circumstances were to include bottle of acid, knives, rocks and iron bars which had to be faced.

We couldn't open the door for about 10 minutes when they finally ran out of glass. When we did open it the entrance and steps were covered in broken glass.

The door also was spattered with some pieces stuck in it and splinters of wood torn out.

Somehow it made me think of a coffin.

Was this just an appetiser – a taste of things to come?

Eddy McDonough, John Pennington and Roy Adams, Harlequin door, 1959

Second from left, Roy, Johnny Penn, and on extreme right, Tommy Barton, 1963 at the Philharmonic Pub

~ 1 ~
Cavern etc

I GOT INTO the Cavern in Liverpool in 1969, it was an exciting place, extremely busy.

The most famous club in all of Liverpool is The Cavern; its association with The Beatles and other Mersey Beat bands doing much for its reputation over the years. But the Cavern was always more than just The Beatles. As such, it was a club that I would have liked to own, but I never thought I'd get the chance. Then one day in 1969, again quite out of the blue, I got word that the owner Alfie Geoghegan was thinking of retiring. I was running the Pyramid in Temple Street a couple of hundred yards away, which was so popular by then that we had expanded into a third warehouse next door and were getting 1.000 people a night. I went to see Alfie and asked him if he was interested in selling The Cavern. He thought about it for a couple of days and he said yes.

It pleased me to become an owner of the most famous music club in the world.

The Cavern was opened in 1957 by a guy called Alan Sytner who previously owned two jazz clubs in Liverpool, the West Coast Jazz Club and the 21 Jazz Club. He was looking for a venue that was different and it was on holiday in France – where he took trips to Parisian jazz clubs built into small caves – that he got the idea. He took over the basement at 10 Matthew Street in the heart of Liverpool and named it after the most famous Paris jazz club 'Le Cavea' and very good it was too. More than two thousand jazz fans packed Matthew Street on the opening night; the opening line up featured the Coney Island Skiffle Group, the Walt City Jazzmen and the Ralph Watmough Jazz Band. Also featured that night was the Merseysippi Jazz Band, which had been going since 1949. I remember calling in on another night when they were on, and whilst standing at the back got chatting to a bloke who seemed to know what it was all about. His name was George Melly, who later became a regular holder of the title Jazz Singer of the Year and one of Britain's greatest jazz figures. Local skiffle outfits were getting opportunities to perform at the Cavern to audiences and on August 7th, 1957, The Quarrymen made their first appearance there. Skiffle became so popular – even among school children – that the club started up lunchtime sessions to meet demand.

By 1959, the Cavern Club had an incredible 25,000 members but Rock n' Roll was now becoming popular and it was inevitable that it would take over, which it soon did. It was in this year that the club was taken over by Ray McFall who was a jazz fan and had been a cashier at the club. He was keen for it to continue in the jazz tradition. But other clubs around the city were doing well with 'beat music' and he realised that to survive he would need to cater for this younger crowd as well as the jazz fans. This he did by phasing in guitar duos as well as skiffle groups on alternative nights.

In May 1960, Ray introduced the first beat group evening – headlined by Rory Storm and the Hurricanes, with Ringo Starr on drums. Rory was to become a real legend in Liverpool, being the first to move from skiffle to Rock and Roll. He had a huge blonde quiff and a personality which was all his own, with a very different style of singing. His characteristic stammer seemed to disappear completely when he started to sing. Towards the end of the sixties Rory's career did a dive and he became depressed. In 1971 he quit and became a barber and later a salesman. At the same time he was getting aggro from local tough guy Eddie Palmer, so it is said: Rory lived with his mother Violet who doted on him. His depression really got the better of him and in his last days he fell to drink and sleeping pills. One day he and his mother were found lying dead in their beds after apparently both committing suicide.

A very sad end to a career and his life.

Another group, which was extremely talented, was the Roadrunners, headed by Mike Hart who now works for the BBC administrating on the pop music side. Another band member was Dave Percy. A few years ago, long after the band finished, my pal Charlie Scott gave Dave a job in one of his bars. Charlie said: "He was a lovely fellow but unfortunately, at every opportunity he would grab his guitar and start playing it!" Needless to say, he didn't keep his job for long. The Roadrunners were way ahead of most bands, including the Beatles at that time. Their main venue was Hope Hall, which later became the Everyman Theatre in Hope Street. Long John Baldry and other aspiring pop stars used to go to see them.

Brian Epstein would see the Beatles perform at a lunchtime session at the Cavern in 1961; they had just returned from playing long hours in the clubs of Hamburg and had become a very professional group and he quickly became their manager. They would play the club 292 times, finally bowing out at their last performance on August 3rd 1963.

This period was undoubtedly the Cavern's heyday; when Liverpool was probably the World capital of popular music. The Cavern's DJ Bob Wooler did much to make sure that big name bands came through the door at this time, including the likes of Gene Vincent, Gerry and the Pacemakers, Cilla Black, the Four Jays, the Searchers, and a little later The Rolling Stones, The Who and the Yardbirds.

In the mid sixties Ray tried to open his own Cavern recording studio but this ended in financial disaster for him and he was later declared bankrupt. The Cavern closed on February 27th 1966. The following day there was an extraordinary event which became known as "the siege of Matthew Street". As two members of the official Receivers Office arrived to serve notice of closure, they found the main door barricaded on the inside with chairs and tables and the side door padlocked against them. Inside was the thumping rhythm of a band called the Hideaways accompanied by hundreds of teenage fans chanting "The Cavern must not close!" and singing "We shall not be moved!" The court officials made a hasty retreat to the nearest police station.

The revolt lasted about two hours until a policeman found a key to the padlocked side door; within a few minutes the barricades had been removed and the protesting teenagers emptied onto the street. They promptly staged a sit down protest and later a march to the Town Hall, although little good it would do anyone. It was more of a gesture than any serious attempt to change matters. But it served to show how much The Cavern played in the public's affections.

It didn't stay shut for long though; Alfie Geoghegan, who ran a successful fleet of taxis, and Joe Davey, who owned the famous all night Joe's Café in Duke Street, bought it and the place reopened on July 23rd 1966. The reopening was such a major happening that the Prime Minister Harold Wilson came to the ceremony along with local MP Bessie Braddock.

Harold Wilson, P.M., Bessie Braddock, M.P., Mary Wilson and Ken Dodd at the Cavern re-opening, 23rd July, 1966.

Until that point, the club had not been licensed and so had sold only soft drinks and crisps, but that went when a license was granted and so the crowd going there became a bit older. DJ Billy Butler became the main DJ and he did a lot to revive the fortunes of the place by booking big bands.

* * *

Taking it over was quite daunting, it was licensed for four hundred people and when it got eight hundred in, it was packed! But we used to get sixteen hundred in and it was almost impossible! We had twelve doormen; we kept a row of chairs in the entrance to sit girls on when they passed out.

Visitors came from all over the world; we had to lead them by the hand through the place telling them: "If you let go, you'll be lost forever!" We operated on two floors – ground floor and basement. On the ground floor, (which was very bare, with black and white lino tiles on the floor) we had the skinheads who danced mainly to pop music. Down in the basement (which was very atmospheric with three long arched brick built rooms, with moisture running down the walls and a smell of cannabis, cigarette smoke and urine) were the troggs – the longhaired brigade. They danced to heavy rock almost exclusively, although I do remember when I booked Gary Glitter the place was a sell out, the centre row of arches had church pews, which had been there for at least twelve years. The stage was in darkness and when the lights came on, Glitter was centre stage with his arms

extract from the Liverpool Echo, date unknown

CLUB OF THE WEEK

Bursting at the seams – so Cavern plans extension

by
Steve Noel

The Cavern ten years ago when the Beatles reigned supreme and the place was packed every night. Nothing has changed. It's still top of the pops.

If there's one club in Liverpool that doesn't need to make a name for itself it must be the Cavern. Yet the "cellarful of noise" in Mathew Street is doing just that.

The place is still a shrine for Beatlemaniacs the world over, of course. They do nicely showing tourists around, selling souvenir cuff links and car stickers, and when owner Roy Adams toured Australia recently he was welcomed everywhere with open arms.

But to thousands of Merseyside pop fans the Cavern is just as well known for its current scene–as Liverpool's leading heavy music club.

Demand for the music is so strong that an extension to the Cavern is under way, which will take the club's capacity to about 2,000.

They work on a policy of encouraging the music as much as possible, and many groups have got their first real break playing at the back of Lord Street.

Many cut out the advertisements for their Cavern appearances and use them to boost their careers elsewhere. Aspiring groups have come from as far as Birmingham, Scotland and London for auditions. Besides the newcomers, the Cavern are proud of the number of top-name groups they have played.

East of Eden used to be regulars and are due back soon. The Pretty Things were on this week and lined up for the future are Vinegar Joe, an Afro-rock band called Danta, a Dutch group, Focus, the top group in Wales, Budgie, and hopefully, Heads Hands and Feet.

The centre room of the club where the stage is, is full of ranked benches left over from the jazz club days, and at weekends the fans queue for them. "just to sit and listen," said D.J. Bobby Rave.

Bobby shares the disc work with Joey Wall, and has been associated with the Cavern for years, managing it at one point.

Apart from the music room, the Cavern has a large bar doubling as the restaurant, and an upstairs disco specialising in soul music.

The restaurant is deliberately unfussy, aimed at simple good value food rather than fancy frills. The most expensive meal is steak and chips at 50p.

The Cavern is open five nights a week, Thursday to Monday. Admission charges vary depending on which groups are playing, but the highest rarely goes above 50p.

The membership, at 50p a time, is enormous, with thousands of overseas visitors joining just so that can go home as members.

In fact, the club is the only one in the country with a special overseas book, giving tourists instant membership rights on production of their passports.

stretched out and his back to the crowd. The music struck up and he jumped around to face the audience at the same time singing:

"Do you wanna Rock?"

There were so many people packed on to the pews, as they all jumped, so the pews collapsed and were flattened. A shame really 'cos those pews were quite historic.

When we took over I noticed the bar staff were mainly beefy middle-aged women. The first weekend I put my sister Freda and a pal Dave behind the bar to help, by the way. One of the women took them to one side and said: "Look there's no tips in here, so you add sixpence to every round you serve, and put it in the jar." They complied over the weekend; their shared tips came to fifteen pounds, which worked out at six hundred rounds! There being forty sixpences to one pound. The other four barmaids obviously kept their own tips. This was only one of the four bars! I changed all the bar staff and Freda took over as manageress. Her daughter Maureen ran one of the bars and Maureen's husband Tony White worked on the door as did my wife Ellen's brother-in-law Joe Quilliam. It helps to keep it in the family.

Freda also has a son named Steve, a six foot two and a half inches tall ex karate man – he was a key man for me, working as a manager in both the Pyramid and Chelsea Reach, my cousin Ray Jones was also a manager in the Chelsea during the twenty years I was involved in it.

Two brothers Mike and Martin Dempsey who'd done some wrestling training with us, were also on the management side, when we closed Mike continued to do door work for me, – a very good experienced asset.

All the drinks were served in paper cups; it was too packed for glasses. When you walked past the speakers it was like a physical blow in the chest, the volume was so high. The head doorman was Paddy Delaney, who'd been there since the Beatles days, he did about sixteen years on the door altogether. Thirteen of them at the Cavern. One night in the Pyramid a group of doormen were discussing Paddy as I passed, saying he wasn't aggressive enough. I turned to them and said to one: "How long have you worked the door?" He said: "Two years," and to the next one, he said three years and the other, four years. I said: "When it comes to the door job you're all red arses! Can you imagine how many people he's chucked out in fifteen years? When you've had as many fights and frights as he's had, you'll learn to be diplomatic!" Which Paddy certainly was, he was very popular and a very good doorman. He was also an ex Irish Guardsman!

One of the main expenses which surprised me was the cost of the paper cups which averaged out at £20 a week. There were no membership cards when I took over, I think what had been left had been taken for souvenirs, so I designed a new card which featured a caveman with a club.

Eventually when I took over the Cavern, I opened an office in Mathew St right opposite the Cavern entrance. I used to go to the office daily, I had a secretary called Eileen who eventually got my paperwork organised. Prior to this, I did everything, paying the bills, keeping the books, the banking and answering letters by hand. I'd leave for the office most days by 10am, sometimes earlier, and because I worked almost every night in one club or another, I was permanently exhausted. I worked three times the hours of anyone I knew. Many a night I would drive home in the early hours, having been on the go since the previous morning. I'd be in sight of my house, and would suddenly find myself bumping along the centre reservation of the dual carriageway. I'd pull in to the side and sleep until the local police would wake me saying: "Come on Roy its 6 o'clock, get this car moving."

One night I called round to the Cavern Club to see how Freda was coping, after which I set off to the Pyramid, which was only a hundred yards away in Temple Street. When I arrived at the bottom of the street by the She Club, I could see something was going on.

There were a lot of people milling around and as I got closer to the Pyramid, I saw the doormen from the She Club, The Yankee Clipper, (Sonny Phillips Club) and the Pyramid club were all strung out along the pavement, their backs to the wall. There'd been trouble with a gang and all hands had come to help. Facing them all on the opposite pavement of this very narrow street was a guy holding a large enamelled metal sign, which advertised Fry's Chocolate.

These signs were heavy, being about six foot by four foot and about three sixteenths of an inch thick. He was scything it holding it flat and sweeping it backwards and foreword screaming.

"I'm goin' ta cut your fuckin' heads off with this you bastards."

He had twenty odd fella's swaying to and fro and looking very anxious. There's no doubt that if he had thrown it he could have done some serious injury the edges of the sign being sharp.

I walked up his side of the street keeping close to the wall. When I got level with him, I jumped forward pulling his right arm backwards making him drop the sign. I put my left arm in a wrestling bar across his jaw. He gave his head a sudden jerk clamping his teeth around my thumb! He was biting hard and the pain was intense. Nobody seemed to be making a move to help they seemed to be frozen to the spot. Then Alec McGowan a club owning friend ran forward to help followed by the others. I ran into the club, all the fight had gone out of me, it was the first time I had experienced the extreme pain of a bitten thumb.

* * *

Here is an article which appeared in full in the American music magazine,
***Rolling Stone**, on March 20th, 1972.*
This is an edited version:

Ferry Back Across The Mersey

BY EARL KIRMSER

LONDON—"Don't believe a word of it," warns the bartender, leaning across the table to pick up some empty mugs. Bill Harry smiles. He's been talking about Liverpool, his days as editor of Merseybeat, and maybe the barman has heard it before.

"I started Merseybeat," says Bill, "in 1961 on 50 borrowed quid. John had a column, 'Beatcoma' which was everything he'd ever written and was the basis for the books. I ran Merseybeat for five years. Eventually we were doing 16 pages and in full colour. It was a paper for musicians until Brian [Epstein] came in on it in 1964 and wanted to cover only the top hits. By that time I'd sold the paper to Ray McFall, who owned the Cavern Club. You know we were the first music paper outside London and it inspired others like Scottish Beat, Midland Beat, and even Birmingham had one too. For the first time there was a new center away from London, in the north of England, and it was us. And the paper was making money, before eventually becoming part of Disc and Music Echo."

"Load o' bollocks," says the bartender, grinning.

These days Bill is a pub raconteur of note. He has an office out of which he handles press relations for a bunch of groups, but the pubs are his real headquarters. Right now he's in a bit of a bind because he's lost his address book. So beneath the row of pint glasses lined up on the table in preparation for afternoon closing time, he's examining the dark reaches of the Soho pub floor with an intense squint. Losing an address book can be a crippling thing in his game.

"Liverpool," Bill continues, "set the pace for the rest of the country and London. It was a seaport like Hamburg, which we call our 'Second City,' and so we got the records from the States first. Everybody knows everybody else then—all the groups and all the fans. We were first with things. A Motown Revue came through as early as '62. Liverpool's Little Harlem, on Upper Parliament Street, had a coloured group called the Chants that were great. Nothing ever came of them—Brian didn't like them—but they still do a bit of cabaret. And you can talk about your Fanny, your all-girl groups. The Liverbirds were ten years ahead of them.

"We had country and western too. It was always big and even now there's about 40 groups working in the general Liverpool area. The biggest are the Hillsiders. They're one of the only British bands ever to have played the Grand Ole Opry. The Spinners are big too.

The pub has closed and while heading for an afternoon after-hours spot, Bill gives his view on the Cause of Death. "London came up and killed it. They came up and recorded *This Is Mersey Beat*—two albums—put on record 40 groups. They distorted it all because the money wasn't in their pockets, and they weren't Liverpool. They wanted control and all the Liverpool groups had to come to London to keep their music alive."

Bill talks of his scrape with bankruptcy that forced him to come to London. His old mate Alan Williams, the very first Beatles manager and one-time operator of The Blue Angel, the famous club on Liverpool's Seal Street, has just been declared bankrupt and he too is now heading for London. How about Ray McFall, the Cavern's first owner?

"Ray's an estate agent somewhere, nobody knows quite where," says Bill. "He had a girl in every city, all sorts of cars, but he's still fighting his bankruptcy.

"He made the mistake of never coming to London, you see."

* * *

Gerry Marsden is on the way to Liverpool. This time of the year finds him doing pantomime (children's holiday theatre)—a three-week season of *Jack And The Beanstalk* in Doncaster, a town in the north Midlands encircled by railroad cars stacked with coal. Gerry is talking in the stale lounge of the Elephants Hotel, an Edwardian building just off the High Street. The shiny apple polish to his cheeks is gone now, and his hair, like everyone's, is longer, but he looks the same as he did no the television show *Shindig*, in the TAMI Show, or in the film *Ferry across the Mersey*. In 1964, Gerry and the Pacemakers had the distinction of a hat trick at the top of the English Charts—"How Do You Do," "I Like It," which Gerry wrote himself, and the Rodgers and Hammerstein "You'll Never Walk Alone."

The Pacemakers are all back in Liverpool running garages, but after the break-up Gerry did *Charlie Girl*, a hit West End musical comedy. He headlined the cast for a straight run of over two years, until the day he caught a sore throat, dropped out for a rest, discovered just a while after the management did that he'd forgotten to extend his contract, and found himself out of the show. Since then he's done some children's television, but he's happier song-writing. He wrote a good number of the group's hits, including the whole score for the film. Right now he is writing show tunes for a West End venture this summer, and some songs for a solo album he's long wanted to do.

After Gerry and the Pacemakers' version of "You'll Never Walk Alone" reached Number One, it was adopted by "the Kop"—the Liverpool football club's homeground rooting section—as their team cheer song. Since then other clubs have adopted it and a vignette of one of these chants is part of the "Fearless" cut on the Pink Floyd *Meddle* album.

Talk turns to the beat groups of old: the Searchers, the Big Three, the Merseybeat Mojos, the Fourmost, the Remo Four, the Swinging Blue Jeans, Rory Storme and the Hurricanes (who gave drummer Richard Starkey to the Beatles), and Billy J. Kramer and the Dakotas. "Billy J. is still doing cabaret," says Gerry. "I haven't seen him in a long time. I'm surprised he never broke out of that." Would Gerry and the Pacemakers ever reform? "No, not really,

Christ! I'd like to go back to the States and do cabaret, but not as Gerry and the Pacemakers … unless it's for something exceptional like £47 million over a three-week period."

In 1963, it was estimated that there were more than 300 beat groups in Liverpool, a city then of 750,000 inhabitants. Each group had its partisan following and many times group and fans formed a company in cottage-industry fashion to support that music. By 1964, Liverpool boasted an active group population of 10,000, though not more than 200 could have been making a living from it. Times have changed and all that's left of that is a memory and a tourist attraction. Gerry Marsden had a laugh on that. "When we were touring the States, the kids would say 'Hi, Gerry, we're saving up to go to Liverpool,' and I'd say, 'Jesus, don't do that—save your money and go to London, then go to Liverpool for a day and see the Cavern, and go back to London, because there's nothing in Liverpool.' It's alright for a day, but they were talking in terms of a fortnight."

The glory that was Liverpool in its high tide days has largely moved the 200 miles down to London.

"The people who we left behind," says Gerry Marsden, "the Ray McFalls, the Alan Williams—they all blew it because they didn't come down to town."

Yankel Feather is one who stayed on. He's a respected artist, a dapperly dressed man with a trimmed greying beard. At present, he's doing a series of drag paintings. Over tea in his Grassendale home in Liverpool, he explains, "Basically I'm a colorist, but I think you tend to excel at what you don't do well. You compensate and so your weakness becomes your strength … I've decided this is my year because I'm the only one with the wit and experience that will do anything."

Is there today the same unified arts scene that seemed to grow up alongside Merseybeat? "There isn't the community any longer," he replies. "Not like it used to be.

"I had a club called the Basement which was for older teenagers–the Cavern was mainly for children. Cilla Black was my hatcheck girl then and she and her husband Bob, who used to lift weights with my bouncers, courted in the club. Brian used to drive around at night with nothing to do. He once brought me 'Love Me Do' to play in the club, but I wouldn't because I thought it sounded like an Arabic dirge. It was the end of what was then our friendship. If only I'd said I loved one of the Beatles, I could've been in on them."

* * *

The Cavern Club is on Mathew Street in the center of Liverpool, in the warehouse section not far from the Pier Head. When it re-opened in 1968 the occasion was marked by a visit from Harold Wilson, then prime minister and, as now, member of Parliament for one of Liverpool's constituencies.

Freda, Roy Adams' sister, runs The Cavern for her brother. He's busy with his other clubs—The Pyramid (formerly The Iron Door), a converted warehouse like the Cavern, with dark nooks and crannies decorated with full-length photos of muscle shows and beauty contests, and two pub-clubs across the Mersey in New Brighton and Birkenhead.

Freda is a pleasant, dark-haired woman and she explains The Cavern's set-up. "We're open five nights a week. Upstairs is a discotheque for the older crowd, the skinhead type who like the bluebeat and reggae. They're a tougher crowd and do a lot of fighting, and sometimes we have trouble between them and the younger, 'heavy' crowd down here, kids we call troggs. They don't mix, which is why we serve up all our drinks in paper cups. Down here we always have live music, and the kids seem to like this 'heavy' music these days … The only old beat band that plays here is Confucious, who are the old Hideaways. And their music changed with their name. Sometimes one of the bands will play a rock 'n' roll number, or we might put on a Beatles record, and the kids really like it, because they've never heard it before, and it's all new to them."

Roy Adams and his re-opened Cavern: now it's full of skinheads and troggs
Photo: Phil Franks

Roy has arrived. He is a hulking, handsome type who looks like he'd be at home beside a Grosse Point swimming pool. "We started this heavy scene a long time ago before the rest of the country." he says. "But to tell you the truth, the kids don't really give a shit what band I book here, they come long just the same. You should've been here Christmas time. This guy who runs a place in Hamburg was with me and the cab we were in couldn't even get down the street here, that's how many kids wanted to get in. We turned more away that night than we let in, and this guy couldn't understand it. Sure, we get American bands who want to come here to play, but they usually want too much money, and as I said, it doesn't really matter who is playing. The club scene is mostly older here now than it was then. We get tourists dropping in all the time. this past year, German, Dutch, and Japanese television people were by, and this summer the Canadian Broadcasting Corporation had a hook-up down here and we did almost a whole hour with them."

Paddy is head bouncer at The Cavern. He came to The Cavern after a stint in the Irish Guards, and long before the Beatles. "I was here when we did trad and everyone had short hair and the short-sleeved shirts … I remember the night this kid with hair over his collar came to the door; he said, 'I'm George Harrison of the Beatles.' and I said to myself, 'That's right, we do have a group by that name on tonight.' Ten years it's been and I keep saying that someday I oughta write a book about it. Ten years and so many names and faces and I can't remember all the names. Somebody should get a place and put a show on and go through the history of it song by song. I think it would do well here. The stuff they play here now is rubbish, just rubbish. But I reckon that trad went underground twice to re-surface successfully both times, so now beat is underground, and it'll come up again."

*   *   *

Penny Lane is a modest middle-class street in Liverpool 15, the Allerton district. If it is a well-visited street, the only sign is the absence of any street marker, which was long ago either stolen or, more likely, discreetly removed by residents. It stretches for about half a mile and is dotted with corner grocery stores, a Polish butcher, a beauty parlor, a wine and spirits shop. No pub, no fish and chippie, no souvenir shops.

Harry Bioletti owns the barbershop on the corner near the bank. But you'd have to step inside to read some of his clippings pasted on a board to discover this is *the* barbershop.

Mr. Bioletti points us along to Strawberry Field. "You ask the Captain there all about it, she loves to talk about the Beatles."

Captain Stevenson of the Salvation Army has only been stationed at Strawberry Field for a year, however, and only knows the legend second-hand. Ken, a staff worker, came here as gardener six years ago, and is more of a veteran. Strawberry Field is a Victorian estate in a residential area not unlike parts of suburban Philadelphia. It was given to the Salvation Army in 1945 and has served as an orphanage for about 35 kids since.

The estate house at Strawberry Field does look like it's forever, but Ken says that it's coming down soon. "They're building the new house over what used to be the garden here, and that'll be ready in September. They've also sold some of what was the playing ground where the kids played football to private developers and that's already been built over as you can see. We have lots of people coming by here and offering to work because of the song. Marge, an American girl from Michigan, is here for a year because she wants to do this kind of work, but she came here really because of the Beatles. We have a Norwegian girl and a Swedish girl here too, and I think they were attracted here by the same thing."

*   *   *

In Liverpool, everybody's second cousin was the original manager of the Beatles. The real one, Alan Williams, is the sort of man that *is* everybody's second cousin. Spread out on the floor of a room in his spacious house in a residential section of Liverpool 8, are the contents of his paper-memories folio. One of the scraps of paper is the charred remains of the Original Contract.

He was Beatles manager from 1960 until the middle of 1961, some 18 months. "In 1960, I booked Larry Parnes and John Kennedy, who were then the kings of rock 'n' roll, for a boxing stadium in Liverpool. They had people like Gene Vincent and Eddie Cochran in their package tour and this was in April 1960, when Eddie Cochran was killed in the automobile accident, and to give it an extra boost — because Vincent was willing to go on with the show — I booked all Liverpool groups like Gerry and the Pacemakers, and Rory Storme, and … the Beatles hadn't really formed then because it was after that show that they came up to me and asked me would I be their manager because they were so impressed by the show. Shortly after that they turned pro. Then I had them for 18 months, when Brian took them over, and I don't think anyone better could've taken them over, because he was one of them.

"I was doing it for kicks," he says. "Because I enjoyed it. I reckon in 1965 it started to go out. And the Liverpool groups have only themselves to blame. The groups got lazy because the demand was on them and they had all the Top Ten hits and suddenly a group like the Rolling Stones emerged. I had a club, The Blue Angel, and all the groups that worked Liverpool used to come on by after hours and have a session. The Stones came and everybody thought they were gonna have a giggle, but the smile was wiped right off their faces when they started to play. I thought that was the beginning of the end for Liverpool. To prove my point now, most clubs in Liverpool are discotheques, because there just aren't enough home groups to go around."

Alan puts more logs into his blazing fireplace. His and the neighbours' kids are in and out, running around.

"I don't mean to sound bitter," he continues in another vein, "But it is sad. All those who were creative and on the scene then, are no longer involved now. It's as if all the heavies are controlling the clubs now and it's purely money — an idea has to be commercially sound. But we had to take risks and we had a lot of fun. These clubs, they bloody well frighten me these days with the heavy boys up front. I had that experience at my old club. The bouncers were controlling the bloody club, and I couldn't tell them who to let in and who not to let in.

"I don't mean to sound bitchy, but you know this year is the first in 25 that I haven't worked a club at Christmas, and my father, who's been in the business all his life and who was with me at the club this was his first Christmas in 50 years he didn't work a club."

So after all these years Alan is going to Town. It's the second time he's been bankrupt, and he claims he got this way because he was bored and there was no challenge. "But I'll bounce back," he says, "because I have before. And that's why I've gone to London. I realise I can't do it in Liverpool and I should've gone to London long ago. We'll probably move down there all together now. Anyway, I don't mind it because Liverpool is dead now, just a concrete bloody jungle. There's no character to Liverpool anymore."

* * *

Clive Epstein runs Clarendon furnishings for the family in Liverpool 13 out on Prescott Road. He was in on the groundwork at NEMS in the mid-Sixties, keeping the books and looking after the conservative end of business for brother Brian. In 1967, after Brian died, Clive was elected chairman of NEMS and carried on for 18 months before selling his interests to Triumph Investment Trust, a merchant banking conglomerate. "What happened to me then." says Clive, "is that I came back to the furniture shops which the family have always had and so I'm now involved with finance and property building. It's not very exciting work, so that's probably what prompts me to say to you that there's a bit of a vacuum in Liverpool. And I don't think its just me. We're waiting for something. I mean, the Beatles, the Everton and Liverpool football clubs were on top at the same time. They're still good clubs and they're still doing well, but there doesn't seem to be the real excitement. Actually Liverpool has a lot of its problems. There's a lot of unemployment and urban re-development is extremely slow. What happened just erupted like a volcano. It erupted in just three months and we were all left goggling and not knowing quite what we were up to."

Clive thinks about it all for a moment. He is tall, well-dressed, and speaks very precisely with little evidence of Scouse in his words. "What happened then was a revolution. We've always been a stronghold over the years for humour and artistic talent, and it's just possible … I mean the kids have suffered here for so long, after all it's not a healthy place for them … and well, perhaps it was just a type of consolation prize for living in Liverpool."

* * *

Six feet eight inch Barry McLelland now worked for me at the Cavern. He was great at sorting out drug problems. He'd position himself where he could keep an eye on the lavatories. If he saw a lad go into a cubicle followed by another guy a few minutes later, Barry would go and look over the cubicle walls where they would invariably be dealing drugs. He'd grab the dealer and after showing him to the other doorman, throw him out. At that time, it would be mainly cannabis, not the problem it is now.

When he was at the Cavern, the doormen used to take the mickey out of him and generally, he took it in good part, but one of the doormen who had a reputation as a hard case used to go too far. Barry confided in me that he was getting fed up with it. Well one night, this guy who I'll call Gary, phoned Barry on the internal phone necessitating him being called up through the crowds from the cellar where he was working. He was given a stupid message calling him a poncy name. Barry was furious and told Gary to cut it out, he'd had enough. Gary said something like: "Oh you're a hard man, get outside and lets see what you're gonna do about it."

6' 8" Barry McLelland in action.

As it happened, Barry had done some boxing when he was younger, he rose to the challenge and went outside. Now Barry being so tall was ungainly but as they squared up to each other, he bent forward from the waist extending one leg to the rear, bending his other leg in front in a classic boxing stance. As soon as Gary moved toward him, he shot his right fist straight out hitting Gary on the jaw knocking him off his feet! The piss taking stopped after that.

He told me later that he was tempted to use his party piece on Gary, which was to lay his arm across the pavement gutter – and stamp on it.

What Gary didn't know was that Barry had some history, in fact he didn't talk about himself much at all, though he had had some colourful experiences, which included being a sparring partner to Sonny Liston for eighteen months.

When he was fourteen years old, Barry was introduced to boxing by the man many considered was a Liverpool legend – Joe Phillips. Amongst other things, Joe had owned eight shebeens in Liverpool's south end. He was the first man to start private hire taxis in that part of town.

Joe was an extremely successful pigeon flyer and it was through that sport that they met. Joe was also a former amateur boxer and with his encouragement Barry joined the Kensington Boxing Club, run by Les Douglas. He was now sixteen years old and had won six schoolboy fights.

He used to go to the P.B.A. Gym in Huskisson Street, Toxteth, where he trained with such good fighters as Harry Scott, Tony Smith and Joe Bygraves, picking up lots of tips.

By the time he was seventeen years old he was six foot eight inches tall, but skinny at thirteen stone, losing his first amateur fight to a six foot five inch policeman.

Barry gave him three stone in weight and the popular opinion was that Barry had won. Eight months later he boxed at the Mather Avenue Police School. His opponent was

Roy Dunne, the National Universities Champion. He had knocked out all the Police boxers and was a six foot four inches, sixteen stone Adonis.

Barry told me, "Les Douglas said: 'Just go forward throwing punches,' which I did. He caught me in the ribs and it hurt – I hit him with a right and he went down – he got up again. I moved in with a left and a right, and this time he stayed down. Even with his great fighting spirit he couldn't get back on his feet for some time."

"During my first eighteen months in Toronto, Canada, I would travel to Texas for six weeks where I spent time in the famous A & B Gym, 110 ?, Travis Street, Houston, Texas – with such fighters as Cleveland Williams who fought Mohamed Ali, and Dave Zigilwich who later on would fight Joe Frazier for the World title, which was amazing as he was only five foot nine inches." "When I first met Dave he'd just come out of the U.S. navy, and we soon became great friends."

A relative of Barry's was very friendly with a guy who'd been in the Police for eight years – he'd moved out to Canada and joined the Police over there.

He invited Barry to come and stay with him, helping towards the rent etc.

Things weren't going too well and one morning he said to Barry: "Look we're both skint – we've got to do something about it, so today we're going to rob a bank." This fellow who I'll call George, was a very forceful character who wouldn't take no for an answer. So Barry got into the car with him and they parked it just round the corner from the bank.

Cavern doormen, 1970's style ~ Joey Quilliam on the right

Barry told me, "It was a bright Spring day in 1964. He parked the car in an alleyway – I had to walk a hundred yards with him to the bank – a thousand things were going through my mind, – like, – is this the first step to the gallows, as topping people was still in force at the time, or am I going to be cut down by Police bullets?"

"He told me to wait outside to stop anyone who tried to grab him on the way out. He pulled out a gun and went into the bank – I waited outside for what seemed like hours but was only about forty seconds, George came running out and ran to the car and drove away. I made my way home by bus and subway."

When he got back George told him that the girl had jumped back and screamed when he handed her the demand note. He'd panicked and ran out.

Barry had some peace for a couple of weeks and then George started again with his crazy schemes. He told Barry he wanted help with one of these and Barry refused. George blew his top and said: "You can't stay here if you're not gonna help."

Barry told me, "I could take no more of living under his roof. I'd been brought up poor but honest, and I had nowhere to go."

"George went to work on the afternoon shift, – I broke my 2.2 rifle down putting the firing mechanism in my overcoat pocket. I sat in a coffee bar for an hour and decided to end it all. I was only seventeen years old."

"I got on a bus and got off by some woods. I set off amongst the trees and sat down on a log, said my prayers and started to cry – God, it's hard to shoot yourself!"

"In the movies it looks so easy. In real life it's another story. I pulled the trigger and the bullet went into my stomach and lodged in my spine. I managed to crawl out and into the road where a car picked me up, it was driven by a doctor who sent for an ambulance which took me to hospital. Just in time, as I'd lost a lot of blood. When I got out of hospital, George said: 'You should have used the 303 rifle and put it in your mouth – that's the way to do it!' "

"I recovered and started work and went back to the gym. A year and a half later I got a charter flight and came home and started work in Liverpool, at the Chequers club."

Local tough guy Eddie Palmer started to come in and intimidate the croupier on the gaming table.

Barry had a word with him and Palmer left saying, "I'll see you later."

The next day Eddie had been out and when he got home, his mother who was a nice lady, said: "There's someone here to see you", – pointing to a car parked opposite. Barry was sat in the car with a pal, Billy Bodell. Barry said: "You wanted to see me later – so here I am, – if you want to fight I'm up for it." Eddie said something like: "You're making too much of it – forget it." Although still very young at nineteen years old, Barry could be a daunting prospect.

After eighteen months he went back to America to resume his fighting career. At eighteen he'd appeared on Granada T.V. being the tallest Briton to have been granted a professional boxing license, in height in World boxing, he was second only to Pottgieter, who was an incredible seven foot four inches. He went to Texas to get his boxing back on the rails. After twelve fights he went to Las Vegas, where he had twenty fights, mainly at the Silver Slipper Saloon and on to Boston, where he lost to Charlie Polite. During his fighting career he met and trained with some great fighters like Sonny Liston, Jerry Quarry, Howard King, George Chuvolo and Harold Johnson.

Barry told me that Sonny Liston was a really nice modest man. He and Barry went to a nightclub one night, where they joined the queue to get in. A steward walked over to them, he said: "I can't believe you two standing here, – why don't you go straight to the front?" Sonny said: "Oh yeah – and how embarrassing it would be for us if the doormen refused us!"

My pal Larry Newport also worked the Cavern door. He was 6' 2" and lightening fast. His reflexes were terrific. He'd place a small coin in your open hand and bet you couldn't close your hand before he took it! As his hand dived into your palm you'd quickly close it. You'd open your palm and there'd be a larger coin in its place! We'd been having trouble with three hard cases from Preston, Larry, myself and another friend Charlie Scott were facing them up. One of them made a move on Larry and within three seconds all three were flattened on the deck, with identical two-inch cuts over their left eye. Larry had done it with his head. We didn't get a chance to move!

Larry Newport

My office was in Mathew St opposite the Cavern about 10 yards from the Cavern door. I used to watch a daily procession of people coming to worship at the shrine of the Beatles! They came from Japan, America, Norway, Sweden, Holland, everywhere! There wasn't much to see! In 1973 Liverpool was in decline, had been for years, inflation was 27% I know because I was struggling with more than one club at that time. I used to say that Liverpool's only hope was in tourism. People thought I was mad, but I'd say: "Think about it, the themes that could be developed here Disney style, which are based on our history. The slave trade, the cotton industry, the music industry, the historic seafaring industry with its nine miles of docks etc. People fly into Heathrow now and get the train from Euston straight to Liverpool to see the Cavern. If a proper theme park was built, they'd have to put a new motorway right into the city!"

Phil Thompson's wonderfully documented book of the Cavern, *'The Best of Cellar's'*, describes very well, the Cavern during my time there.

The following is an extract from the book.

By the late 1960's, the Cavern had not only a new audience, but a new owner. Liverpool businessman Roy Adams took over the club.

Jack Smith was a Cavern regular during the late 1960's and his first memories of his first visit to the club in 1969 gives one an idea of the changing scene at the Cavern as the end of the decade approached. "I was pissed off with the Soul scene at the Mardi Gras club, that was becoming rather 'thuggish', and I decided to become a member of the Cavern club. I had heard from various sources, notably workmates older than me, about the slippery steps and the gloom on entering the club. But it was different from what I had been told. As I paid my entrance fee, watched over by Paddy Delaney, I was struck by the warm air wafting out from the doorway, and the old entrance with the slippery steps that once led directly into the cellar had now been closed. As I walked into the club I was distraught when I saw that the place was full of Mods – the very people that had driven me out of the Mardi Gras! However, it was soon pointed out to me that the place to be was across the floor and down the stairs that led to the basement. Across the floor I stumbled, to glares from the Mods, and descended into a Bohemian basement of tranquillity and wonderful strangeness. The D.J., Billy Butler was playing the terrific sounds of the Doors, the Stones, Procol Harem and the Velvet Underground. There were also incredibly sensual women and two live bands, from London, – no less! One look around and I was hooked. The pungent smell of incense burning and the aroma of smouldering reefers was evident. There was still the original stage, with the graffiti on the wall and rows of chairs in front of the stage, but I don't think any of us gave a thought to the old days. The Beatles had been and gone at the Cavern, but just like in their days at the club the walls still felt slimy. There was a pungent fruity stale smell and clinging damp that permeated down to your socks. I can remember my Mum barging into my bedroom on a Sunday morning, throwing open the windows and regaling me with her usual,

"You've been to that smelly cellar again – Pooh!"

Although the Halcyon days of the Beatles at the Cavern were now a fading memory, the beginning of the 1970's saw the club continuing to provide a good standard of musical fare. Roy Adams continued the Cavern tradition of bringing top acts from outside the Merseyside area to the club. Focus, Thin Lizzy, Vinegar Joe, Status Quo, Gary Glitter, Wishbone Ash, Supertramp and Judas Priest were just some of the top names to appear at the club in the early – 1970's.'

John Unsworth was a regular during this period and he would attend the club five nights a week, and he told me: *"The floor of the Cavern seemed to be an inch deep in sweat – I dread to think what it really was that we were paddling around in – but I enjoyed every minute of my time at the club. Admittedly there were drugs like LSD and Cannabis floating around , but no more than any other club during this period. The*

RAVE AT THE CAVE

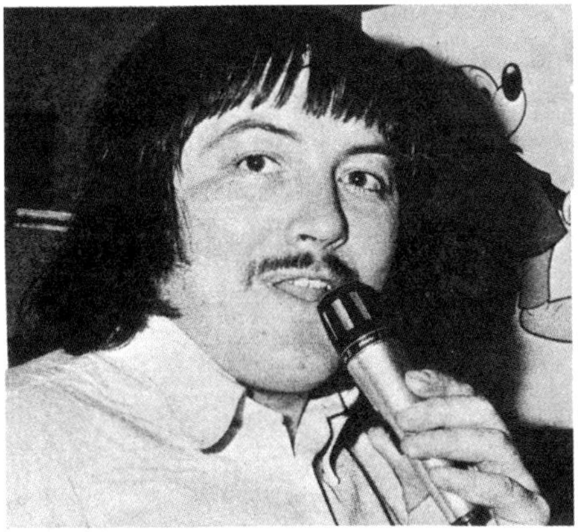

THERE'S a permanent fixture at the Cavern, and it's called Robbie Rave. He's the guy who plays all the latest music for you and he's been doing that since '61'. Robbie talked to our humble reporter (*that's me)* about some of the problems of being a D.J.

Robbie said his main problem was getting new releases accepted by the kids, and trying to get people to listen to local talent. Robbie reckons that a lot of local groups deserve to get a break. Though Robbie reckons that one local group *Strife* will certainly make it, since it all seems set fro them to cut a disc (lots of luck guys). Robbie is also pretty enthusiastic on an American band by the name of *The Eagles*, they've cut an L.P. in America and they also had three hits and at the moment they're planning an English tour, Robbie reckons they'll hit it real big.

Robbie is a D.J. and a half, he's a guy who knows his music and what people want to hear and I want to wish him lots of power to his stylus.

RON VAUGHAN.

majority of Cavern members were there for the excellent music and we were rarely disappointed. As soon as the doors to the club were opened, there would be a mad scramble down the stairs to get a good seat in front of the stage. The seats there were just like church pews and were soon filled up. The D.J.'s were backstage and you couldn't see them, but you could tell who they were by the way they introduced the bands. At the stage entrance all the groupies would hang out, and these girls could tell you anything you wanted to know about the bands that played at the Cavern. There were coach trips organised to Pop Festivals and all the Cavern members knew each other. It was really like one big happy family. The café at the club was the place to chat, because it was the furthest place away from the music. I remember that Molly the cook, did great egg and chips. There was one local band who were very good, called the Klubbs, who were on most nights. Everyone looked forward to hearing them and they always gave a good show. They later changed their name to Strife. When the original Cavern closed and moved across the road to the other side of Matthew Street, most of the regulars moved elsewhere, because there just wasn't the same atmosphere there."

* * *

The club was so busy I decided to extend the basement sideways to next door. I made the applications and got on with it and was actually decorating with a Black Magic theme, the inspector came and inspected the new concrete stairway, he said the bottom step was minimally out something like a quarter of an inch. He instructed me to completely rebuild it; although I'm sure I could have rectified it, this staircase was solid concrete – a hell of a job. So we got on with it. A few weeks later I received a letter from the council informing me that I had eight weeks to vacate the premises as British Rail were taking it over. I got on to them and they informed me that they had written to the Cavern several times with the notifications.

I presume mail had gone to the previous owner who kept stum! I managed to get a bit of a delay on the order and wrote to various celebrities like Cilla Black, The Beatles and others, and heard nothing! Letters were coming in from all over the world. Offering me support and begging me not to let it close, there was nothing I could do. In the last weeks, groups were clamouring to play the Cavern. One band, the Yardley's actually came over from America with all their gear, just to play. They continued to keep in touch with Freda for years after. T.V companies came to film the place and in fact, I still have a 16mm film, a copy of which was the fee I charged to let them film the Cavern. That was a Dutch film Company and coincidently the featured band was Amsterdam Lil.

The final night of The Cavern would be on Sunday May 27th 1973.

In the days before the Cavern's last night, I was quoted in the Echo: "It's going to be a sad and nostalgic occasion. I would like to see part of the cellar preserved as a tourist attraction. I think it could be done and would be worth the effort." But that plea too would fall on deaf ears.

I had special tickets printed up with some of the names of the most popular bands who'd played there over the years, proclaiming: "End of an Era, the last night of the Old Cavern, Liverpool's world-famous club." Inside we printed the names of the final bands to grace the stage: "One last attempt to bring this famous roof down will be made tonight by: Strife, Hackensack, Harpoon, Supercharge, Bilf Slat and the Yardleys". The DJs for the

This week-end the old Cavern closes for good and members move to a new cellar on the opposite side of Mathew Street. This article looks at the club's future in the age of the teeny boppers...

Will there be a new Mersey Sound?

by Alfred Green and Peter Trollope

extract from the Liverpool Echo, May 1973

ORIGINALLY the Cavern was a raw, primitive place. It made no pretence at sophistication in either the facilities or the music it provided.

The hypnotic beat of the Mersey Sound was the only intoxicant dispensed on the premises and, at that time, it was all that was needed by the young disciples of the embryo pop stars.

Since then, the Cavern has changed its style as well as its sound. The members moving into the new cellar, on the opposite side of Mathew Street, are at least a couple of years older than their predecessors.

They believe in another style of music, the "progressive" style and "heavy" sound typified by groups like Ten Years After, Pink Floyd, Focus, King Crimson and Yes, currently regarded as one of the brand leaders.

The new Cavern members also like Bacardi with their Coke and gin with their orange juice. They represent the generations between the Beatles and the Jackson Five.

"We shall not be catering for the other facet of the pop scene – the teenyboppers," says Mr. Roy Adams, at present master-minding the switch from one cellar to another.

● *Keith Chegwin: Will he put the Mersey Sound back at the top?*

"This is our scene – 18 plus – and we will be giving them the sort of music they like in surroundings which will be bigger and better than the original Cavern, but with just as much atmosphere."

The new headquarters, once part of the old fruit exchange, are steeped in history, some of the cellar walls having been built by French prisoners during the Napoleonic wars.

"I've also discovered that the first horse-drawn railway vehicles used to come in where the new main hall is going to be," says Mr. Adams. "They came in from Mathew Street and then went to Victoria Street and eventually to Park Lane depot."

Capable of holding around 2,000 people, the new Cavern will have two levels – both below the ground – providing a separate disco as well as the main area for live performances.

"The main cellar offers better vision than the old one, although we have retained the pillars because the fans seem to like them so much. A specially designed sloping roof above the stage should help to give better acoustics," says Mr. Adams, who puts the cost of the conversion work at around £35,000.

Will the new Cavern produce a new Mersey Sound? Mr. Adams smiled cheerfully and answered: "I hope so. There is still a lot of local talent around which is just coming to the surface, and we like to give talented but unknown groups, a chance."

Following the departure of the Beatles from the active pop scene, the younger fans found themselves without any identifiable idols.

Then came Slade, the Osmonds, David Cassidy, the Jackson Five and T. Rex, filling the gap left behind by the gradual switch to a more serious style of music.

The teenyboppers were too young to appreciate the progressive and heavy groups that fascinated their elder brothers and sisters.

A song called "One Bad Apple", by the Osmonds, started the new bandwagon rolling and the timid cries at concerts grew into a shriek when Marc Bolan swopped his acoustic guitar for an electronic one, and switched on the new generation.

Slade appeared from out of nowhere. They had previously tried to cash in on a skinhead image, and just discovered in time that the youngsters needed heroes not anti-heroes.

The kids knew exactly what they wanted. It didn't matter that they might never be able to touch Donny Osmond. They had plenty of pictures of him – and he was singing for each of them.

Tin Pan Alley detected the smell of gold in the air again – just as it had at the Cavern, a decade earlier. Fan clubs sprang up again, and the age of some of the performers produced yet another phenomena – the weeny-bopper, aged between seven and 12 years and just as well informed as the older fans.

The Osmonds and the Jackson Five had their own idols for the weenies – Jimmy and Randy – and Britain suddenly found Ricky Wilde, the son of singer Marty Wilde. It s unlikely that the new Cavern will become involved in this scene, but Liverpool is about to stake a claim for the hearts of a new generation of fans with 16-years-old Keith Chegwin.

He was born on January 17, 1957, has never been to the Cavern and does not remember much about Beatlemania. But down in London they reckon he is about to answer the dreams of the teenies and weenies with his first record "I'll Take You Back" which is to be released on June 1.

Keith, a twin, was first discovered singing on the programme Junior Showtime when he was 12 and since then has appeared in a number of films, including Roman Polanski's version of Macbeth.

But it is his singing career on which his highest hopes are pinned at the moment. "I love singing and appearing on the stage," he says calmly. And I think I can identify with the fans, because I'm their age and know exactly how they feel and the music they like."

Will the Liverpool group Strife take the new Cavern into tomorrow's headlines? Or will it be Keith Chegwin who puts the Mersey Sound back at the top of the charts? Or will it be someone still waiting to be discovered?

Anyone who knows the answer to these questions, and has a little bit of luck, might end up as rich as the Beatles and leave Merseyside with another legend for future generations to remember.

● *A smile for the future from Roy Adams in Mathew Street. The old Cavern is on the right and the new premises on the extreme left.*

End of an Era

BEATLES - GALLIARD - TOBIAS WOLFE - DOGFEET - WOODFALL - AMSTERDAM LIL - PATTO - BUTCH - POSSESSED - PARLOUR BAND - JERUASALEM SMITH FLYING HAT BAND - KLUBBS - EAST OF EDEN - YARDBIRDS - PRETTY THINGS AMON DUUL - GARY GLITTER - HELLO SAILOR - WILSON PICKET - FOCUS GEORDIE - BLACKFOOT SUE - ARGENT - ROLLING STONES - VINEGAR JOE - BABE RUTH - STATUS QUO - SWINGING BLUE JEANS - GREASY BEAR - THE ESCORTS FREDDIE STARR & THE MIDNIGHTERS - GERRY & THE PACEMAKERS - RORY STORM & THE HURRICANES - CILLA BLACK - HERMANS HERMITS - BILLY J. KRAMER - BEN E. KING - SONNY WEBB & THE CASCADES - WAYNE FONTANA & THE MINDBENDERS - THE SEARCHERS - JOHNNY KIDD & THE PIRATES - BUDGIE STEVIE WONDER - CHANTS - FREDDIE & THE DREAMERS - THE UNDERTAKERS WILD TURKEY - CAPABILITY BROWN - ALEX HARVEY BAND - INCREDIBLE HOG SATURMALIA - ETC. - ETC. - BEATLES - GALLIARD - TOBIAS WOLFE - DOGFEET WOODFALL - AMSTERDAM LIL - PATTO - BUTCH - POSSESSED - PARLOUR BAND JERUSALEM SMITH - FLYING HAT BAND - KLUBBS - EAST OF EDEN - YARDBIRDS PRETTY THINGS - AMON DUUL - GARY GLITTER - HELLO SAILOR - WILSON PICKET FOCUS - GEORDIE - BLACKFOOT SUE - ARGENT - ROLLING STONES - VINEGAR JOE - BABE RUTH - STATUS QUO - SWINGING BLUE JEANS - GREASY BEAR - THE ESCORTS - FREDDIE STARR & THE MIDNIGHTERS - GERRY & THE PACEMAKERS RORY STORM & THE HURRICANES - CILLA BLACK - HERMANS HERMITS BILLY J. KRAMER - BEN E. KING - SONNY WEBB & THE CASCADES - WAYNE FONTANA & THE MINDBENDERS - THE SEARCHERS - JOHNNY KIDD & THE PIRATES - BUDGIE - STEVIE WONDER - CHANTS - FREDDIE & THE DREAMERS THE UNDERTAKERS - WILD TURKEY - CAPABILITY BROWN - ALEX HARVEY BAND INCREDIBLY HOG - SATURMALIA - ETC. - ETC. - BEATLES - GALLIARD - TOBIAS WOLFE - DOGFEET - WOODFALL - AMSTERDAM LIL - PATTO - BUTCH - POSSESSED PARLOUR BAND - JERUSALEM SMITH - FLYING HAT BAND - KLUBBS - EAST OF EDEN - YARDBIRDS - PRETTY THINGS - AMON DUUL - GARY GLITTER - HELLO SAILOR - WILSON PICKET - FOCUS - GEORDIE - BLACKFOOT SUE - ARGENT ROLLING STONES - VINEGAR JOE - BABE RUTH - STATUS QUO - SWINGING BLUE JEANS - GREASY BEAR - THE ESCORTS - FREDDIE STARR & THE MIDNIGHTERS GERRY & THE PACEMAKERS - RORY STORM & THE HURRICANES - CILLA BLACK

LAST NIGHT OF THE OLD

CAVERN

LIVERPOOL'S WORLD-FAMOUS CLUB

SUNDAY, MAY 27, 1973

TICKET £1·25

One last attempt to bring this famous roof down will be made tonight by

STRIFE

HACKENSACK

HARPOON

SUPERCHARGE

BILF SLAT

YARDLEYS

THE WORLD'S MOST FAMOUS CLUB

D.J.s

ROBBIE RAVE **RICKY McCABE** **BILLY BUTLER**

JOEY WALL

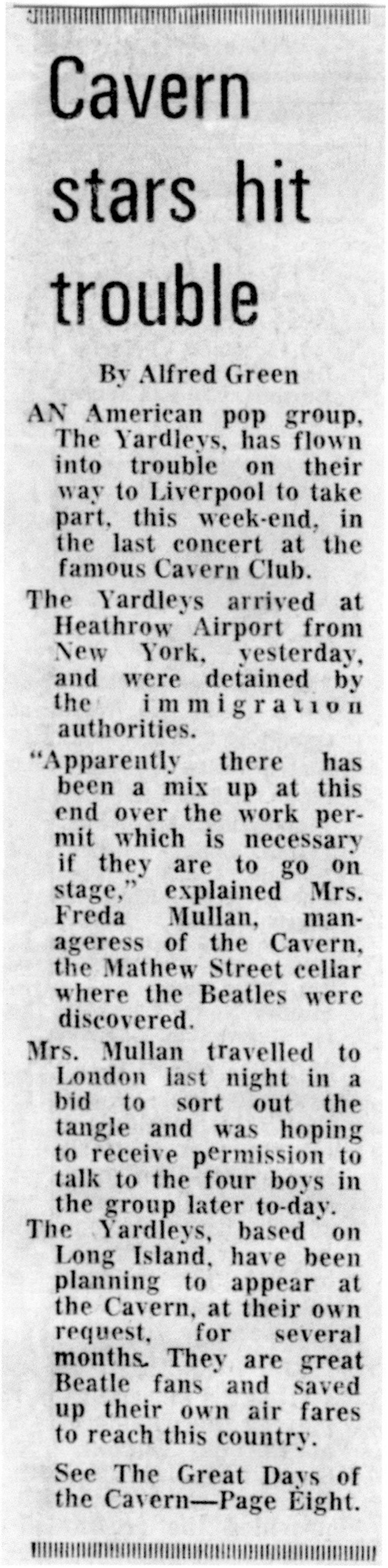

Cavern stars hit trouble

By Alfred Green

AN American pop group, The Yardleys, has flown into trouble on their way to Liverpool to take part, this week-end, in the last concert at the famous Cavern Club.

The Yardleys arrived at Heathrow Airport from New York, yesterday, and were detained by the immigration authorities.

"Apparently there has been a mix up at this end over the work permit which is necessary if they are to go on stage," explained Mrs. Freda Mullan, manageress of the Cavern, the Mathew Street cellar where the Beatles were discovered.

Mrs. Mullan travelled to London last night in a bid to sort out the tangle and was hoping to receive permission to talk to the four boys in the group later to-day.

The Yardleys, based on Long Island, have been planning to appear at the Cavern, at their own request, for several months. They are great Beatle fans and saved up their own air fares to reach this country.

See The Great Days of the Cavern—Page Eight.

evening were Robbie Rave, who was our house DJ at the time, as well as others who were regulars including Ricky McCabe, Joey Wall and Billy Butler. Each ticket cost £1.25.

But on the back of the ticket, I offered a glimmer of hope to the crowd: "Start of an Era: The New Cavern is still in Matthew Street only eight yards away at No. 7 – watch press for announcements". I had taken out a lease on a building directly opposite. I would call it the New Cavern.

Before that though, we had just one more night to get through at the Old Cavern, and what a night it was; the place was absolutely packed nd the street outside was too. It seemed that we had reporters and film cameras everywhere. The bands played all night, the music was loud and no one wanted to go home. In the end I think we shut the doors at six o'clock in the morning.

Now you might think that we were all sad that night, but that's not how I remember it at all. Because we were getting ready to open the New Cavern, all the conversation was about the future and not the past. Someone said: "At least the toilets won't flood when the tide comes in!"

*   *   *

I've never forgiven the Council who were obviously aware what was happening for making me rebuild that staircase! I took on the premises across the street in the old Fruit Exchange, and set about building the New Cavern. I converted both the ground floor and the basement – a big job! I particularly remember having to create access through one of the basement walls to the lavatory areas. These walls turned out to be seven feet thick, metal filings had been mixed in the composition of the bricks. We found that hammers and chisels, and even mechanical drills, made no impression. After four men had spent a week working in pairs with practically no effect, I had to call in Blaster Bates who eventually succeeded with it actually creating a short passageway through the wall. Apparently French prisoners built these walls during the time of the Napoleonic War, some of the prisoners being housed at St Nicholas's church at that time. They certainly knew a bit about making bricks!

The New Cavern featured bands like the Runaways, which was an all-girl band, average age 16, very raunchy – we had to have the doormen up front to stop the lads from storming the stage whilst the girls taunted and beckoned them. I booked Wizard to appear one night and the place was packed out. Due to a cock up at the docks, their gear had been misdirected on their return from a continental tour. This meant they had to hire equipment for their gig. They arrived in a very disgruntled mood. When they appeared on stage, Roy Wood wasn't wearing his customary make up, which was a main feature of his act. They also cut their act down to forty-five minutes and refused to do an encore! This infuriated me, as I was paying them £1,000 plus VAT, a lot of money in 1974. My two youngest children wanted to get the bands' autographs, so I knocked on the dressing room door leaving the children with one of the doormen. One of the roadies opened the door with a "Whadya want?" loud and aggressive.

Freda, Roy's sister

I said: "I want to see Roy Wood".

"Well you can't!"

I shoved him out of the way and stormed in. I saw this pathetic white skinny figure, seated with his chest on his knees, looking completely spaced out. I thought, my God, it's true about these guys – wonder what he's on!

I said to the roadie: "Where's Roy Wood?" – he pointed to this wreck, and I stormed out, completely disgusted.

A short while later I booked American band the Chilites, their attitude was the complete opposite of Wizards, they felt privileged to be appearing in Liverpool's Matthew Street and couldn't have done more to please. A terrific act.

During the mid 1970s, government minister Michael Heseltine was sent to Liverpool to assist in regeneration of the city. Various projects were set up including the wonderful buildings set around the Anglican Cathedral which are I believe retirement and student accommodation and the Liverpool Garden Festival not forgetting the Albert Dock complex. Local architect David Backhouse came up with the idea of rebuilding the original Cavern as the central feature of a new tourist attraction in the Mathew street area. Royal Insurance were the backers. David brought in a very talented Architect called Dominic McCannon to assist him in the project. Dom was a friend of mine having met through him doing designs and plans on some of my varied little projects. The old Cavern had been demolished a couple of years earlier so they had a vacant plot to work on, currently used as a car park. When the machines were brought in to scrape the surface to investigate the foundations, they exposed three yawning holes about four or five feet across which they decided to investigate. David Backhouse first and then Dominic, were lowered down in a bucket to see what was below. Imagine their astonishment when they discovered three

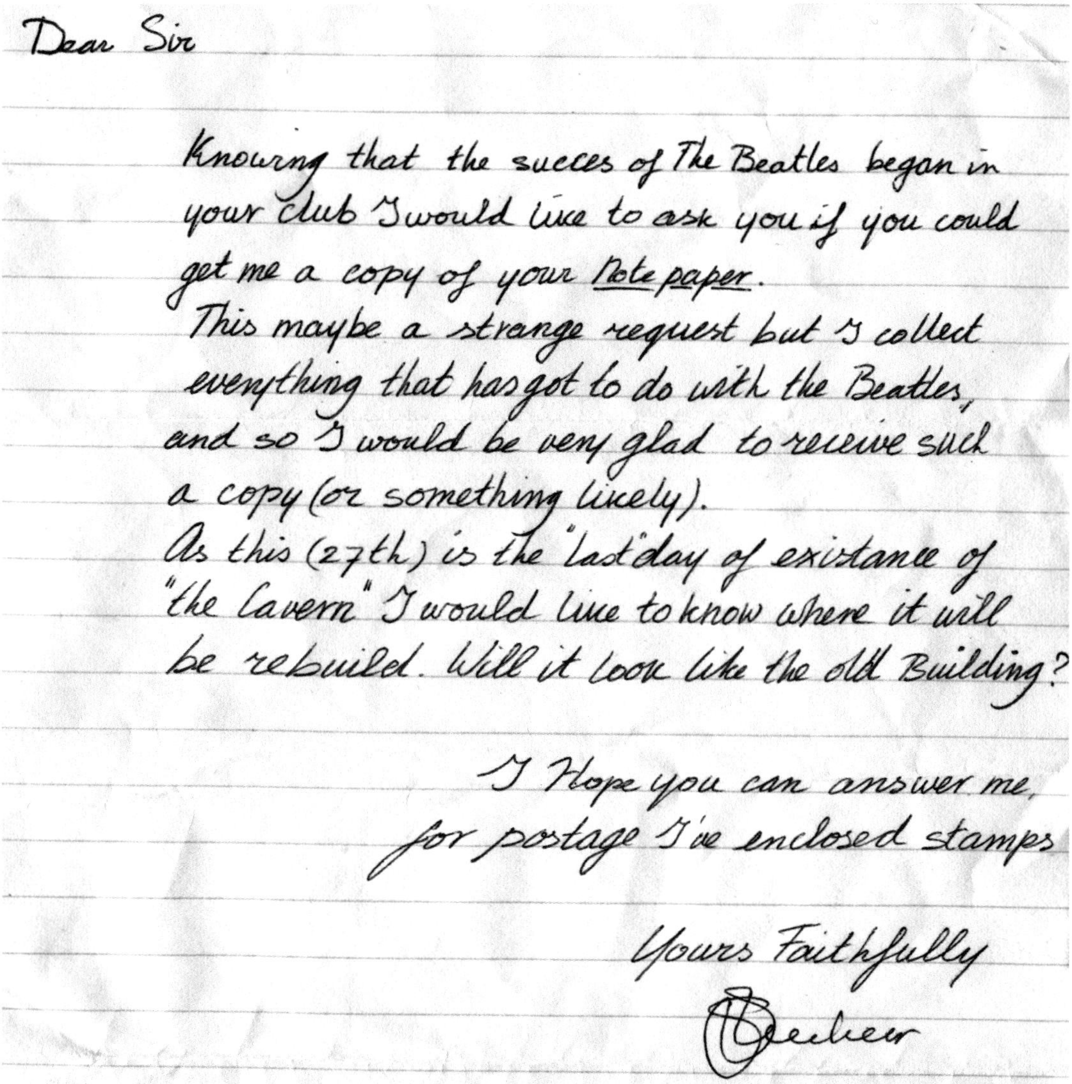

Dear Sir

Knowing that the succes of The Beatles began in your club I would like to ask you if you could get me a copy of your Notepaper.
This maybe a strange request but I collect everything that has got to do with the Beatles, and so I would be very glad to receive such a copy (or something likely).
As this (27th) is the "last day" of existance of "the Cavern" I would like to know where it will be rebuild. Will it look like the old Building?

I Hope you can answer me,
for postage I've enclosed stamps

Yours Faithfully

tunnels hewn out of solid rock. These tunnels were thirty-two feet high and sixteen feet across. They also contained water. They were roughly two hundred feet long. Royal Insurance supplied lights and canoes and arranged to have it filmed. Dave climbed into a dingy attached to a rope and set off along one of the tunnels, however as he approached the dark and unknown, he panicked a bit and yanked on the rope and they pulled him back.

They presumed that these tunnels provided access from the river Mersey to the auction rooms and the fruit exchange across what used to be Mathew Pluckington Street, now Mathew Street, they also found some wooden structures down there which were presumably used to load the barges. A manhole has been retained close to the new Cavern, which still provides access to the tunnels; this could be another attraction for brave tourists.

A local historian Jack Cooper thinks its unlikely that barges would have been used because that would require horses to pull them, he also thinks that access may have come from the Pul pronounced Pool, located in the Whitechapel area which was a series of very basic docks starting at what later became the Custom House. It was destroyed by bombing in the second world war – its now Liverpool's main Police Headquarters. These docks follow a slightly erratic pattern right up to what is now Whitechapel. Jack also told me that there used to be a major shop years ago, which had buildings facing each other each side of Whitechapel. They were joined by an underground tunnel, which was lit by a single gas lamp. If there was a high tide and the tunnels flooded, the shop manager used to swim to the gas lamp and put it out because of the danger of escaping gas should the water put it out.

Apparently, there are still many tunnels in that area of the city. Incidentally, the brown moss formed on the walls by the damp was known as Lire the ancient English name for brown – Hence LIREPUL! (brown walls)

The new Cavern archways were constructed at right angles to the original necessitated by the air vent put in for the new railway line. Dave Backhouse brought in various Cavern personalities to sign the wall behind the stage inviting everyone he could think of connected to the original Cavern. Unfortunately, he forgot about me the last owner of the original Cavern.

The current Cavern which was rebuilt on the original site is still vibrant – being successfully run and promoted by C. S. Tours – owned by Bill Heckle, Dave Jones and George Guinness.

They also have a wall with the names of all the groups who played the old Cavern carved into the bricks and the names of various owners. They've got fourteen owners names, but I can only think of five from the original club.

Alan Sytner 1956
Ray Macfall 1959-66
Joe Davy and Alf Geoghegan 1966-69
Roy Adams 1969-73 (New Cavern 1973-76)

How I came to be on this prestigious list is my story.

Cavern advert, taken from NITE-OUT No. 10 – "The Paper that stays awake all night"

article and picture from the Sunday Times, February 4th, 1973

Rubbishing the Beatle shrine

By David Blundy

BEATLEMANIA began to twitch back into life in Liverpool last week as ageing fans campaigned to save the Cavern, birthplace of the Beatles and the tunes the world danced to in the Sixties.

The only new sounds likely to emanate from the Cavern in 1973 are the roar of bulldozers and the rhythmic rattle of pneumatic drills. British Rail, planning an underground loop line, will be sinking a waste disposal shaft through the place where the young John, Paul George and Ringo strummed their first notes.

The Cavern is a small, dark hole in the wall off Mathew Street in the centre of Liverpool. It smells dank, the bare brick walls are pitted with ancient slogans *(Up with CND; I Love Paul)* and at least one rat scuttled out of the gents on Thursday evening. But the owner, Roy Adams, feels it ought to be a Grade 1 listed building at least on a par with Liverpool Cathedral.

"We get more visitors down here than the Cathedral does," says Adams. "We get Americans, Canadians, Japanese, French, Dutch, Germans. There's no justice in it."

He says he would have put up a more vigorous fight but British Rail's notice to quit was delivered a year ago to the wrong address and he received it only recently.

"The kids are signing petitions and they even offer to stage a sit-in when the demolition men start work," he says.

The Beatles, after the rounds of Lancashire dance halls, came to the club in 1961. They played there 292 times, mostly at lunchtime, for about £1 each a show, which was 13 shillings more than Cilla Black got for looking after the cloakroom.

Patrick Delaney was chief doorman then. A broken nose, a cracked rib, a split lip and 12 years later, he is still chief doorman. He remembers the time Paul McCartney tried to borrow a halfpenny off him for a cheese roll. "I lent him a penny. He's never paid it back actually."

Bob Wooler, resident DJ at the Cavern for eight years, introduced every one of the 292 Beatles performances. "They'd take it in turns to be late for a performance. Their act was a calculated affront to the Establishment. The kids loved it," he says.

"The club was so packed in those days steam would rise out of the ventilators into the street. People had to be lifted over the heads of the crowd into the lavatory." The adulation was so great that in 1965 people bought bits of the original wooden stage at five bob a time.

The Mersey Sound began to fade towards the end of 1965 and in the following year the club went bankrupt and closed down for two months. It was reopened with great ceremony by Harold Wilson, then Prime Minister, and the late Bessie Braddock, who were both made honorary Cavern Club members.

The Cavern still plays a nostalgic half-hour of Beatle music at midnight but most members prefer to rave to other Liverpool groups.

The Beatles themselves are showing less concern than British Rail over the club that helped to make them rich and famous. Ringo has said he might make a sentimental journey. Paul McCartney has expressed an interest. Not a word from George or John.

"British Rail have been very decent," says Adams. "They are trying to find a way of saving the club. The only possibility is shifting the disposal shaft and putting a concrete roof over the club. That could cost us £20,000."

"All we need," says Bob Wooler, "is a little help from our friends."

A long, long time after the Beatles: Wild Turkey, one of last week's groups at the Cavern

HISTORIC CAVERN CLUB GIVEN 3-MONTH REPRIEVE

LIVERPOOL, England—The clock was seconds away from striking midnight February 10th when a man in evening dress took the microphone from the lead singer of the rock group. "May I have your attention for a moment," he half-asked, half-ordered the crowd of teenagers. "Complete silence, please." The kids complied, many of them recognizing the man as club owner Roy Adams.

"We have heard today from British Rail that we have a three-month extension on the Cavern," Adams announced. Cheers rose from the 2000 young people in the place. Great Britain's mass audience and music papers, meanwhile, began rewriting the premature obituaries they had published about the club where the Beatles played 292 shows in the early Sixties.

British Rail is constructing an underground in Liverpool, and an excavation shaft will plow through the Cavern sometime later this year. Adams said he had a new site picked out, "but it will take me five months to fix it up. We've got to find a place for the kids to go during the two-month interim." The place may well be his own Pyramid Club, five minutes away from the Cavern.

Adams, 40, is a physical culture devotee who insists he is not a rich man despite his three clubs, 20-room home and Bentley Rolls. He also is less emotional than some people who are clamoring to save the spot that spawned the Beatles.

"You have to think of the future of the city and the development of the area," he said. "We're out of character."

To say the least. The Cavern is extremely grotty, a dirty surface floor beneath an abandoned warehouse on a narrow side street.

"But even if we moved," Adams added, "the original cellar room where the Beatles played could be preserved. The city could keep it as a monument. It's already a tourist attraction."

Manageress Freda Mullan, Adams' sister, confirmed visits to the club during the previous week by Argentinian, American, Dutch and Spanish pilgrims, along with the usual quota of Britishers.

Before Adams' announcement, US and European press photographers visited the club for "last-minute" pictures, and SAVE THE CAVERN! petitions and letters poured in from around the world. A letter from Cuba, written in Spanish, thanked the club for making possible "The Chicagos." Another fan wrote: "Would they let British Rail go through Shakespeare's birthplace?" A letter in Disc concluded emotionally: "Lennon wept."

Alan Williams, an early Beatles mentor, received the Cavern news in stride. "You should take the ferry across the Mersey while you're here," he advised a visitor. "They're getting rid of that next."

—Paul Gambaccini

Cavern has a week to find new home

The proprietor of the Cavern Club, which gave birth to the Beatles, last night began a frenzied search for new premises.

For the world-famous warehouse premises in Mathew Street, which wrote a new chapter in Liverpool's history, is to come down to make way for part of the city's new underground rail loop.

The club will close next Wednesday unless its owner, Mr. Roy Adams, persuades the authorities to let him stay there until the bulldozers actually move in.

But if the shock to th thousands of r was hardly le Adams, for a serving notic in the dark ten months longer than necessary.

When notices to quit were served on adjoining properties 12 months ago, the owners of the warehouse mistakenly notified a previous owner of the Cavern Club.

Mr. Adams heard the news only in November, final confimra-

he said last night. "We have members all over the world, and we have tourists calling her con stantly.

'I have been asked about the Cavern in Australia, Singapore and Japan, and broadcast about it in Canada. In the past two years alone we have had eight foreign crews here."

keep

Adams, and a home would be found for the membership. But the £10,000 ploughed into the Cavern over the past 18 months will be written off.

And the club that started the Merseyside explosion, immortalised in book and song as "A Cellarful of Noises," will be marked by nothing more romantic than an extraction duct into the underground tunnels.

articles from the Liverpool Echo, 1973

Cavern Club to close

LIVERPOOL'S famous Cavern Club is to follow two of London's Sundown chain in closing. The Sundowns — at Brixton and Mile End — closed last Thursday.

The Cavern, which was the spawning ground of the Beatles and other groups from the Merseybeat era is to be demolished to make way for an underground railway line.

Owner Roy Adams said last week: "We've got to go — there's nothing we can do about it. We are definitely staying open until the weekend of February 3 — after that we're living from day to day."

Bands booked to appear at later dates will be asked to play at the near-by Pyramid Club, one the Iron Door, original home of the Searchers, and Billy J Kramer. A new Cavern Club will be opening somewhere in the city centre.

The two Sundowns have been handed back to Rank Leisure Services, the company that owns them.

But the Sundown Edmonton will continue to operate, because it is still attracting large crowds. It is not yet known how existing bookings will be affected.

John Conlan, General Manager of the Sundown group told the MM: "There are not enough big names around to enable us to keep three theatres running — it is this that has caused the closure of the other venues. As yet, we have no plans for re-opening them."

Playing for kicks—by Paul

"IF IT had been physically possible, I would certainly have gone along to the old Cavern to kiss it goodbye," said Paul McCartney, whose fame, with the other Beatles, started in that arched cellar, now to be destroyed.

But Paul, with his new group, Wings, was in Liverpool for only 24 hours, performing two shows before 5,000 people at the Empire on Friday; and next day they were due in Leeds.

"When I heard the Cavern had to go in the near future, I wanted to take the group with me on a farewell surprise visit for an hour, after our Empire show. But there just wasn't the time available.

"I'd have loved to have done it. After all, for The Beatles and a lot of other folk who eventually made it, the Cavern was where it all began. Even if we did work more for the kicks than the money in those good old days."

● *To Beatle fans the Cavern soon became a shrine in those heady days of the sixties.*

To open cut here

Prease tell me about CAVERN CLUB and

about BEATLES!

I will PAY mony about it. (STAMP's mony)

So Prease tell me!

I'm Japanease girl and Beatles Fian. (PAUL McCARTNEY's best)

Prease tell me about CAVERN CLUB and BEATLES!

Prease wrishe back.

I'm Waiting for your Letter!

1975 JUL. 13

Dear Sir.

I am a boy, 18, I attend a school for accountants (sigh!),
I am a boy, 18, I attend a school for accountants (sigh!),
I play the guitar and I am a super Beatles fan.
I've found your name in a Italian magazine where there was
an article about the "Cavern" how it's today.
So I decided to write to you for asking if you can help me.
Can you ask for a boy, if he want to become my pen-pal?
In your club there are a lot of teen-agers ev'ryday, so you
can do it easily. Can't you?
If you can't find me an English friend, please, give me an
answer at least. Excuse me for my bad English!
Thank you very much! Grazie infinite!!

Salutoni
CIAO

Your sincerelly

Francesco Cavallini

extract from the Liverpool Echo, May 23rd, 1973

When Cilla would give them a song at the drop of a hat

The Beatles were the biggest stars to emerge from the Cavern. But that smoky cellar in Mathew Street also launched Cilla Black, Gerry Marsden and Billy J. Kramer.

This is the third article about the exciting days in that "cellarful of sound" which closes for demolitionat the week-end.

by George Harrison

AFTER a boys' club charity show I had attended in September, 1957, I wrote in my Mersey Wall page in the Echo: "One of the acts was a rock 'n skiffle group, a quartet of youngsters from dingle, headed by 14-year-old Gerry Marsden as guitarist-vocalist. With a bit of experience, these lads, particularly the bubbling Gerry, could be top class. They provided some of the gayest entertainment I've struck in months."

When Gerry left school and went as van-lad for British Rail, he and his group worked nights in dance halls, clubs, and, of course, at the Cavern. By now their name was Gerry and the Pacemakers and their throbbing tempo, with Gerry as vocalist, started to earn them the kind of Liverpool reputation the Beatles enjoyed.

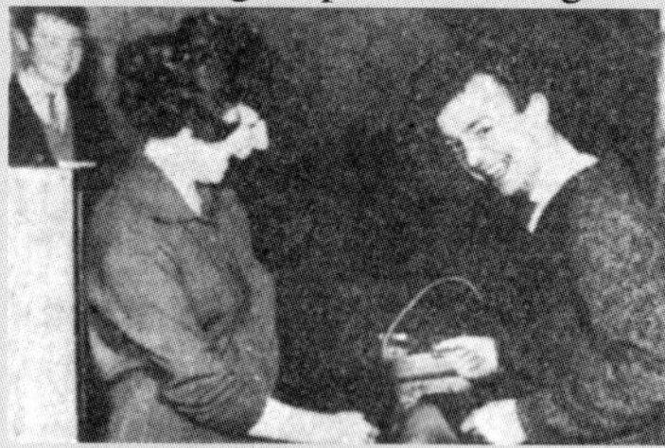

Dancing at the Cavern – Cilla Black and Gerry Marsden

The Remo Four

Says Gerry: "They were great days at the Cavern. We joined the Beatles in lunch-time or evening sessions and, at the drop of a hat, young Cilla would bet on stage with us and sing. She worked there as a hat-check girl."

When Brian Epstein signed up to manage the Beatles, Gerry went to see him and asked if he would manage them, too. He agreed and as success began rolling for the Beatles, it rolled for the Pacemakers.

The cavern fans were wildly delighted that their judgement had again been proved right to the rest of the country. The first three records made by Gerry and the Pacemakers ALL went to the top place in the charts, a record in itself.

Remember them? The first was "How Do You Do It?" Then, late in 1963, they took a chance with a totally different song, a straight ballad–"You'll Never Walk Alone".

Not only did this beautiful number hit the top; it also became the theme song for Liverpool's great Kop choir at Anfield. To be followed later by practically every football club's supporters through the land. But it still belongs to the Cavern and the Kop.

While all this was going on, the "Cellarful of Noise" kept bringing out new Merseyside talent. To Brian Epstein goes the full credit for spotting the well-hidden potential of Miss Priscilla White, the hat-check girl with the auburn hair and the perky smile.

At the Cavern one afternoon, in August, 1963, when she jumped up to sing, Brian stood enthralled and pictured what she would look like on giant London stage with full production around her.

He took her on one side and told her he would manage her. Says Cilla (Brian's first managerial decision was to change her name to Cilla Black): "I couldn't believe it. The idea of working for Brian, with the Beatles and the Pacemakers, just turned me on."

A month later the gal from the Cavern made her first record. The following February she recorded "Anyone Who Has A Heart", and it soared to No. 1 in the hit parade.

Rather sadly, she told me not long ago: "I don't think I could go back to the Cavern, although I loved the place. I'm a bit too old for it now." What? At 29 this month.

Ronnie Owens, who ran a popular group under the name of Lee Castle and the Barons, confessed, "Although everybody thought the world of Cilla, I don't think anyone really believed that Epstein could make her into a star. Here favourite number was 'Fever', and she sort of squeaked the top notes. But all the groups used to know this and we helped her out by hitting it loud."

● *Does the face behind the counter seem familiar? This picture of Cilla Black dates from the time when she worked at the Cavern, where she was spotted by Brian Epstein and launched on her way to stardom.*

Loud was the Cavern's rhythm slogan. The music had to bounce off the cellar roof and through the arches to make the kids appreciate it. Rory Storm and the Hurricanes had the touch. So did the Swinging Blue Jeans who had a following of fans as great as those of the Beatles for a long time.

Brian Epstein's "stable of stars" grew steadily as success in recordings came his way. A very warm-voiced Bootle boy named Billy Ashton, singing under the name of Billy Kramer and backed by a group called The Coasters, had won Cavern acclaim. They took the top award as the best non-professional group in the area and Billy thought they ought to turn full-time professional.

But the boys in the Coasters considered it too risky, as they all had good jobs and played only as a side-line. The man who had guided them through their career to date, part-time manager Ted Knibbs, agreed with Billy and unselfishly offered to see Brian Epstein and talk to him about taking over Billy's contract, as Brian was more likely to help the lad with his future as a solo singer.

Ted Knibbs was as good as his word. He, Brian and Billy Kramer met in the Nems office in Whitechapel. There was £50 outstanding to Knibbs for expenses he had incurred on Billy's account, Brian agreed to pay that and thereupon took over Kramer's sole management.

His first act was the inspiration of putting a "J" into the name and making Billy Ashton into Billy J. Kramer. But Ted Knibbs told me later, when Billy had become famous, "I never did get that fifty quid from Brian."

Under the Epstein banner, Billy J. was whipped away from Liverpool to record in London. He leapt to the top with "Do You Want To Know A Secret?" then toured America and Down Under with tremendous success. The cavern saw him no more, except when he popped in to say hello.

He became No. 1 in the hit charts three times in one year, 1964, and the Cavern crowds gloated in his triumphs as he was "one of ours!"

That fierce belief of everything Liverpool being the greatest, so far as the fans were concerned, carried the old Cavern through a decade of good and bad. With so many would-be stars battling for a place in the sun, many had to fall into the shadows. And they did.

Scores of groups of varying talent took the stage, hopefully dreaming that they, too, would be discovered and lifted to fortune. But the vital spark had gone from the cellar. There was no more gold left there to find.

extract from the Liverpool Echo, April 5th, 1976

The only sound is silence in the cellar full of noise

JIM MANSELL ON THE END OF A CHAPTER IN POP MUSIC HISTORY

MATHEW STREET will never be the same again. On Saturday night Liverpool's world-famous Cavern Club will close its doors for the last time. Sadly, it will mark the end of a glorious chapter in the city's history–but the memories, Beatles and all, will linger on.

The Cavern sign, says the club's present owner, Roy Adams, will be taken down and sold. But never ever will Liverpool forget that raw, primitive Mersey beat sound and atmosphere which floated up this cobbled city centre lane to stop the music world in its tracks.

Dwindling attendances have forced the closure from the weekend of a club whose name is probably known to more people than, say, Buckingham Palace.

The original Cavern was demolished in 1973 to make way for Merseyside's rail loop line. To maintain the famous tradition , the club was moved across the street from No. 10, but sadly, the decline in its popularity began with the decision to move the Beatles' operation to London.

January, 1957, saw the start of it all when the Cavern became a jazz centre. Some of the top bands of the day played there–Chris Barber, Humphrey Lyttleton, Acker Bilk.

The transformation came at the turn of the last decade when it became a beat club. The birth of a sound and a centre which was

● *Recognise them? Yes, its Cilla Black and Gerry Marsden dancing at a lunchtime session at the Cavern in the days before their professional singing careers began.*

● *The Cavern in action. Now it's almost all over.*

to become a shrine for teenagers from all over the world was about to take place.

Brian Epstein was the man who ensured a safe delivery for the package which teenagers had been seeking. They wanted a sound that was different. They wanted a new set of stars to worship. He ensured that the Beatles and the Cavern provided just that.

He took this raw-bone group of Liverpudlians and turned them into the hottest property that music has ever known.

Mathew Street and the Cavern were alive with thousands of youngsters hypnotised by the glamour of it all. They were swept along by the new atmosphere, Cliff, Elvis and Bill Haley had to take back seats. The Mersey sound had taken the unsuspecting pop world by storm.

But what was so magical about this cellar called the Cavern Club, the hole in the Liverpool ground which launched so many stars? Why did the Cavern provide a way of life for hundreds of Merseyside youngsters?

A hideaway, an escape…

Ray McFall, who put on the first all-beat session at the club in May, 1960, believes it was due to the atmosphere.

"It was very loud and hot and humid. It wasn't just a club. It was something to do with the cellar idea. Going down below ground was a bit like people of old getting away from authority in the catacombs.

"It became a hideaway, and escape. it was the sort of place that adults would never go to and that was what the teenagers wanted. They wanted a place they could call their own and where they could their own kind of music and meet their own age group."

But if the Beatles, who played at the Cavern 292 times, promoted it to the No. 1 beat club in the world, other famous names helped to maintain that position. Gerry and the Pacemakers, Billy J. Kramer, The Searchers, Swinging Blue Jeans and The Fourmost all swept from the Cavern to the top of the pop world. And what about the hat-check girl called Priscilla White? She was spotted in the club by Brian Epstein, became Cilla Black and within a month had a No. 1 hit record with "Anyone Who Had A Heart".

When the original Cavern closed in 1973, Paul McCartney, who'd formed his own group, Wings, by them, following the Beatles break-up, said he'd wanted to go on the final night "to kiss the old Cavern goodbye."

"After all, for the Beatles and a lot of other folk, who eventually made it, the Cavern was where it all began. Even if we did work more for the kicks than the money in the good old days."

Ironic, isn't it, that at a time when the Beatles are enjoying a tremendous revival the sign that promoted their fame the world over will be lost to the city landscape to become just a fabulous memory.

THE CAVERN CLUB
OF LIVERPOOL

Saying goodbye to The Cavern dressing room

Start of an Era 1380

THE NEW

CAVERN

IS STILL IN

MATTHEW STREET

ONLY EIGHT YARDS AWAY

AT No. 7

WATCH PRESS FOR ANNOUNCEMENTS

~ 2 ~
Wartime

MY FIRST MEMORY is of both excitement and wonder. It was early in the Second World War, and I was seven. The Government had advised the public to shelter under a table or beneath a staircase in the event of an air raid, as they had not yet built any shelters, so when the sirens sounded, my sister Freda and I were dragged out of bed to join my mother, my auntie and grandma under the stairs in my gran's little terraced house. I thought my Auntie Nell was a heroine when she ventured out to crouch under the table to make a pot of tea. "They don't understand," said my mother, Molly, indicating Freda and me. We looked at each other and said: "Oh yes we do!"

Once inside our hideout, and later when the shelters were built, we would start to hear explosions and the sound of aircraft. German planes were easily identified by the drone of the engines, which would be two seconds loud and one second low – loud, low, loud, low, and so on. British planes had an even, smooth drone, probably because they were not carrying bombs. The explosions would get nearer and louder and every now and then came the screaming of a bomb just before it exploded, which meant it was very near, probably passing overhead. We would duck involuntarily.

Dusk brought the yelling of the air raid wardens, who patrolled the streets bawling: "Put that light out!" on spotting the merest chink from a window. Cigarette smoking in the street was banned and everyone had heavy blackout curtains on their windows, with the panes criss-crossed by brown sticky tape to lessen the amount of flying glass. Men not in the Forces took over duties as firewatchers, patrolling the flat roofs during the night. Eventually every street in Liverpool had a brick air-raid shelter with a flat concrete roof. They were about nine feet high and eight feet across and placed end to end down the centre of the street for the full length – enough to accommodate everyone who lived there. It must have cost millions and created a city within a city. They also doubled up as our playground, as there was nowhere else to play during the War.

We lived at 33 Galloway Street, a street of terraced houses that was typical of that part of Wavertree, Liverpool 7, except that the frontages were of yellow brick instead of the usual red. The road was cobbled and the pavements had Yorkshire stone flags. Girls would number the stones irregularly with chalk and play hopscotch,

Outside 108 High Park Street ~ Roy, 18 months old

Roy and Freda with Daddy Jack, New Brighton Beach.

following the numbers hopping on one leg; if they stood on the black line between the flags, they lost points. Skipping was also popular. Freda and I used to listen out for the ice-cream man who came around on a motorbike shouting, "Ice cream-io", though most ice-cream men had a three-wheeled bicycle with boxes in front reading: "Stop me and buy one." There was also a little dairy on the corner of Galloway Street where my mother would send me with a jug for a gill of milk, ladled out of an urn.

We made our own amusements. There was a lamppost every fifty yards along the pavement, each eight foot tall and made of cast iron with an iron bar near the top that protruded two feet each side. They were for the gasman to lean his ladder against when cleaning the glass or changing the gas mantle but the kids used these lamps for climbing and swinging from the bars. Sometimes they would make a maypole out of it with a rope. The lads could make a pushcart from a plank of wood and two pairs of discarded pram wheels; the front wheels would be attached to a short length of plank with a bolt through the centre attaching it to the main plank. With string each end, it could be steered anywhere.

My life may have seemed typical of a Liverpool city kid at that time, but in other ways it was unconventional, though I did not realise it at the time.

My father, Jack Adams, worked for the Admiralty, having been a petty officer in the Royal Navy Reserve. His speciality was boom defence, placing deterrents against seaborne invasion, such as massive nets in which to trap submarines. The strands of these nets were six inches thick and made from a form of rubberised canvas, and hung from green glass balls that floated on the surface (after the War these balls became collectors items). My father designed one of the nets used. They also had heavy wooden rafts with rows of two-foot long spikes sticking out on an angle, placed offshore just below the surface to stop invading landing craft. Before the war, Freda and I were taken to watch my father drilling the crew on the aircraft carrier Ark Royal at Portsmouth; he also took us on board a submarine.

Jack and Molly, with me, age 4 in Southsea.

My father had had a colourful childhood. His own father was in India during the Raj, and two of my dad's brothers were born in Hong Kong. At ten years old he developed alopecia and lost all of his hair. **There was a photograph, which his stepmother had insisted be taken – he'd rested his chin on his chest, he was so self-conscious.**

His mother had died when he was five years old and his father remarried. His stepmother immediately sent my dad's sister Freda and his brother Roy into an orphanage, where they stayed for ten years. I discovered only recently that his sister Freda was still alive; she'd had ten children and many grandchildren, a whole family I didn't know about. I was fascinated to discover that amongst the grandchildren were more than one boy called Rowland and also two or three girls called Freda.

His stepmother had a party for one of her own children and had locked my dad in his room so nobody could see him; he climbed out of a window and down a drainpipe, where she was waiting with a stick. He ran away from home and stowed away on a Norwegian fishing smack. They discovered him two days out at sea, laid him across a hatch cover and beat him with a codfish. Undeterred, he pursued a seagoing career; he circled the globe three times on one ship. He was pretty well self-educated and learned to speak several languages, including dialects such as Swahili.

While working on a trawler, he met and became a lifelong friend of my Uncle Sonny, my mother's brother, which led to him meeting my mother. When my father and Sonny were working on the trawlers as young men, one thing they liked to do on going ashore was to sit outside a bar and play their mandolins. People would throw them a few coins and when they had accumulated enough of the local currency, they'd go inside and have a few drinks with the locals. It wasn't the case that they were desperate, it was just a bit of fun and they got a kick out of it.

Uncle Sonny watches Jack in a supporting role, 1933, between trips.

However, on one occasion they were in a bar in Spain doing just this when someone took exception to them, probably some local buskers. A fight started and Sonny and Jack flattened a couple of them. The bar owner called the police, who arrived in some force. As the police came in, Sonny and my dad ran out the front door, which had large, D-shaped handles. My dad shut the doors after him, putting his arms through the handles clasping his hands while Sonny made his escape. When the police stopped pushing he let go and tore after Sonny.

When they got to the ship they hid in the anchor chain locker. The police could not find them and left.

On another occasion Jack and Sonny were at sea and on night watch together in a terrible storm. Jack was on the deck and steering the ship and Sonny was below stoking the boiler. As the boat was pitched and tossed around, Sonny was taken with a severe bout of stomach cramp. He managed to yell up to Jack who rushed down and started to massage the cramped area. Sonny was doubled up with the pain, Jack spent the night scrambling up on deck checking the steering, rushing back down below stoking the boiler and seeing to Sonny. He was certainly glad when the relief watch took over.

As it happens my dad Jack had quite a musical talent, as well as the mandolin and the guitar he was a good trombone player, and reckoned he could knock a tune out of every instrument in a brass band, he had a good baritone voice and was with the Royal Naval Singers of *HMS Danae*. I still have a slightly broken 78 disc of him singing a solo *'Old Faithful'* accompanied by a blind pianist. His family were into brass bands and his nephew was bought out of the Army by Watneys Brewery so that he could be their bandmaster. My dad got me interested in a wide variety of music and even now I'd be hard pressed to say which type of music I like best.

In my earlier years he was always abroad, often for eighteen months to two years at a time and coming home only for a couple of weeks in between. Freda and I were approaching our teens before we got to know him. As the War developed he was shipped out to Sierra Leone in West Africa, which was known as 'the white man's grave', and my mother took her two children to live with my Gran in High Park Street. Later on, my mother's cousin Cissy, my auntie Nell and her son Ray joined us and we rented a larger house at the top end of the same street. This house was three-storeys high and one of a row

Jack, the one with the monkey.

of adjoining houses each with fifteen-yard-long front gardens, the only ones in the very long street. We used to climb up to the disused top floor and look out of the window from where we could see the city buildings blazing after the air raids. High Park Street was the first street in Liverpool to have amber lights, which my Gran hated; she said they made everyone look ill. My father would send me photos from Sierra Leone of the natives he worked with. One of whom was an African Chief known as Tommy Yellow. I used to try and draw these guys and thought it strange that men worked with no shirts on.

The War of course disrupted many families. Living in Liverpool, such an important seaport and therefore a prime target for the Luftwaffe, the effects of the conflict were all around us. My father once asked a shipmate to deliver a present to my mother when he came to Liverpool, and she took me on the tram down Park Road to the Adelphi Hotel to meet him in the bar. Well, I don't think he was best pleased when she arrived with a little 7-year-old in tow and after a few minutes we were walking back down the Adelphi steps into Lime Street with an air raid on. All trams stopped and we had to cross the road to where Lewis's building had stood until a few days before; in its place was an enormous pile of smouldering ash, surrounded by a high fence. No street lights were on but everywhere was lit with the criss-crossing searchlights, bombs exploding and 'flaming onions' dropping into the street like balls of fire; they may have been incendiary bombs. Much of the sky was blanketed out by the dozens of barrage balloons. My mother held my hand as we inched along the fence with our backs to it. We walked over a mile through that air raid to my gran's house in High Park Street.

Jack Adams, 1947

The attack on the Twin Towers in New York on 11 September 2001 has made a lot of people realise what people in Britain, particularly England, had to suffer during the 1939-45 War. Bombs came down like rain, particularly in the major cities, nightly for five years. At the time of the atom bomb, the Germans had just started to use their new weapon against us, the V1, or 'flying bomb' (popularly known as the doodlebug), which was like a small, pilotless aeroplane. Our school had been bombed, so the kids were distributed around the area to people's houses for schooling. They were only terraced houses, which would give up their front parlour for lessons two or three half days a week.

To help the war effort, every building that had iron railings had them removed to make munitions. Lots of wonderful buildings lost their valuable railings; the sad thing I understand is, they were never used. Even the US Government took 500lbs of keys from the Chicago Historical Society to swell their scrap metal pile; these originally came from old European dungeons. People were told to bathe once a week and use only four inches of water to save fuel. After the war a lot of people went to Australia having developed this bathing regime over five years, and the Aussies dubbed them the dirty Poms. '*If you want your money to be safe, hide it under a Pom's soap*', went the joke. Had they experienced the Blitz, they might have understood.

Lord Woolton, the head of the Board of Trade, came out with some other bizarre rulings. His department informed the Wholesale Textile Association that men's socks must be made five inches shorter than normal; the new sock would be only nine inches long instead of fourteen-and-a-half. They also banned the manufacture of ice cream, in view of the urgent need for economy in manpower, transport and packing. An appeal went out to save rubber; they said two rubber jar-rings from every home would supply 1,000 Churchill tanks with rubber equipment, a pair of old Wellington boots would make a Mae West lifesaving jacket and every ton of woollen rags would make 500 battledresses for the troops. Big restrictions were placed on the use of paper and long letters were scrapped. Even toys at Christmas were rationed; customers who would normally spend £1 per head on the family were restricted to one shilling and sixpence.

Sweets were practically non-existent, the ration was so small and the choice so limited. A little shop at the top end of High Park Street started selling small squares of flavoured ice wrapped in tissue paper. We thought they were delicious at a penny each; they were obviously the forerunner of the lolly ice. Nobody owned a fridge; if we had, we'd have realised they were just frozen lemonade. Beef was so scarce that they started to sell whale meat in the butcher's shops, and even that was rationed. We never took to its fishy taste.

My gran came in one day very excited. She had managed to buy two tins of pineapple chunks off a spiv. They were in a plain metal tin with no label. We couldn't wait to have

Munitions factory Dinner Break ~ Mum (Molly), second row from front, second from left.

some. It turned out that the tins contained chunks of turnip soaked in sugar and water, but we enjoyed them anyway. Food became more and more limited as the War progressed. There was no imported fruit, and oranges, bananas and grapes were not seen for more than five years. About three years after the War was over, I was on a visit to Liverpool from Felixstowe and saw a crowd gathered around a shop window. It was Coopers in Church Street, which was a wonderful delicatessen in peacetime. I went over to have a look and standing on a bowl in the centre of the otherwise empty window was a pineapple! Just seeing one was a thrill; the younger kids had never seen a pineapple, or a banana for that matter.

Our local cinema was the nearby Cameo picture house. One day my mother sent me off on my own to see the matinee. I paid and went in, calling into the lavatories before seeing the pictures. It was packed with kids who were peeing against the wall. Not knowing any better, I joined them. A massive hand grabbed me by the scruff of the neck and steered me out of the door, shoving me into the street. I shuffled home crying to my mother because I had paid and not seen my favourite female actress Anna May Wong, a

Chinese female detective, and Buck Jones, the top cowboy of the day. The Cameo became infamous ten years later in 1949 after a double murder was committed in there. There was a massive enquiry and 75,000 people were interviewed. George Kelly and Charles Connelly had apparently tried to rob the takings and shot the manager and his assistant. Kelly was hung for the murder; Connelly pleaded guilty and got ten years. **As a child you are oblivious to such things, but Liverpool was a very tough city**. There was a notorious gang during the War known as the Peanut gang. My grandfather came home from work one day and said this gang had thrown a fellow through a shop window, in front of a queue who were waiting for a tram. They used to wear peaked flat caps, which all workers wore then, the difference being that they had razor blades set into the peak.

My mother's father, Jeremiah, or Jerry, was a big, broad-shouldered man who worked as a cooper. He could direct you anywhere in Liverpool by the pubs: "Straight down to the Vine, turn left at the Flat Iron ..." and so on. He always wore boots and Freda and I would compete to undo the laces on a boot each to earn our Saturday penny. My Gran also wore button boots and dressed in black, which the older women all did. She would cross the road nightly to fetch my Granddad a large jug of Guinness.

My Gran came out of her front door one day, looked up and saw the front end of an enormous barrage balloon was hanging down the front of the house. She panicked and ran through to the back, only to find the tail section completely covering the back yard. These things were about sixty feet long. In September 1942, twenty houses in Medlock Street, Kirkdale, were completely wrecked by a loose barrage balloon which bounced from one to the next along the whole street and finally exploded on the roofs, starting fires. People in bed had to scramble to safety out of wrecked bedrooms and into the street shelters.

My mother took a job with my two aunties, Cissy and Nell, in the Navy, Army, Air Force Institute (NAAFI). They wore uniform and set out daily to *HMS Wellesley*, a building in Wellesley Road used as a transit stop for sailors going to war. Going to work early in the mornings after the nightly air raids, they saw some terrible sights. Once they saw a young baby splattered against the stone wall of the reservoir at the top of High Park Street. On another occasion, a landmine had gone through a window and the front part of it had landed on an armchair; the rest of it was sticking out of the window. These bombs weighed over 1000lbs and came down on a parachute.

After the air raids the kids used to collect shrapnel – there was plenty of it about.

One day I was playing in Wavertree Park where they had two giant cast iron cannons which we used to clamber over and mess about on, they were about fifteen feet long. I heard the air raid siren and dashed off down Spekeland Road towards home. Halfway down the sloping road, the air raid wardens were rushing people into a shelter. I didn't want to go into a shelter which could be for hours so I broke into a run towards home, which was nearby. I tripped on a jagged piece of a bicycle wheel rim that had been cut in half. As I stood on the end of the rim the other end went into my calf. It made a wide, deep cut about two and a half inches across and a half inch wide. The wardens came over and threw me onto the back of a flat backed coal wagon and carted me off to Smithdown Road Hospital to get it stitched. This left a large wide permanent scar, it being in the calf muscle. I called it my war wound!

A couple of years later, when I wore boots all the time, as practically all the boys did, we used to have a horseshoe-shaped piece of steel on the boot heel with steel tackets or studs on the soles which we were very proud of. we were able to run and slide along on them.

The steel on one side of the plate on my left heel wore down very thin. As I was running somewhere one day the steel plate swung around so that the steel razor edge was protruding out from my boot. Consequently, as I was running, it managed to slice through my calf muscle three inches below the bike wheel injury. These two injuries affected my right calf muscle ever after.

* * *

I used to look down the front page of the *Liverpool Echo* on a Saturday morning where every column listed all the cities cinemas in alphabetical order, they covered the entire front page and of course that, like all the papers was a broadsheet. I ran my fingers down the titles till I found the word *Tarzan* and wherever that film showed, that's where I'd go, provided it wasn't too far. I think that's how I discovered muscles. To get into the matinee cost a half penny or a jam jar or a ball of silver paper, all to help the war effort.

The women in that area used to go to the wash house in Steble Street every couple of weeks to do the family washing. There was also the swimming pool and the washing baths, where you could climb into a lovely deep bath of water and have a soak – none of the houses had proper baths with running water, just tin tubs. I sometimes hung around waiting for women with their clean washing and offered to carry it for them. The going rate was about tuppence. I was ten years old and had to carry one bundle about a quarter of a mile and the woman gave me only a penny. Some of the bundles were large, as much as you could wrap in a sheet, and most of the women took old prams to put them on. The other swimming baths I went to sometimes, was in Cornwallis Street, which was nearer to the town centre. I liked it because it was the only saltwater baths in the city. The boys and girls had their own separate pools. Consequently not many bothered with swimming trunks, they could hire what was known as slips, for a couple of pennies. The slips were a light piece of canvas about five inches wide, which was suspended from a cord round the waist, it hung down the front of the body and passed between the legs and up to the rear of the waist. These things were ugly and cumbersome. I tried them once and made sure to bring my swimming trunks in future.

Sometimes I would go into town on the tram with a friend, Carl Daley. We would go to what was known as the 'back of the market', which was a couple of streets of market stalls by the Royal Court Theatre. I bought a pigeon there as a pet. I took it home and put it in a pigeon box where I fed it daily and cleaned it's bed. After a couple of weeks I let it out for some exercise. I never saw it again and realised it had probably flown back to it's owner.

Great business when your stock replenishes itself! **We learned a few tricks ourselves, too.** A black guy who lived in our neighbourhood asked Carl to buy him a dog at the market and gave him five bob. We were upstairs on the tram when we saw a pack of dogs in the street chasing a young bitch. Without a word, we both galloped down the stairs, jumped off the tram and chased after the dogs. We caught the bitch and took it to the guy. He was so pleased he gave us an extra half crown.

Carl got a Saturday job in the market selling a 'miracle' chrome paste that he would demonstrate to prospective customers. You could apply it to any metal and it would polish up with a fabulous chrome finish. It sold like hot cakes; fellows were using it on the tanks of their motorbikes, making them look like new. Unfortunately, it wore off after a few hours.

* * *

As Liverpool continued to take a battering, Freda and I were sent to North Wales as evacuees, to a place near Wrexham called Coed poth. We didn't like it there much. I thought the Welsh people were cruel because they wouldn't let me listen to *Happidrome*, my favourite radio programme, on a Saturday night. They also made me go outside every time I wanted to blow my nose when I had a cold. My mother, who used to visit us twice a week from Liverpool (a horrendous journey which used to take hours), realised I was unhappy and took us back to Liverpool. Later on we were sent back to Wales with another party of evacuees. This time we went by train and bus to Holywell on the Flintshire coast. We were wearing labels and each carrying a small cardboard box hanging from a string over the shoulder, which contained our gas mask. At a village hall, local people came and picked out who they wanted. I was lucky because I went to a couple who had no kids. The man of the house had a motorbike that he would sometimes give me a ride on and also kept two pet badgers, which he kept in a cylindrical metal box and would exercise on a lead. I never discovered why he kept them.

My father returned to Liverpool but not for long; he was posted to Rosyth naval base on the Firth of Forth, so we all moved up to Scotland with him until the end of the War. We lived first at Kirkaldy and then Rosyth and I went to a succession of schools. They could be hard going up there. Whilst at school in Kirkaldy, I walked into class after lunch one day, as I sat down I placed a matchbox on my desk by the inkwell. We used to get two matchboxes and join them by pushing thread through a hole in the side and tying it to a matchstick inside. We'd hold a matchbox each standing ten feet away from each other and talking into our matchbox. In our imagination they were phones joined by the thread. This was the game we'd played at playtime.

As I sat down placing my matchbox down, the teacher said: "Adams – come here, – what have you got there?" I picked it up and showed her it. She said: "Take it to Mr Collins, and tell him I caught you playing with it in class."

Mr. Collins had come into the class that morning – he was a nice looking smart suited man who won us over immediately with his smile. To us he looked much better than the old lady who's place he'd taken as school head. I happily went along to Mr Collins' study, giving him the message. He went to the drawer and took out a strap I'd not seen before, but was soon to learn about. The strap was about three and a half feet long and quarter of an inch thick. It had two cuts in the end about ten inches long, giving the strap three tails. He told me to hold out my hand to the side and brought it down from shoulder height across my palm. He then told me to hold out the other hand, doing the same again. I was terrified and horrified; I was only nine years old. He then went through the same procedure again, making it twice on each hand. To this day I don't understand why he did it; he had to be a sadist.

That was the first time I experienced the belt, tho' certainly not the last. Sometimes they'd use it on the legs. I only came across it in Scottish schools. Some of them did use the cane, the same as in England. We moved from Kirkaldy to Rosyth. We stayed in the same house for all the time we were there, a solid building with a prim and proper little garden at the front that looked like one of the new prefabs which were springing up all over the country. The houses on that new estate in Rosyth looked so much like kids play houses that it was known locally as 'Dolly Town'.

About a quarter of a mile down the hill from our house was a Prisoner of War camp full of captured Italians. It was just a collection of wooden huts in a muddy field with corrugated tin roofs. There was no barbed wire to keep the prisoners in because there was nowhere for them to go to. The fifty or so inmates were also pretty happy to be out of the war and to be well fed three times a day. I used to go down to the camp with a pal to look at the prisoners. It was clear on my first visit there that they were a friendly bunch, well dressed in their Italian Army denims, and most of them spoke English to a greater or lesser degree. My pal and I used to go into the huts and I think they liked our company. Inside they were pretty bare, with bunk beds around the sides and a stove in the middle of the room which was kept piping hot. On one occasion I tripped over the edge of the stove and put out my hand as I fell forward. The whole of my palm pressed on the red hot chimney pipe and I let out a yelp of extreme pain that I had never before experienced. All the skin on my hand blistered up and then peeled away, leaving a bloody mess. The prisoners gave me first aid and made sure I was all right. For weeks after that incident they were helping to dress my hand with new bandages and were concerned that it would heal properly, which it did thanks to their attention.

I knew that they had a little wind-up gramophone player in one of the huts, so to say thanks, I raided my father's record collection for the only piece of Italian music that he had. It was an old 78' of *'O Sole Mio'* and when I took it along, they were delighted. They played that record until I thought it would wear out.

Eventually towards the end of the war they were all shipped out, presumably home to Italy, and the huts were left bare. I wandered around the camp looking for souvenirs but all that was left was some straw. At home I kept a rabbit in a small hutch, so that afternoon I grabbed an armful of the straw and carried it home for my pet's bed. Later that evening I was sitting down to dinner with the rest of my family when there was a knock at the door. My father answered the door and was taken aback to see two policemen standing there.

They came in and said to me: "Have you been down at the camp today?"

"Yes I have," I replied: "I brought home some straw for my rabbit."

"We know," said the bigger of the two policemen, "we followed a long trail of it all the way to your front door."

I was summoned to the police station at nine o'clock sharp the next morning. My father took me down and I was marched into the sergeant's room and made to stand in front of his big wooden desk. My father sat in a chair behind me as the sergeant delivered to me the biggest bollocking of my life. I recall phrases like "this is how it all begins" and "life of crime" and things like that being shouted at me. I wasn't even ten years old: a bit of an over-reaction to a handful of straw.

I was travelling twelve miles daily to Dunfermline High School, but for some reason my Dad moved me even further away, to High Valleyfield. High Valleyfield school had a high percentage of poor mining village kids.

When dinnertime came, the kids would line up in single file against the wall and would press sideways into the wall, at the same time pushing forward, the idea being to squeeze out whoever was in front of you. The younger ones were inevitably the victims, always getting in late. After the meal, kids would scramble onto the long bare board tables and scrape the plates with a spoon for any scraps left over, especially if we'd had 'stovies', which was mashed potato with beans mixed in. That was the most popular dish.

In the winter they gave us three weeks off for 'tattie' picking. We would pile onto a wagon or an old bus before daylight and go into the frozen countryside, where we would be unloaded into a potato field. There would be a row of canes down the middle of the field about forty feet apart. The areas between the canes were known as 'stents' and each kid had his own to work. The tractor would come along and plough up a furrow of potatoes and our job was to pick up the tatties and throw them into a basket. Unfortunately when the spuds were ploughed up, they'd be flung out in two different directions, so they'd be spread out for about six or seven feet. Before you'd got a quarter of your stent picked, the tractor would plough up another row, and so it went on. The worst part was the cold in your fingers. Once the field was ploughed, we would line up in twos with a basket between us, picking up the remaining spuds. It was backbreaking for children, and my first experience of real manual work. There was no escape; you had to stick at it.

My mum used to get homesick for Liverpool and a couple of times travelled back to see my Gran. Then mum decided Freda and I could make the journey on our own. The trains were always full of troops and we spent most of the eight-hour journey standing or sitting on the soldiers' kit bags. Freda was in charge, being a bit older than me (she was about 12 years old). Mum couldn't bring us because she was working in a munitions factory.

My friend Carl Daley had a pal called John Walsh, who was such a rough diamond we called him Claude because it was so unsuitably posh. I actually lived in Scotland at this time, and whilst on visits to my gran I used to spend time with Carl, who was a respectable lad. One day Claude came round and mentioned a gorgeous woman he'd been watching. This young woman used to go to the pub off-license in High Park St. most evenings, for beer and cigarettes. He said: "Come with me and I'll show you".

It was early evening and we watched her under the amber lights – high heels clicking – the girl came walking up the street wearing a sweater, which was a popular fashion at the time. Claude said: "You two wait here", (we were stood at the end of an entry on the opposite side of the street). He trotted across the cobbled street to an entry which was alongside the pub. The girl came out of the off-license and jiggled her way up the street. As she got close to the entry, Claude ran out and grabbed one of her breasts in each hand, giving them a shake and a couple of squeezes. As the girl shrieked, he turned and legged it down the entry with her yelling after him: "You dirty little sod!!" – still holding her beer in one hand and cigarettes in the other. Carl and I did an about turn down the entry, shocked by his audacity.

There was a shop on the corner called Harold Stead's. We used to go to Harold's when we got our pocket money and buy a penny Vantas, which was a drink in a bottle, a little like Coca-Cola. Harold used to give the bottle a little shake when taking the top off, and shake the drops at us, saying, "Go and wash your Sunday face." His

standing joke. One day Claude said: "Let's go and buy a couple of Vantas, – I want to play a joke, so when you get yours, ask him what the time is." So we went into the shop and asked for the drinks – Claude got his first. As he served mine I said: "What's the time Harold?" He tutted and shaking his head went into the back of the shop. As he went through the door, Claude shot round the counter and grabbed money out of the open till. He took off with it immediately. Harold told me the time and I also left. I don't think I ever saw Claude again after that.

One thing I liked to do when visiting my Gran was to go down Windsor Street and look in the junk shop windows. I was fascinated by old things – even in my Gran's house I was always rummaging through the drawers looking for old penknives, coins, pens, anything that took my fancy. I never changed, and as I grew up I retained my interest in all things old: buildings, furniture, pottery, paintings and so on. Antiques becoming something of a passion in my life.

Another passion was horses. On one visit from Scotland I went to the circus in Sefton Park with my young cousin John Morris, who was only seven at the time. Halfway through the performance they brought on 'the unrideable mule', which was bareback with a simple halter, no bit in its mouth, and challenged anyone to ride it for a prize of ten shillings. The challenge was to remain on its back for two minutes. Lots of people had a go, mainly youngsters, and the mule was flinging them all over the place. The main difficulty seemed to be in mounting it; people were unseated before they actually got settled on its back. I waited until the mule came close to the box section that formed the circus ring and succeeded in leaping the gap onto its back. The mule proceeded to buck and fling itself about but gave up after two and a half minutes, according to the Ring Master. I went back to my seat and the show continued. John and I had more or less given up on getting the prize when, just before the finale, I was called into the circus ring and they made a big show of presenting me with the ten shillings.

We were on another visit to Liverpool when the War ended. VE (Victory in Europe) night was 8 May 1945. Everyone in the street started walking towards the city centre. When we got to Park Road, there was a terrific mass of people converging from all the side streets. Freda and I were in the middle of the crowd, all singing. When we got to town, people had arrived from every direction and were climbing lampposts and buildings, even though a lot of the main buildings had been reduced to high mounds of glowing ash. The noise of cheering and singing was tremendous.

Time to celebrate - no more munitions, it's all over - Molly is on the left.

~ 3 ~
Moving South

THREE OR FOUR years later we moved to Felixstowe, which was a place I loved.

There was a small dock where Boom Defence equipment was kept and the Harwich ferryboat used to pick up passengers.

Dad was in charge at Felixstowe Dock and had about thirty men working for him directing their efforts from a little office on the quay side.

The kids started to call me 'Jock' because I now had a Scottish accent! I went to Felixstowe Grammar School where I felt distinctly out of place. All the boys wore smart grey jackets and trousers whereas I had an old jacket and well-worn corduroys. I also had thicker hair than the other boys who all had neat haircuts. Because of the different style of education in Scotland I'd landed in a class that was further ahead in some subjects and behind in others, and I couldn't cope. I was also painfully shy and spent the whole of the first term looking down at my desk; – outside of the classroom I couldn't even identify my own classmates.

I pestered my mother to get me a grey jacket like the other boys, so we went into Felixstowe High Street and in Burtons window was a grey jacket at a special price.

This jacket turned out to be a silver grey and was a different material to the other boys' jackets. It also had a faint broad brown shading like a stripe down the back which only showed in the daylight outside, the stain came from it being displayed in the direct sunlight in the window. My mum bought me a pair of grey flannel trousers to wear with it. They didn't match very well and made me even more self-conscious.

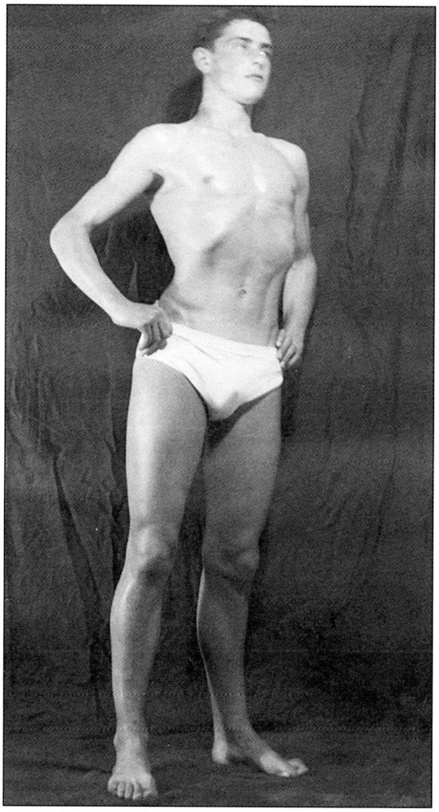
Roy, age 15 ~ 5' 11¾"

One lad picked a quarrel with me and at the height of the argument he said: "What do you know with your cheap jacket and twenty five bob flannels?" It was true because they weren't Worcester flannels like the rest of the kids wore. This was on the playing fields at the back of the school. I saw red and dived on him dragging him down onto the grass. We rolled and wrestled about throwing pretty ineffectual punches until I finally pinned him down and made him apologise. It turned out that he was a bit of a bully so I gained some popularity with the other kids. However when I'd stood up I found my jacket was covered in green grass stains.

My mother cleaned it as best she could but I was really self-conscious wearing it and continually put pressure on her. She complained to my dad and he said: "I'll make you a jacket!"

Roy, age 17, with Uncle Sonny

He dug out some material, which was navy blue, measured me up, got the sewing machine out and made the jacket. Although he did a pretty good job it was obviously home-made. The pockets were squares of material stitched on in a sort of blanket stitch and the shoulders had no pads plus it had no lining. I was mortified having to wear it, though the kids at school didn't say anything.

I'd started wrestling at lunch times with a couple of the lads at play-time, we didn't know what we were doing but enjoyed trying to throw each other around. So when lunch time arrived I went on the field in my home made jacket and started the wrestling. It ended in five minutes when the pocket of my new jacket was ripped off. I felt a mixture of horror and relief. I obviously got lots of stick from my dad, but it could have been worse, I think he realised that the jacket caused me embarrassment.

During the summer weekends I started working on the beach for a guy called Basil Bugg! He ran boat trips around the bay and out to the light ship which was three miles off shore. I progressed on to Ipswich School of Art and spent the entire eight weeks summer breaks working on the beach which entailed walking up and down on the shingle in bare feet touting for customers, when we got a boat load of twelve people Basil would cast off for the lightship. While he was away I would row groups of farmers and the like around the pier, which was the second longest in Britain after Southend, for the princely sum of five shillings a boatload. When I would see him returning in the distance I used to keep watch for the beach inspector. If Basil was carrying more than the twelve passengers allowed, on sighting the beach inspector I used to close the beach hut doors, which faced the sea and Basil would give them an extra run around the bay until I opened the doors giving the all clear. It was a steep shingle beach and we had a landing stage about forty feet long on metal tractor wheels which we had to keep pushing into the water as the tide receded. At the end of the day the stage would be maybe sixty yards down the beach and it was my job to turn the handle on the winch and pull the stage back up to the prom, the wheels being well down into the shingle it was like a rowing exercise in reverse and it really muscled up my back. One morning on arriving for work on the beach with my dog Rusty, I saw a very lovely blonde sitting on a towel on the shingle. I went over and advised her to move to the other side of the beach hut away from the landing stage cable. I was totally smitten and had great difficulty concentrating on my job. Her name was Eve Williams. She was a dancer in the summer show at the Pier Pavilion, which was two hundred yards away from our beach site. She was sixteen years old and I was fifteen. We

Left to right: Terry Freeman, Tony Partridge, Bill Langlois, Dave Bowdige and Roy

became an item and spent every spare moment together all summer.

She would come to the beach every day and Basil would sit in the hut ogling her. He'd say to me: "Chroist boy, if Oi was ten years younger, Oi'd give you a run for your money! If Oi'd known then what Oi know now." I thought – *I wish he'd tell me what he knows now!*

There was a guy called 'Sparky' who had a loud, booming voice. He never rested – all day; he'd be up and down the beach offering trips around the bay or to the lightship. Round the bay was a half-hour trip; to the lightship was an hour. Sparky used to live out of town in Trimley, so he'd travel in on the bus. He worked the weekends for Basil. He never wore a shirt, just a singlet, with a seaman's cap and his trousers tucked into his Wellingtons. He had been an amateur boxer. It was a secret ambition for me to eventually have a build like him. Being of the tall, skinny variety, it had to be an uphill struggle! Years later, when I had a family, I visited Sparky and Basil. Sparky made a fuss when he saw me. He said: "Basil's just offshore in the boat". I swam out to the boat, about five hundred yards. As I grabbed the boat, Basil said: "Here y'are Jock, just scrape those barnacles off from under the stern", handing me a scraper – I hadn't seen him for fifteen years and he didn't even say hello!

I went to Felixstowe Grammar School and on my first day, I walked into the dining hall. There was a long table with about 20 lads sitting with their backs to me; they all wore grey uniform blazers except one who had a brown jacket on. The first thing that struck me was that the shoulder blades of these lads were about three inches apart except for the lad in the brown jacket; his were a good six inches apart. It was hard to believe this broad back belonged to a thirteen year old boy. His name was Tony Partridge, and he and I became good friends and still are though he's lived in New Zealand for the past forty years. Tony and I lived on opposite sides of the town, and each morning before school we would run about two and a half miles to the top of Bent hill the halfway point, we'd

Tony Partridge, 1949

shake hands and turn and run home again, this was our training for the school cross country race. Tony eventually went to Dartmouth College of Navigation eventually getting his masters ticket and met a girl Helen, who became his wife in New Zealand. He was the master of the biggest ship to sail from Auckland to Liverpool in the 1980's, which was a high tech container carrier. In our early teens Tony Partridge and I used to sit on the edge of the promenade after working all day on the boats, and sing the latest songs by Danny Kaye from the film *'Up in Arms'*. He came over from the States to the London Palladium, where he was a sensation. After his main act he simply sat and talked to the audience. His particular humour and witty asides were such that they didn't want him to leave. His act went on for nearly three hours.

One day whilst on the promenade, Tony pointed out a guy who was walking in our direction. "Wait till you see this fellow Roy, he's one of my favourite people – his name's Bill Langlois. Bill was a seaman; he always wore a neat fitting seaman's peaked cap, very good looking with a great personality. He had a wonderful deep, almost musical voice, similar to Dean Martin but with a real Suffolk accent. In the winter he'd go out on the fishing smacks or the shrimpers or on the longer trips on merchant ships. But in the summer he loved to work on the beach. The finest boat on Felixstowe sea front was the *'Viking'*. It was in a different class to the boats Tony and I worked on, and Billy being the top man was it's helmsman. We loved him because he was amusing but also serious and we learnt a lot from him. He was thirty years old, twice our age, yet very boyish.

Roy with Diane and Sparky, 1966.

One day he took us to the local dump where we collected a couple of sackfuls of old po's or chamber pots. We'd no idea what he had in mind until we returned to the prom late at night with them. He took one of the po's and climbed up one of the twenty foot lamp poles that ranged along the prom every thirty yards. He placed the po on top of the lamp, after which the three of us climbed the poles, putting a po on top of each one, right along the promenade. The local council were not amused, tho' lots of other people were.

Bill then had another idea, he got a flat topped barrow and decided to put it to some use. He put trays of fruit on the barrow and started selling fruit just by the prom. Tony, myself and our other pal Terry Freeman were then commissioned to go out in the evening and scrump apples, pears, peaches and plums, etc., from gardens and orchards all around the area, just to keep the stall going.

Fortunately, Bill soon tired of this and went back to skippering the *'Viking'*. One day he met a beautiful country girl who was in Felixstowe for the day. She lived in Martlesham and Bill started cycling over there every evening to see her. I think it was about seventeen miles away, and he'd cycle home the same night so he could make work in the morning.

They eventually married, and I went into the Army, and when I next visited Felixstowe after leaving the Army, I searched for him. It was years before I discovered that Bill was living down South in Shrivenham, Wiltshire. I was now living in Liverpool and went down there to visit Bill and Maud his wife. They now had thirteen children and were on hard times. I got them fixed up with a house in Liverpool and transported them all there. Bill came to work for me for a while until he got sorted. Maud was never happy being away from her farm life and eventually after about ten or fifteen years, they went back to her home territory. Bill died eventually, but Maud is still going strong and still working the land. Bill – I'll always remember as one of my heroes.

Incidentally, one day when working on the beach, Bill was approached by an agent of some sort, who marketed Capstan Navy Cut tobacco. He'd decided that Bill looked like the archetypal ideal seaman with his cap and handsome yet rugged face. He sent a photographer up from London to take pictures. With going into the Army, and not being a smoker, I never saw the finished product.

One afternoon I was approached by two middle-aged ladies who wanted to know what time I was going to pull the landing stage up. They told me they walked the length of the prom from their hotel every day, just to watch me winding up the stage.

While I was talking to them, two men came across and during my conversation with them, they asked me what I did when not working on the beach. I explained that I went to Ipswich School of Art. The next day they came to see me again and introduced themselves as Carl and Roger Yale, songwriters, based in Denmark St., London. They'd written a song called *'The Dreamer'*, which was being launched on the B.B.C. Light Programme by Leslie Hutchinson, also known as Hutch. Unusually for that time, he was a popular English black singer who's trade mark was a white handkerchief which he always used to wipe down the piano keys and the piano stool before sitting down to play.

Carl and Roger told me that they needed a design for the cover of the song sheet which would be displayed in record shops, Woolworth's etc. This was the main method of publicising songs in those days. There were very few record programmes on the radio. There was *Housewives Choice*, every weekday morning, from 9 till 10 a.m., and Jack Jackson's popular one hour show on a Saturday night at ten 'o clock. I used to stay up till midnight on Saturday to hear the top twenty records with Ralph (Muffit) Moffat, on A.F.N. – the American Forces Network and later on, Radio Luxembourg. The good thing was if you bought a record, you knew it would be popular for a couple of months so you got your moneys worth. There'd only be three or four new releases over that period, so each new record had an impact. However, the most popular programme was lunchtimes *Workers Playtime*, a variety programme, comedians, singers, and most bizarrely, as it was for radio – ventriloquists! Most music programmes throughout the day featured live orchestras and bands, very few records.

Anyway, the Yale brothers asked me to design the song sheet, which I did. How it fared, I've no idea as soon after I was in the Army.

My other pal at that time was John Hopson whose ambition was to become a vet, when we were about fourteen and growing bum fluff on our upper lips Hoppo came to school one day with his top lip cut to ribbons, he'd decided to shave his moustache off. I asked what went wrong and he explained he'd used the blade to castrate a rabbit first and he should have done it the other way around. He now lives out in the bush in New Zealand raising and slaughtering his own pigs for a living surrounded by about twenty wildish dogs.

Another incident that happened in Felixstowe when I was about sixteen – I was walking along the deserted prom in the winter and was taken short. I went into a public toilet and dropped my pants, as I sat down I saw an eye watching me through a hole in the partition wall, as I noticed it, the eye vanished, then it appeared again and I gave it a mighty punch. There was a squeal from the next cubicle. I pulled my pants up, ran outside, and saw the town Nancy boy mincing along the prom as fast as he could. He wore a loose silk neckerchief, which flapped around, his left arm glued to his side as far as the elbow the lower arm and his right arm which held a big handkerchief held aloft, both swinging rapidly to give him impetus. It was strange sight, which really made me wonder what he was about.

I'd first become interested in physique when I was about thirteen years old when I started drawing cowboys and Indians and African natives etc. Then of course at Art school I used to draw from Greek and Roman statues. In fact, I went to see my first physique contest at the local theatre in Ipswich and was very impressed by the winner. He was the first live bodybuilder I'd seen. His name was Tony Chandler and he was elected Mr. S.E. Britain 1947. A short while later I saw a guy on the inside cover of a *Health & Strength* in a classic relaxed pose. His name was Hubert Thomas and his physique reminded me of the statues I was drawing at Art School. He was placed third in the 1950 Mr. Universe.

My sister Freda met a soldier called Dennis who was stationed near Felixstowe, he was a physical man with a good build (particularly his forearms) who taught me to throw the discus and javelin.

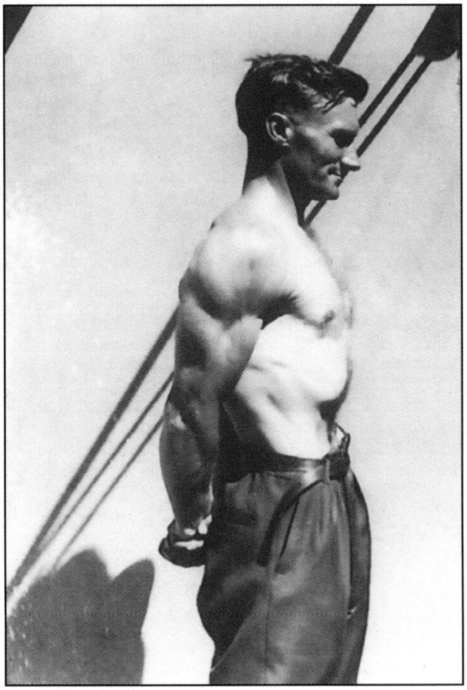

Dennis, my early mentor.

He told me about Dynamic Tension, a system which had been developed and promoted by an American called Charles Atlas. In its most basic form Dynamic Tension is using your body's own weight and muscles as resistance over a particular muscle set; for example flexing the forearm up to curl the bicep whilst holding hands and resisting with pressure from the opposite arm. Over time, the muscles would tone and build in size and strength. Sicilano was to build one of the finest physiques of his day and changed his name to Charles Atlas.

In 1921 Atlas heard that Bernard McFadden, the publisher of *Physical Culture* magazine, would sponsor a body building competition entitled 'The World's Most Perfectly Developed Man'. The pageant was held at Madison Square

Garden in New York City. He won the contest that year, and again when it was held in 1922.

I started to do Dynamic Tension because it was convenient to do anywhere and was always a good stand by when weights weren't available.

I got hold of some home made dumbbells and started a bit of weight training with them. Dennis had a hero at his camp, a PTI called Al Murray, who Dennis told me, was very fit and strong with great arm development. Around this time I was walking along the promenade at Felixstowe in the rain and I picked up a page from *Health and Strength* magazine, which was lying on the prom. On the top left side of the page was a picture of a man in a double biceps pose. I stared at it! How can a man look so perfect? He was extremely handsome of face but the body was equal or better than any artist's perception of muscular proportion. The caption read STEVE REEVES of Oakland California. I turned the page over and there was a full-page picture of a blond haired man of equally impressive muscularity without the aesthetic proportions and his caption read Jack Delinger of Oakland California! I thought that's got to be the place to live Oakland California! I was about sixteen at the time.

That year 1948 John Grimek was to win the first Mr Universe with Steve Reeves in second place – third place was Andre Drapp a classic French physique with superb abdominals!

Forty-five years later, in 1993, I was to go to the Oscar Heidenstam dinner in London where Reg Park our greatest bodybuilder was being honoured and who should I be sitting next to but Al Murray. I couldn't wait to send a photo of Al to Dennis who now lives in

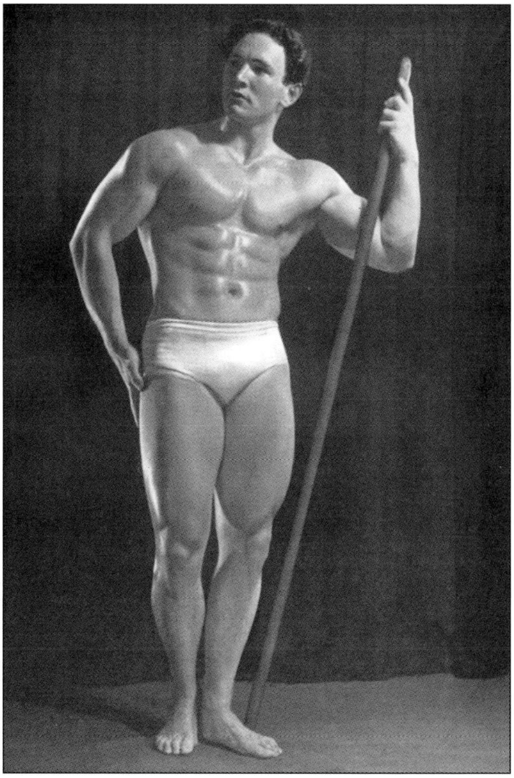

The well proportioned, six foot, three inch Hubert Thomas. Photo: Graham.

Tony Chandler (courtesy of Health and Strength magazine)

Germany! Al Murray became a well known physical culturist eventually becoming the British Olympic Weightlifting coach,) Dennis had also told me about the great John Grimek from America who had an amazing depth of muscle and besides being superbly strong retaining terrific agility, often finishing his muscle presentation with the splits and a back somersault off the rostrum. At the same dinner, I met John Grimek for the first time. I had obviously watched his career over the years in the various physique magazines, particularly the *Strength and Health*, the popular American magazine, which was attached to Bob Hoffman's York Barbell Company. John was the main promoter of Hoffman's bodybuilding products. For twenty years he was the founding editor-in-chief of *Muscular Development*, a top US magazine. His articles on bodybuilding were renowned. He was still writing with bodybuilders' advice as a regular subscriber for Bob Kennedy's *Musclemag International* right into his late eighties!

Meeting him was an experience to treasure, as was meeting Steve Reeves when he was honoured at the O.H. Foundation dinner in 1994. John didn't come to that dinner – he'd hurt his leg on his previous visit and it had troubled him ever since. He'd told me that he'd continued heavy squatting in his workout well into his seventies; this was when the leg trouble started. His doctor said: "John, you really must stop the heavy squatting at your age" – so he did stop. I asked him what weight he'd been using – he said: "Around the 600 mark! I did actually do 640 before packing in. I was aiming for 700 and I would have made it!" I asked him how long ago that had been and he said: "Oh, about eight years ago" – which meant he'd been seventy-five when he stopped squatting!

In 1998, NABBA (National Amateur Bodybuilding Association) celebrated the 50th anniversary of Mr Universe. John Grimek missed it. He would have been eighty-eight years old. Unfortunately he was not well and was unable to travel.

John Grimek
Photograph by Cliff Oettinger from Body Culture, December 1950

Photographs of Steve Reeves

Top left: Britain's first sight of the young Steve Reeves at the 1948 Mr. Universe contest (courtesy of Health & Strength magazine)

Pencil Drawings from 1954-55
by the Author
Opposite: Steve Reeves
Below: Reg Park
Lower right: John Grimek

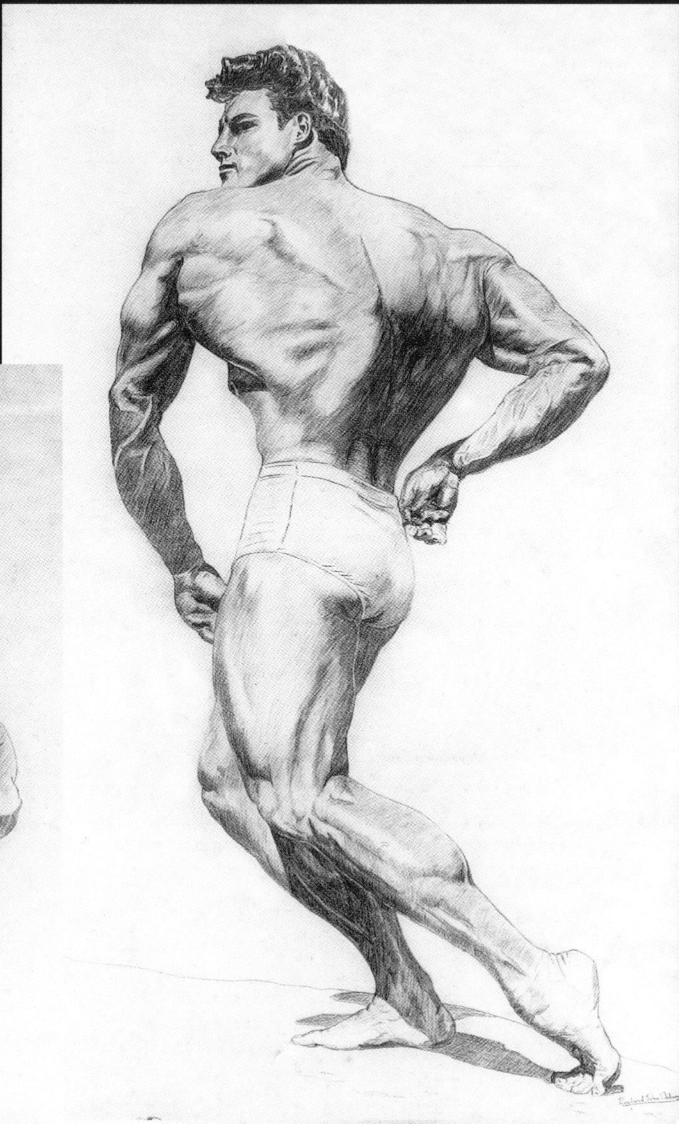

~ 4 ~
I Get Called Up ~ (Germany and the Tower of London)

IN 1950 I WAS called up to do my National Service in the Irish Guards, after six months I signed up for the extra 3 years because my parents were living in Ceylon and Freda was married and living in Paris.

I had a friend in Felixstowe called Jack Stuart. He and I were both keen on training mainly running at that time. When my mother left to join my father in Ceylon, I went to live with Jackie and his mum. She used to talk all the time about her eldest son who had died; poor Jackie hardly got a look in. He got called up for his national service being a bit older than me. Within a couple of months he had done his square bashing and was sent to Germany. He wrote and told me he'd become a dispatch rider, riding his motorbike up and down the country and really lapping it up! However, one day he'd been sent on a job a fair distance away. It was in the summer and he stopped and drank from a stream, when he returned to the battalion he took ill and died. The girl who nursed him was a Felixstowe girl. I was left on my own with his mother who in spite of Jackie's death still went on about her wonderful older son.

One morning at breakfast she said: "Oi a'd a terrible emmorage last noight." Proceeding to explain how ill she felt. I didn't know what she was talking about but had a vague idea. I couldn't wait to get away and into the army! I had a large black dog called Rusty who was known by everyone in Felixstowe, they would even let me take him in to the local theatre.

I also had a girl friend called Peggy Carmichael; she worked as a beach photographer for a local business called Mr Snaps. She was extremely attractive of course having powerful but shapely legs. She always wore the briefest of shorts, which showed them to good effect. When I was called up she offered to take my dog and keep him for me until I was demobbed. I was sent down to Caterham in Surrey. She packed her job in and followed me there with Rusty. It was eight weeks before I was allowed out to see her. She had a real problem because she wasn't earning enough money to keep herself and the dog. A young officer in the depot heard about the situation, she'd turned up to try to see me with Rusty in tow. He was on duty in the guardroom he reported the situation to his superior officer and offered to look after

Roy, aged 17, with Peggy Carmichael.

Rusty for me, which he did. I was in the army for twice the expected time and lost touch so I never saw Rusty or Peggy again. For all I know, she and the Lieutenant could be living in married bliss in the Home Counties!

I remember when I turned up at the barrack gates, a giant lance sergeant looked down at me. I was wearing an old brown pinstriped suit a green chequered shirt, and brothel creeper shoes, my trousers were turned up exposing my multicoloured socks, the barrack buildings were at the far end of the drive which was about a quarter of a mile long, each side of it was a massive parade ground with squads of soldiers being screamed at by their various NCOs and marching in different directions. The lance sergeant said: "Yes Sir, what can I do for you?"

I said: "I'm a new recruit," his voice changed dramatically. He screamed at me.

"Stand to attention when you talk to me. Go to the far end of the drive and report to the company office. Right turn, quick march, swing your arms to shoulder height front and rear, left right, left right!"

He watched me all the way, yelling as I went. It gave an inkling of what was to come.

Next morning we were issued with our uniforms and suits of denims. One of the lads was twenty-one stone Jim Nolan – a six foot five inch giant who'd come straight from an office job. They had nothing to fit him. They managed to cock up some denims for him while a uniform was made, just as well cos' he lost two stone the first two weeks. They marched us to some huts for haircuts. When we halted outside a squad came clattering down the steps. Their heads were shaved bald, they had dark bags under their eyes and their sleeves and denim trousers were half-mast. I said to Ronnie Wells who I'd palled up with: "Ooh look, the Gamma people", (characters from a sci-fi film of the time) and we both laughed.

The same lance sergeant who I had met at the gate came over and grabbed me by the ear, he dragged me up the steps into the hut where two (barbers) were waiting for me. "Ya see this c…. here, he likes takin' the piss give him a special!"

I had very black hair, which they shaved off leaving my head a see through shade of blue. They then chipped at it with the shears leaving white patches all over; I looked like a spotted dick pudding! He then took me to another hut to have my teeth checked. The so-called dentist said: "You've got a perfect set of teeth." He then grabbed an instrument and yanked one of my teeth out. He held it in front of my face telling me: "Don't worry, there's nothing wrong with this tooth, I need this for a set I'm making!"

We had a lad called Wilson in our squad; he was smaller and thinner than anyone else and not very bright. The guardsman in charge of us whose job it was to show us how to clean our kit, make our beds etc, was called Potter, he had to be addressed as trained soldier. If you wanted to go for a pee you would have to march up to him, halt, stand to attention and say, "May I go to the lavatory trained soldier," sometimes he would say: "No Fuck off!" and you'd have to try later.

There was a fireplace at one end of the barrack room with a leather couch with brass studs all around it. Potter used to lie on this couch picking his ears with a matchstick. He would constantly pick on poor Wilson. One time he said: "Wilson, bring your John Ls over here, meaning his underwear. He then examined them and said: "What's this?" Pointing at a mark on the inside of the pants. "Its Kiwi trained soldier."

"That's not Kiwi – it's shit! You two – take him outside and scrub him"

Outside was a six foot wide passage way with a sink at one end and open air at the other, it was November and very cold, they scrubbed the poor sod with a floor scrubbing brush till his skin was raw, in cold water. There was a small hot water geyser over the sink and one squaddie was designated to get up at five thirty a.m. half an hour before reveille and fill a fire bucket with hot water for the trained soldier.

The rest of us washed and shaved in cold water.

Eventually Wilson was discharged without ever going to the battalion.

We were sent on to Pirbright barracks and then to Pickering in Yorkshire. Pirbright was compared to the depot a much more civilised place. There was actually a radio speaker in the room. Jim Glynn a six foot two ex-boxer from St Helens, called me over to the speaker, which was not very loud: "Ee Jock come and hear this."

We both stood close to the speaker and heard the wondrous sound of Mario Lanza singing *'Be My Love'*.

This was a voice with muscles, when his first film was released people flocked to see it. He probably did more to popularise opera than anyone before or since.

After three months at Pirbright, we went to Pickering – way up on the Yorkshire Moors. We did battle training there, marching at least eight miles each way each day, to and from the various locations in the middle of nowhere. We had a guy called Hall in our squad – he was unique in that he was married with a child. He was small for a guardsman and always seemed to have a bland smile on his roundish face. We were allowed to go into the village one night to a dance, where we all stood around in our army boots drinking. One of the lads took up with the village scrubber. She took him into the local cemetery where he had sex with her. He then passed her on to his mate, eventually a queue was formed in the cemetery and most of the squad had a go – I'd left early, I had been on guard duty and was in bed when they returned to tell the tale. About an hour after everyone had settled down to sleep, I awoke to the sound of Hall putting his uniform on. I asked him what he was doing. He said: "I'm going back to that village to find that bird and have another go." He'd had two goes the first time round. He came back somewhat disgruntled about an hour later, she'd long gone.

He had to be on parade about three hours later. The bromide they'd put in our tea didn't seem to work on him!

One high spot I remember in the guards was on a PT parade when the sergeant referred to me as "you muscle-bound fucker" which was meant to be an insult, but pleased me no end! When we joined the battalion in Germany I befriended a fellow called Tommy Nolan who boxed at light heavy in the boxing team. We went on a battle scheme to Sennelager and were living under canvas. One evening we all were allowed to go to a commercial beer tent and mix with other regiments. A group of us sat around a big table drinking and having a singsong. On the next table were the Grenadiers. One of them took exception to me and started an argument, as I rose to the occasion, a pal sat next to me muttered "Watch yourself Roy, he's their heavy-weight boxing champion." Next thing this guy challenged me to go into the woods and fight him. My pal whose name was Cornelius Michael Patrick Rooney intervened and said: "He's only a kid don't be picking on him"

Irish Guards P.T. Parade at Pirbright Training Camp ~Roy 2nd row down, 3rd from right (no shamrock)

whereupon Tommy Nolan jumped to his feet and said: "Ill fight you!" I felt humiliated because I was nearly nineteen although I was relieved.

The two of them then vanished into the trees. Five minutes later Tommy appeared and swaggered over to the table, he'd sorted the other fellow out! Which amazed us all. Tommy used to show me photos of himself in Dublin in a suit with a black shirt and white tie and also a trilby hat and raincoat, collar turned up gangster style. On the rare occasions they let us go into Dusseldorf Tommy and I used to go with the boxing team. We'd all go down to a bar and order pints all round of the very strong German beer, when we'd downed it and called for another pint they refused to serve us – they'd been instructed to only let us have one drink. So we'd all open our hands and let the glasses drop and smash on the floor, whereupon there'd be murder and eventually the police would arrive and move us on to do it somewhere else.

The Germans called us the boy soldiers, as the average age was only 18. Because the occasions when we got out were rare, trouble in the town was very minor and infrequent, however one of our squad was a very pleasant Irishman called Mick Cleere, he was twenty-six years old and we called him the old man, I can remember out on field training back in England on the Yorkshire moors after our route march in full kit we would carry out battle tactics all day some of which would entail carrying a colleague up hill on your back. Both of you wearing full battle kit and rifles.

(I actually drew the short straw; I had to carry the heaviest recruit in the battalion, nineteen and a half stone Jim Nolan!). We could obviously handle this, being as fit as we were but I remember Mick struggling up a hill and thinking: "It's a disgrace making a man of his age do this!" Anyway, Mick befriended a guy called Pat O'Dell and one night they went into Dusseldorf together. They went into a bar and ordered a drink, when O'Dell finished his drink and demanded another, he was refused and produced a gun which he levelled at the barman and demanded the money from the till.

The barman said: "Don't be silly, give me the gun".

Mick said: "Give it to him" and O'Dell shot and killed the man. His defence was that Mick had spurred him on to do it. This was nonsense as Mick was a gentle fun loving bloke who wouldn't hurt a fly!

Tommy Nolan and I also went into town and we were sat in a bar having a drink and Tommy turned to me and said: "I love you Jock" and gave me a little tap on the jaw. I said: "I love you too Tom," and tapped him on the jaw.

(I thought it was an odd thing for a man to say but he was a tough guy so I thought it was OK.) He then hit me a bit harder, so I hit him a bit harder. He said: "Come on, let's get out of here". So we went out into the freezing cold, we were wearing our greatcoats and our caps with the slashed peaks, which rest on your nose. He was striding along with his collar up, very purposefully.

I said: "Where are you going?"

He said: "You laced me in there."

I said: "Well you laced me!"

He said: "Well we've got to sort it out, we've got to have it off."

The houses all fronted onto the pavement, and we came to a sort of cul-de-sac of houses forming a square.

He said: "This'll do." He hung his hat on a doorknob and rushed at me, I grabbed the lapels of his greatcoat with my left hand and hit him with my right, right between the eyes. I leant back out of his reach and then pulled him in and hit him again, each time I hit him I just kept leaning out of his reach, I really took advantage of my reach and height being six foot two inches to his five foot ten. Meanwhile people were opening windows and yelling at us. Then a police car pulled up and four German policemen got out.

Tommy said quickly to me: "Right, I was attacked by some Germans and you stepped in to help me and they ran off." I knew his game: he didn't want anyone in the battalion to know that baby faced Adams had given him a hiding. They locked us up in the cells at our barracks to await complaints from the Germans who we'd supposedly been fighting. We were there for about 10 days.

On the third day, Tommy was sweeping out the guardroom and singing *'The Old Refrain'* a favourite song of his in his very nice tenor voice. He got to my cell door and called me. He said in a singsong voice: "Put your hand through the grill" which I did. He said: "That's it, give Tommy your hand." whereupon he grabbed my hand and stabbed a table fork right into my palm (one of the prongs had been bent back, leaving just three, making it easier to push in). I obviously yelled, and he shook a finger at me and said: "That'll teach you to black Tommy's eyes!"

It hurt like hell because the prongs went in deep, but I wasn't really annoyed, in fact, I thought it was amusing really. After all, I'd taken advantage of him when I fought him!

In the next cell to me was Pat O'Dell. He was awaiting trial for murder. I said: "What do you think will happen?"

He said: "I'll swing and Cleere'll swing with me!"

I thought you miserable bastard cause he could have got Mick off. They both got life, which they served on the Isle of Wight.

After we got out of the 'nick' I walked into the NAAFI and was immediately surrounded by blokes asking what had happened to the Germans, one said: "How many were there Roy – there must have been a few of them to do that to Tommy!"

I obviously couldn't say what had actually happened. Years later two real hard case brothers called Quinn came to see me in a nightclub, they'd been in the Guards with me. The conversation turned to Tommy Nolan and one of them said: "I believe you gave Tommy Nolan that hiding in Dusseldorf?" I asked him how he knew and he told me that Tommy had told him all about it, asking him to keep it quiet. At least he told someone the truth.

I appeared on work parade one morning wearing the correct dress, which was denims. Unfortunately, I'd lost a button at the bottom of my jacket and stitched it on with black cotton, having no khaki cotton left. The sergeant spotted this and gave me seven days C.B. (confined to barracks), which meant that I had to report every hour (outside of parade times) to the guardroom. It was a freak occasion because I was the only one on C.B. and everybody wanted my services because there was a brigadiers' inspection next day. When I reported to the guardroom, the sergeant said: "Go round every wash room in the barracks and collect as many razor blades as you can find and report back here". When I got back with five razor blades, he pointed to the wooden floor. He said: "Start over there and scrape the floor white!" After an hour, my fingers were cut to ribbons and I hadn't done two square feet, so he said: "Go up to the company office and scrub the whole floor". The company office was thirty-five yards long with about twenty desks in it. I scrubbed the lot, moving desks as I went. I got back to my bunk at 1.00am and had to start on my kit for next morning. It was a Saturday, and after morning parades I reported to the guardroom. I was sent to the cookhouse. There was a yard at the back of the kitchen covered in snow. There was a brick-built hut five feet high by five feet wide. In the hut were five one hundredweight bags of spuds and a forty-gallon drum of icy cold water. The cook gave me a knife and said: "Peel that lot, when the drum's full I'll give you another". There was nowhere to sit, I couldn't stand up, so I had to bend over for hours and peel those spuds. My hands were frozen as well as everywhere else. When I'd finished, it took hours before I could straighten my back. That was a bad day!

One night I awoke to the sound of boots in the corridor outside the barrack room, we were in ex Gestapo barracks, which had marble corridors. The duty sergeant came in and said: "Adams, company office, grab your cap and boots." He then marched me down the corridor and across the barrack square in my pyjamas to the company office. An officer was waiting, I had to march up to him and salute. He then handed me a telegram informing me that my father had died. Not a word was said except for the sergeant who yelled: "About turn, quick march." That's how I heard of the death of my dad who was only forty-six. I applied for compassionate leave which was refused – I was somewhat disenchanted with the situation, and showed it in my general behaviour, so much so that the adjutant sent for me. "What's happened to you Adams? You've always been a reasonably good soldier, but lately you're always in trouble, what's the problem?"

So I told him my father died: "I applied for compassionate leave which was refused. My mother had to sail home on her own from Ceylon which took six weeks, now she's living on her own in Liverpool and I can't see her!"

Within four weeks orders came through to transfer me to London so that I could visit my mother. I was posted to the Tower of London as mess orderly to the Tower Guard, which meant I was responsible for seeing to their welfare when on Guard duty.

I took over from a Grenadier guardsman called Rigby, who explained the job to me. He said: "Look your boss is quartermaster Major Rolfe of the Royal Fusiliers and he doesn't want any grief with complaints from guardsmen so he's given you a job as ration stores man. You've got a 3-ton truck with your own driver and you go to Woolwich arsenal twice a week and pick up the rations for all the personnel at the Tower."

He showed me the ration stores which was in the casemates, which is almost like another moat after the main outside moat of the Tower. It's like a street with buildings built into its walls. My ration store was through a door set into the wall and was dungeon like inside, I noticed two very worn and polished flag stones in the floor which were red sandstone the rest of the floor being grey stone, I pointed to them and asked why that was. Rigby said: "Oh there's a dungeon under there, a hundred men of the Black Watch were put down there after a mutiny and suffocated!"

In the early 1700's there was a Scottish Jacobite rebellion in which the Black Watch played a major part. In 1743 there was a mutiny in the Black Watch which would almost certainly relate to the incident in the Tower, giving this story credibility, Flora McDonald was imprisoned in the Tower at this time.

On my first weekend leave I took the train North to Liverpool to see my mum. She had got back safely from Ceylon but had very little money. During the six week trip at sea across the Indian Ocean and through the Suez Canal she did nothing but worry about how she was going to be able to afford the usual end-of-voyage tip to the cabin crew. She bought a small terraced house for £350 which was all the money she had in the world in Hawkstone Street in Liverpool 8 which was very close to Princess Park. It was quite a change because for the last couple of years she'd lived a life of luxury in Ceylon with servants catering for her every need. But her two sisters were living close by in Liverpool so she wasn't completely alone.

Well – I became the man to know in the Tower, being in charge of the food in the army puts one in a very strong position, even the sergeant major used to get a loaf off me each day. Because I was the only Irish Guardsman in the Tower, I was called Mick, although the Irish Guards is actually a British Regiment formed by Queen Victoria in 1900 to commemorate the bravery of the Irish troops in the Boer War.

Being my own boss, I was able to get the tube twice a week to Ralph Samuels' gym in Fulham where my old mate Kish trained, it was mainly a gym for hand balancers but they did have a weight section with an Olympic barbell. I trained there for a couple of years, taking a particular shine to a girl called Pat Toby who was the fittest looking girl I'd ever seen. She was always in *Health & Strength* magazine, featuring in various balancing stunts with Ralph Samuels and other gym members, in Ralph's regular column. Her legs were the female equivalent of Steve Reeves – hard to explain, but I suppose I'm talking about classical lines.

With Terry Freeman, 1949

I turned up one night for a workout, and Ralph and several other regulars were waiting for me. They presented me with a beautifully scripted certificate congratulating me on reaching the age of twenty-one. It was signed by all the gym members. This really meant something, as I didn't have any family to celebrate my Twenty-first Birthday with. My only sister Freda, was living in Paris and my mother was in Liverpool. I've still got the certificate, It's a prized possession.

Another high spot I remember at Ralph Samuel's gym was two workouts I had with Universe contestant Monohar Aich in 1953. He caused a sensation when he first entered the Universe in 1951, because, although he was only four foot eleven inches tall, he

Nigel Kishawi at Rhyl, 1953

had seventeen and a half inch biceps. I remember him doing triceps dips on the parallel bars – he did about six sets of two hundred reps., at a terrific speed! Most of his other exercises were similar, as far as I can remember he did very few exercises using weights.

His Indian colleague, Monotosh Roy, came on stage at the contest, with an eight foot long razor pointed spear. He wedged the handle against the floor, placing the point against his throat and with arms outstretched, pushed his throat forward until the spear handle bent into a 'D' shaped bow! Those guys were really something!

Kish's full name was Nigel Kishawi. He'd finished his army service and was in and out of various adagio and balancing acts, eventually marrying Miss S.E. Britain 1952, Val Mansell and forming a successful act called Kish and Valaire. They eventually became international, performing as far away as Japan and eventually settled in Australia. Kish and I met in Felixstowe where he had finished up after his father had kicked him out for writing on the walls of a public toilet. 'Wogs go home.' This was ludicrous and harmless really because his parents were upper middle class people in Egypt and his father was an Arab and his mother English.

He'd worked his passage on a ship to England and when I met him he was wearing an overcoat made from an American army blanket and he wore Zoot suit trousers wide in the legs tapering in at the ankles and brothel creeper shoes which were leather shoes with inch and a quarter thick soles, he also sported a D.A. (Ducks Arse) haircut and to my pal Tony Partridge and I (we were only sixteen) he was an entirely exciting character. People in England were still wearing short bum starver jackets and fashion was non-existent so soon after the Second World War.

He got called up for national service, where he very quickly became a PTI. He had an extremely shapely natural physique and when he came home on leave he demonstrated his newly acquired skills in hand balancing, somersaults etc. Later on he was heavily featured in a book by John Barrington called *Anthropology and Anatomy*. Barrington said Kish's physique was 95 percent perfect proportion, to be bettered only by Steve Reeves at 98 percent!

Well, I started going to the Serpentine in Hyde Park on a Sunday where Kish and other show biz people used to go. There was the equivalent of a concrete beach by the river where we used to practice various stunts, balancing, adagio etc as well as swimming. Kish and I were approached on several occasions with various offers to test for parts in shows

Roy at the Tower of London, 1952

and films. I remember in particular *South Pacific*, the touring version – the show in which Sean Connery launched his career, and *Wish You Were Here* at the Garrick Theatre and also to test for a film with my hero at the time Burt Lancaster in *The Crimson Pirate*. I of course could take up none of these offers being still in the army.

One day, I went down to the West End just to take in the sights. I paid six bob for a seat in the cinema in Leicester Square to see *Quo Vadis* with Peter Ustinov at the matinee performance. When I came out, I saw a portly character with a flowing scarf carrying a book – and who should it be but Peter Ustinov! As I turned a corner into Leicester Square I noticed that the corner shop, which had very large windows, was a photographers called Landseers.

I had to look twice after glancing in the window. There was a life size photograph of a man with a magnificent physique. It had been cut out so that it appeared to be freestanding. The picture was of Reg Park –

* * *

I walked on and, outside the Union Jack club, bumped into a mate from my battalion in Germany, Clayo Clarkson. He first caught my attention in Sennelager when we were living under canvas. I crawled out of my bivouac one morning and saw this six foot two inch broken nosed fella who was busy shaving and singing a Doris Day number. He turned to me and did a little dance saying in a scouse voice: "Ah, I wish I was at the Grafton." This tickled me.

I'd been away from Liverpool for some years. When I bumped into him he told me he was skint and starving, his uniform was crumpled. I said: "Come on, I'll sort you out."

I took him into the kitchen in the Tower. There was a load of trays of rabbit breast on the stove, row upon row of them. I said: "Help yourself Clayo." Then I fixed him up with a bed for the night. He still talks about it. Clayo is still singing. He did do door work in the late fifties and sixties.

Five or six years ago I bumped into Clayo one day in Liverpool, (although we'd kept in touch we only met occasionally, with him living on the Wirral side of the Mersey), he'd just been to pick up some compensation money. I asked him what that was about and he told me he'd read an article in the paper about money which the Army had set aside for compo claims. He'd been having trouble with his ears, tinnitus, which he decided to claim for. He made the claim saying it was due to the rifle training in the Army. They tested him and gave him a payment and a small pension. Although I don't go along with the compensation culture, I decided to have a go because I had a genuine grievance. I claimed for the perfectly healthy tooth they'd yanked out. My dentist, who I'd been going to for thirty years, wrote saying that I still had the remainder of my teeth intact and he could not imagine a condition at that time which would have required my tooth to be extracted. I also claimed for tinnitus, which they didn't accept, however, they did pay me £4,500 for the loss of my tooth. Thanks Clayo!

The Edwardian style came into fashion in 1953 and I had an Edwardian suit made, prior to this I had a navy blue barathea suit made at Cecil Gees in London which I wore off duty with a black shirt and white tie and slip on shoes with a chain across, and boy did I think I was the bees knees, until one night Id left a girl friend in Sloane St Chelsea and walked all the way back to the Tower having missed the last tube.

I decided to try to climb in to the Tower as it was all locked up. I climbed down into the moat, which was about twelve feet deep there was no water only grass! It was about fifty yards across and I started to climb up one of the massive cast iron drainpipes which had a coat of arms cast into them, these pipes were a good fourteen inches across and about twenty inches where the coat of arms was. I had reached about fifteen feet when the pipe started to come away as I grabbed the coat of arms.

I pushed myself away from the wall and fell, landing face downwards on all fours, I tried to move to one side but the broken pipe struck me on the backside slicing through my nice suit trousers leaving a foot long cut in my right buttock, the scar stayed with me for

In the bar at London's Norwegian Embassy – Roy with the white tie, Mildred in front to his left.

years! I had to make my way out of the moat and lay bleeding on one of the benches they had by the railings with some newspapers I gathered from the trash bins to keep me warm till the Tower opened at 6 a.m.

Being locked out like this was not unusual for me, as the girl friend wouldn't let me stay with her. She used to let me lie on her bed with her and kiss and cuddle but only on the condition that I kept my trousers on. This was acceptable behaviour in those days. I met her whilst strap-hanging on the tube one day, it was packed and she was about ten feet away, I caught her eye and she smiled. I was in uniform and worked my way towards her, I leant down and asked her if she had a nail file, she produced one from her bag with a quizzical expression. I leant forward again and asked her: "What's your phone number?" Taking my shoe off at the same time, she told me and I scratched it on the instep under my shoe, starting a relationship which lasted until she went home to Norway about eighteen months later.

Anyway, one night I decided to try my luck at getting in the Tower. I hammered on the door and a Yeoman Warder called Paddy shouted: "Go away."

I said: "Its Mick let me in."

He said: "The Ceremony of the Keys is over, nobody gets in."

I said: "OK Paddy, remember that when you want bones for your dog." Next thing the bolts were drawn back.

"Get in quick – this never happened."

See what I mean, the power of food control!

I befriended some of the Royal Fusiliers in the Tower and occasionally went to their manor (as they put it) for a night out. One night we went to a dance, which was above a grotty pub at the Elephant and Castle. When we went in it was to me then a strange scene. All the girls wore tight skirts almost to their ankles, on their feet they wore flat black soft shoes no heels, the lads had long jackets and zoot suits trousers, both lads and girls had D.A, haircuts.

I asked a girl for a dance and she said: "I only do ordinary."

I said: "what's ordinary?"

She said: "Like this." She took my hands and held my arms down by her sides and proceeded to shuffle her feet without raising them from the floor, everyone else did the same.

I said: "What's this?"

She said: "We call it the creep." That's the first I'd heard or seen it and not long after that it swept the whole country. The song, *'Walking Is A Thing That No One Does – Everybody Does The Creep'*, went into the hit parade.

We picked up three girls and took them to the pictures. There was a picture on about the French Resistance; we took little notice because we were snogging the girls. Then on the screen, a girl came running out of the woods yelling.

"The Germans are coming! The Germans are coming!"

One of our lads called out, "Sod the Germans I'm coming!"

I remember a barber's shop in the East End, which had photos of a local lad called Arthur Mason who had aspirations to go into films, he knocked around with Spencer Churchill, a bodybuilding icon, and a hard case called Bobby Ramsey. Arthur married film starlet Vera Day, after which they moved to the U.S.A.

I got to know a boxer whilst in the Tower called Sammy Bonici; I remember the Boxing news said he was the greatest thing since Nel Tarleton. I don't know what became of him.

A lot of these Fusiliers were East End villains, and being impressionable I got friendly with some of them. Somehow or other I had become the owner of a 9mm automatic browning pistol. To this day I don't remember where it came from. I mentioned it to one of the guys one day and he asked me if he could borrow it. I said yes and thought no more about it. A few days later, one of the other guys showed me the cover of a newspaper with a photo of a detective; he had a wound on his forehead where a ricocheting bullet had caught him, fortunately doing no harm. The guy with the paper said: "That's where your gun finished up."

I never saw the gun or the guy who borrowed it again. His name was Edwards. It was nearly fifty years ago!

The Korean War was on at the time and the Tower of London was used as a transit stop for guys going to Korea, Sometimes three hundred and fifty would arrive and I'd go to Woolwich for the extra rations. I'd be issued a weeks rations but these guys were usually gone after two days and I'd be stuck with the extra rations. So on a Sunday I'd take some butter, sugar and tea down Petticoat lane and flog it. This gave me some money and I was able to get myself the aforementioned civvies. With my Edwardian suit, when I visited Liverpool, I was ahead of fashion.

The guard's officers were wearing this style and quite often I'd get a butt salute from the guardsmen on duty! All the boys down the East End used to congregate on Sundays down Petticoat Lane and hang around in their suits, unfortunately their numbers increased so much they got in the way of normal business, so the stall holders started to creosote the fences which they liked to lean against on a Sunday morning. After a few suits got ruined they moved somewhere else. In Liverpool they weren't as concerned about smartness and were more interested in being in fashion, the style became bastardised, trousers narrower, jackets longer, the Teddy boy had arrived!

With Kish, 1953

In 1953 I was sent on demob leave and went to Rhyl in North Wales where Kish was in the aqua show, which was attached to Prince Cox's Circus. Another charismatic diver was Johnny McGrath who was also an excellent visual comedian. Off-season he, like Kish, did

My 'Full Gainer'

a dual balancing act with his wife, Jackie Lambert, who was billed as Tarzan Junior led the aqua show. Jackie was a superb diver who did the actual dive off Manhattan Bridge for Johnny Weismuller in Tarzan's New York Adventure. He was also an excellent trampolinest and a great comedian. He and I got on well and he said he wanted me in his show. I told him my diving was very straightforward and not something people would pay to see. He said: "I want you because you look good and I'll show you some dives. Come on over to the boards." He said: "Run along the 1m spring board, at the end kick your right leg into the air as hard as you can, at the same time flinging your head back."

This I did and executed a reverse dive from the front. Now he said: "Go up to the 5m board and do it." This I did and hit the water flat on my back and it hurt!

As I swam to the side he said: "Why didn't you straighten out when you saw the bleedin' water."

I said: "Because you didn't tell me to."

He said: "OK go again and get it right." I did and did a perfect full gainer.

"Ok now go to the top board and do it."

Well, I got to the top board and stood at the back gathering my courage, all the girls from the show were sat opposite on the other side of the pool. So I gritted my teeth and did it! Now he said: "This time you do the same but as you somersault your arms and legs must continue in a running

Johnny McGrath, Lady and Kish.

motion." Well, I managed it and thought never again, and he said: "Right, that's in the show twice a day!"

Three of us started the show all diving together spinning over in a running motion, as time went on he taught me various stunts and I enjoyed it. Then I went back from leave and did about five months before saying farewell to my happy times at the Tower. I would have signed on for another five years, but I knew if I did they'd send me right back to the battalion.

In 1957, Johnny McGrath was in a show with Kish and Jackie Lambert. They were doing a ten-man stunt comedy dive. Johnny was at the top of the ten-man pyramid and was wearing a cap with a long peak. When he hit the water, it got under the peak and jerked his head back breaking his neck. He's been in a wheelchair ever since. He became a theatrical agent and developed a feisty reputation – not surprising! His wife continued for a while with another balancing partner who was trained by Johnny, keeping that side of the business going.

Left: Pat Toby on the beach

Below: Typical bathing beauty contest, holiday camp, 1952, Pat is second from left

Reg Park in Hawaii

~ 5 ~
Gyms and Gym Heroes

WHEN I WAS in London I went to the 1953 Mr Universe competition it was held at the Palladium in those days. A high spot was a young serving sailor in the US Navy who beat all the other amateur contestants by a mile. His name was Bill Pearl. When the professionals came on, it came down to four finalists. Johnny Isaacs, Arnold Dyson – Spencer Churchill and Jules Bacon. I knew all about Spencer Churchill, he trained at St George's club in Putney near to Ralph Samuel's gym where I trained. I'd never met him, but like every other bodybuilder in the country I was a great fan of his. He was a friend of Reg Park and sometimes they trained together. Well, Spencer looked spectacular, I'd never seen anyone look so good, like Reeves he has an aesthetic quality as well as amazing shape, very broad shoulders and an amazing bulky yet streamlined appearance with an extremely narrow waist. Well – they announced the 4th place winner first, Spencer Churchill! No one could believe it, they handed Spencer a little shield, which he flicked with his thumb. Spencer had some years before entered a South East Britain competition, A little man walked down the line telling everyone how to pose. He was Laurie Webb. When he got to Spencer, Spence asked.

"Are you judging?"

He said: "Yes."

So Spence said: "Well I'm off", and walked off the stage. It was a NABBA competition and he was never forgiven. In future competitions it was rumoured that a NABBA official would tell the judges he (Spencer) had a curvature of the spine when he did his characteristic relaxed pose, in which he looked terrific. Spencer took to carrying a Doctor's certificate, refuting the slur, but he still won no major contests as a result of his black listing. To fans of Spencer, this ranked with the non-appearance of Elvis in this country – as an injustice!!

Kish told me that when he went to Oswestry upon going into the Army, he was walking between wooden huts with steps to the doors. A guy was sat on a step with his elbow on his knee and Kish said he couldn't believe the forearm on the bloke. He had a small wrist with a terrific muscularity all sinews and veins, Kish walked back twice to have another look. That soldier was Spencer Churchill.

Upon leaving the army I came back to Liverpool where my mother had bought a little terraced house so that I'd have somewhere to go on leave. She was living for the day when I came home, so I thought I'd come to Liverpool for a few months and go back to London.

The first thing I remember on arriving in Liverpool was to look for a Gym. I remember going to one at Boaler St school a couple of times and was very impressed by a black bodybuilder called Basil Grant, that was back in 1954, and I was amazed to discover that he was still training and competing twenty-five years later and still looking terrific. I then joined the Victor barbell gym in Anfield, which was immediately next door to Liverpool Football ground. I'd not seen such an orderly gym before with graded dumbbells on racks and upright barbells around the walls with a sit up and chinning room etc. I thought this place is ahead of its time. Its only since reading Alan Radley's *History of*

Paul Wynter at Vic's Gym

Physical Culture and seeing pictures of gyms a hundred and fifty years ago which made me think again. Some of these gyms were massive, people trained in squads they had spectators viewing boxes along the sides three tiers high! I did go to Bill Watson's gym for a while whilst in London. Bill lifted in the Olympics. I remember his advice on bodybuilding: "train as much as you can, and eat whatever you can get your hands on.' He didn't have any benches in his gym, we did press on back off the floor!

The Victor gym was my only source of leisure in those days; money was scarce so it was the only respite from work. The most popular guy in the gym was John Pennington nicknamed Fatso, but he certainly wasn't fat. He had broader shoulders than anyone else and he was an acclaimed wit, the place was full of real characters and training was better than a night out.

The owner Vic Imundi had built the gym as a labour of love, he ran a busy café and his pal Bill Newton ran the gym. Vic used to bring a bodybuilding celebrity each year when he staged the gym contest; we had Reub Martin, Reg Park, Paul Wynter, Spencer Churchill, John Lees, Paul Nash and Dennis Wynn etc. Of all the black bodybuilders I've met over the years, the physique of Paul Wynter was, and is, one of the most impressive. Like Reeves, he combined a perfect proportion with terrific bulk. He was also extremely strong. When he visited Vic's Gym in the 50s, I remember him doing lying dumbbell flying exercises using two Olympic bars with 140lbs on each! (Also a Reg Park feat) He also did a single arm overhead press using an eleven-stone man! Now in his sixties, he is amazingly unchanged, still doing three and four hour workouts four times a week!

John Pennington, Vic's Gym, 1953

When I think about it now, none of the guys who trained at Vic's were interested in entering physique competitions. We just trained to get stronger and improve our bodies. I can't remember anybody in the

Bob Hickson, Roy, Denny and George Rowan

Bert Owens and Bob Memery

Eddie McDonough, 1961

Roy with Earl Maynard (Mr. Universe), 1956

earlier years that I trained there actually training for a physique competition, apart from the annual gym contest, which was an in-house thing.

We did have one member who was selected to enter the Mr Universe competition one year and that was George Rowan. I don't remember how that came about, but I know he was not a regular physique contender. Bodybuilding nowadays seems to be all about winning competitions at any cost. We did, however, have a very competitive strength set team.

At the time that I joined the Victor Barbell Gym in December 1954, having finished my time in the army, heavy squatting was not really popular with the bodybuilders, though it flourished later on. However, I arrived at the Gym one evening and saw Julian Creus, ex-Olympic lifter, doing squats in a makeshift garage in the back yard. I was surprised to see this little man with enormous thighs doing sets of twenty repetitions at a good pace with 300lbs on his back!

This inspired me to look at my own paltry efforts in this department. I have to say I was never a great squatter, having a terrible style. Amazingly, I did for a short while become holder of the club's record (not counting Creus') with 360lbs! Along came a new member, cyclist Bob Memery, thin upper body, terrific thighs and calves. After a few weeks he approached me, the 'squat champ', and asked if he could train with me on the squat. The club competition arrived. I decided to go for a final lift of 400lbs, having done it in training. I started with 380lbs and failed – twice! Bob, however, got 380lbs on his final lift! A proper strength set team was put together concentrating on curl, bench press and squat. Under the guidance of Bill Newton, who ran the gym with Vic Imundi, the team eventually beat all comers, travelling all over Britain. They went to Los Angeles in 1971. When they returned, Bob said to me: "Roy, you wouldn't believe those Yanks, they were injecting themselves between each attempt!" One said to me: "Why don't you guys try this gear?"

I said: "What for? We beat you anyway!" Bob Hoffman, the famous York Barbell owner, sponsored this trip.

They went to the World Team Championships in 1973 at Harrisburg, Pennsylvania, and won that! Joe Weider, the famous physique magazine owner, was good enough to sponsor them for that trip. The other two members of the team were Bert Owens and Bob Evans. Bob regularly bench pressed 350lbs at less than 11 stone. Bert regularly exceeded 400lbs on the bench press and took the British record with 440lbs. Both these fellows worked hard as joiners and could only train three times a week!

On 2nd March 1969, Bob Memery did a full squat with 610lbs. One judge, whose name was Jock Slithers, said: "No lift."

Bob, with the weight on his shoulders, said: "Why?"

"You did'ne go down low enough," was the reply.

Bob went down again and said: "Is this low enough?"

"Yes," came the reply. He then stood up with it – two repetitions with 610lbs at 12 stone in weight, a new world record! He was to do 640lbs later. I've known him to do 36 reps with 300lbs, 21 reps with 400lbs, a one-minute break then 12 more reps! He also did 12 reps with 500lbs only to be beaten by Bert Owens who did 13 reps. Bob Memery and

John Lees at Vic's Gym

Bert still train at Vic's Gym (48 years at time of writing!), though in different premises now. These fellows have never had special diets or supplements worth mentioning!

At the time of writing, Bob Memery has just celebrated his 74th birthday. He's recently started to do a few press ups to keep fit. He's just completed 74 reps to celebrate his birthday!

Eventually, in the late sixties, I started to run competitions in a couple of the clubs, both for beauty and physique, and they were rather successful. One competition I called the Mr and Miss West Coast, another Miss Pyramid. A stunning beauty called Jennie McAdam won the Miss West Coast and made the nationals as Miss W.C.! As Miss Pyramid, which she also won, I entered her in the Miss Night Club of Great Britain. She won it – her prize was £1,000 and I received the latest transistorised TV. Another girl whom I coerced into entering, borrowing a pair of shoes and swimsuit for her, went on to win 'The Most Wanted Girl In The World' for a £10,000 prize! – The biggest prize in a beauty contest! Her name was Tricia O'Donnell.

When Reg Park came on his second visit in 1954, I decided to do a drawing of him and get him to sign it. I didn't have time to finish the legs but took it anyway. Vic introduced me, and I was overwhelmed and couldn't speak at first. Reg said he loved the drawing and asked me to do some of the bodybuilding exercises for the *Reg Park Journal.* This I did and he paid me five bob a drawing. I found them difficult to do as I had no model and had to use my imagination. I used to deal mainly with Reg's dad who looked after the business, which was mail order, selling equipment, weights etc.

Reg travelled all over Britain doing appearances in gyms large and small, community centres, halls etc. You could call on him anytime and if available he would jump on a train and arrive. Not like nowadays, when you have to give them six to eight weeks notice so they can prepare themselves! Reg would start off by sitting and talking, answering

Reg Park in 1949, aged just 20, having become Mr. Britain

questions, after which he'd lift weights, often attempting maximums, then he'd pose, his size and muscularity unsurpassed.

Wag Bennett, the well-known owner of Wag's Gym in London, told me how he'd met Reg. He was going to the Weightlifting Championships at Earls Court, which was part of the Olympic games in 1948. Walking in front of Wag, who was with Bob Woolger (his future father-in-law), was Steve Reeves, John Grimek and Bob Hoffman with the York Barbell Team. A young man fell into step with Wag and started talking. He looked at Reeves and Co and said: "I'm going to win that Universe contest one day." Wag was eighteen at the time; Reg was twenty, having just finished his army service.

Reg started to train for the Mr North East Britain and won it. He then moved to London to the famous Viking Gym, owned by Henry J Atkins. Reg stayed at the house, the gym being in the house. Wag told me he and the lads in the gym used to give Reg their milk ration to help him bulk up. Reg won the 1949 Mr Britain title, with Paul Newington second, beating the massive John Lees into third place. In 1952, the year after he won the Mr Universe title, Reg invited Wag to go to Leeds to train with him – Wag was training for the Mr Britain contest. He must have been a good training partner for Reg – I was told he'd bench pressed 500lb the previous year on his twenty-first birthday! I think Reg Park was the only other person to bench press that amount at that time! Reg had booked him into a well-known hotel in Leeds, which was popular with celebs.

Reg asked Wag "Would you like to see the gym?"

Wag said: "Oh yes please, I sure would", so Reg got the key and they walked to the end of a row of houses, where there was a row of tin-roofed garages. Reg inserted the key into the door of the end one saying: "The beauty of having the end one is there's a window!" Wag told me. When I looked inside, I couldn't believe it. It was a one-car garage, the floor was dirt with no covering, and the bench was bare wood with some sacks. There were big weights strewn around and candles everywhere.

I asked: "What are the candles for?"

Reg boomed: "For night training of course."

Reg Park, 1962, weighing 240 lbs.

I couldn't believe he built his physique in conditions like these, but he did!

Wag came second in the big man's class at the 1952 Mr Britain, Eric Eastham pipping him at the post! Wag Bennett had a brother-in-law called Howard who was a bit of a tearaway as a lad, eventually being put into a Dr. Barnardo's Home. At sixteen years old they shoved him into the Navy. He grew into a fine man, winning the Mr. Navy physique competition and later in Singapore, – the Navy's Best Built Man.

He missed Reg Park by one week in Singapore. They'd all been reading about Reg and he was looking forward to meeting him, but was transferred the week before Reg arrived. Back in London he was offered a casting for a part in the touring version of the musical *'South Pacific'*. He couldn't take it so he passed it on to his old bunk mate from the Navy, Tom Connery. Tom landed the job in the chorus and toured with the show. After eighteen months, his part was upgraded and he changed his name to Sean. He had appeared once before on stage, in Edinburgh, in the musical *'Sixty Glorious Years'*, starring Anna Neagle. He'd had a walk-on part as a Guardsman.

Spencer at Vic's Gym, 1952

A couple of years before, when *'South Pacific'* was at Drury Lane in the West End, they had a gym under the stage. Reg Park told me that he trained there when preparing for the Mr. Universe. Larry Hagman and Sean Connery trained at the same time. Larry Hagman being the son of Mary Martin, star of the show.

Wag Bennett has known so many people in his career as a gym owner. People from all walks of life trained at Wag's gym, including underworld figures, such as the Krays, the Richardsons and the Tibbs. The gym is still going to this day – with Wag still running it. We dine together once a year at the O.H. physical culture dinner in London. Last year, March 2002, Wag and his wife Diane, were guests of honour, which meant we couldn't sit together.

At the 1966 Mr Universe, Wag was judging. One of the contestants was the young Arnold Schwarzenneger. Arnold came second, being beaten by Chet Yorton. Afterwards, Wag spoke to Arnold who was sitting looking very depressed at being beaten. Wag explained to him that his calves had let him down. Arnold tore the lower legs off his track-suits so that his calves were always on show, (this was Reg Park's suggestion). He started to train at Wag's Gym, and Wag and his wife Diane put him up. For a while he slept on the couch! After that he became part of the family, coming and going as he pleased. Wag asked him one time what his ambitions were.

Arnold said: "I want to become the most successful bodybuilder in the world and get into acting and become the most successful film star."

Wag said: he thought, in your dreams! – Arnold proved him wrong!

Arnold mentioned to Wag that one of the reasons he came to England was to meet Reg Park, his hero. So Wag arranged for them to attend a seminar in Leeds, organised by gym owner Tony Charna. The reigning Mr Britain, Dave Johns, did the physique-posing routine and Arnold did the talking along with Wag. Afterwards, Tony arranged a meal for them, which they devoured with relish! They then were invited to Reg's house where Lydia, his mum, had prepared a meal for them. Lydia knew her job when it came to feeding muscle men! She served roast beef and Yorkshire pudding in the traditional Yorkshire way – the pudding was massive, covering the whole plate, with the meat etc on top! They daren't mention the fact that they'd already eaten and had to get on with it. Wag said they managed to clear their plates although they were absolutely bloated!

A visit to Southport Baths, 1955.
Left to right: Harry Williams, Denny Rowan, Irwin Brooks, George Rowan and Roy Adams

Waterloo Summer Fête, 1963
Lads from Crosby Gym ~ Tony Buck, centre; Roy Adams on the right

A back shot of Roy, 1953

Reg Park wins the 1951 Mr. Universe contest

Many years later in the 90's I would go with Sheilagh my partner up to Leeds to meet Reg and his lovely wife Marion when they visited from South Africa. Lydia would cook and I'd insist on sitting in Arnold's chair (my claim to fame). Reg still works hard training people, which he loves doing in South Africa, he's also an expert on remedial training and has helped many well-known rugby and football stars. His son Jon Jon runs World Gym in Los Angeles and his daughter Jeunesse works hard for the 'Save a Tree in Africa' fund amongst other things. She is a friend of Nelson Mandela and was South Africa Environmentalist of the Year in 1999.

Reg Park was, and still is, a phenomenon in more ways than one. One of the most remarkable things about him is the fact that he didn't actually start serious training with weights until after he'd seen John Grimek beat Steve Reeves in the 1948 Mr Universe – he was then 20 years old. Obviously he was already a very physical man – he'd just come out of the army where he was a PTI sergeant. He was a good track athlete and also played a lot of football in his teens. When he saw the Mr Universe in 1948, he vowed one day to win it. Within a year he won the Mr Britain title and in June 1950 the Mr Europe title. After winning the Mr. Britain, Reg's parents sent him to America, – as a twenty-first Birthday present. Whilst there he stayed with a Dr. Tilney and met Joe Weider, who helped further motivate Reg's training, posing, etc. He returned with a Californian tan and a type of trunks with a high waist and high cut at the thighs, which gave Reg a new look, apart from the benefits of the superior food and protein drinks available in America.

In September that year, he won America's Best Developed Athlete. This was incredible because the Americans had many supremely developed bodybuilders, whereas

Early Days: Terry Philips shows great potential

in England we still had food rationing! It didn't actually end until 10 years after the War in 1955!

In 1950, Steve Reeves came over for the Mr Universe – there's a story that as he walked from the Palladium in the afternoon after the judging, one of the major stores had just closed and as the female staff emptied out and saw Reeves they stopped in their tracks, actually stopping the traffic! They'd never seen anything like him, with a terrific face, dark hair which had an auburn shade to it, a California tan and broad shoulders with a full drape plum coloured jacket and Hawaiian shirt! The whole bodybuilding fraternity was besotted by him.

This was what Reg had to compete against in 1950 after only two years serious training on weights. Nobody wanted to see Reeves beaten, including me! Reeves looked terrific on the night, though it's generally accepted that Reg was actually in better condition, Reeves having been unwell the week before. The next year when Reg won it, there was without a doubt no one in the world who could have beaten him.

Mareon and Reg Park with Sheilagh on a visit to Reg's mum in Leeds, 1990

Steve Reeves landed a bit part in a film called *Athena* with Debbie Reynolds and Jane Powell which the whole gym went to see. He then played Hercules in the film *Hercules Unchanged* which, pound for pound was the most profitable film ever made, probably because it was the first film promoted on television. The film makers actually got him to slim down for the film thinking that his physique might make the average male filmgoer feel inferior! He progressed onto a successful film career.

Reg Park also made six Hercules films, he didn't slim down his herculean physique and certainly looked the part, which he actually played very well.

I think Reg's achievement in developing that physique was unequalled by anyone. He obviously had great genetics, but not the genetics of Steve Reeves, who had a natural balanced physique, which included highly developed, well-structured legs. Reg had to spend many hours on his legs, doing calf raises with 1000lbs on his back to develop his great calves. The difference between his legs in the Mr Britain competition and the Mr Universe competition tells the whole story. Nobody to this day has equalled his achievement! Chemically developed physiques don't count! I'm not knocking people on steroids. I think it was inevitable that they would become popular – anything to speed up the agonisingly slow process of building some muscle, was bound to be – it took years before anyone started to look outstanding physique wise, unless you were a Reg Park! Of course, one reason for this was our lack of knowledge about nutrition. I remember someone mentioned amino acids once! Casilan came out in the early 60s – I tried it and mentioned to Bill Newton that at four shillings a pack it was very expensive and only lasted a week. He said: "You're wasting your time – you need a pack a day!" That was the end of that!

When I was putting contests on in the early sixties, I did see a sudden dramatic change in the physiques of some of the entrants. I stopped doing it. It was no longer a level playing field.

I've remained friends with Paul Wynter, John Lees, Earl Maynard, Hubert Thomas and Spencer Churchill to this day, Rueb Martin sadly died in 1997. His wife the beautiful ex-Windmill Girl Beryl still attends the Oscar Heidenstam dinner in London.

We could only train three times a week in Vic's gym because the format used to be a rest day between workouts, so the gyms only opened three evenings a week, opening more nights would probably not be worthwhile as bodybuilders were like vegetarians and train spotters e.g. cranks, so there were not that many of them. Consequently our workouts were for at least three hours at a time. As boxers like Joe Bygraves and Randolph Turpin started to use weights people began to realise the benefits and the sport gained credibility.

Vic's Gym, 1960. Back row: Gilly Neal, Roy Adams, Tony Coburn, Brian Hilton, Frank Duff, Doug Tomala.
Front row: Jimmy Davis, Arthur Vacakazzi, Eddie McDonough, Ray ?

Reg Park and Dennis Wynn at Vics Gym, 1953

Reg poses with Vic watching, 1953

I meet Steve Reeves, 1994

With Reg Park, 1988

With John Grimek, 1993

~ 6 ~
Labouring Days

AFTER LEAVING THE army, I tried to find work. I was walking along Old Hall Street in Liverpool and noticed a sign – 'Liverpool Warehousing Company'. I was with an ex army pal Joe Lees so we went into the office and asked for work. The guy said: "Stand under the clock across the street 7.45am on Monday and you'll get some work." So we stood there with some other no hopers on the Monday and were picked out for some work. We didn't know that the stand as they called it was the pits. You were promised only one days work at a time, the pay was lousy and work hard, 3 cwt bags of Cuban sugar, cotton seed and bales of cotton all day long with one 10 minute break in the morning.

When we arrived for work on Monday, everyone would be standing outside the warehouse, shoulders hunched against the cold. The foreman would arrive to let us in giving us our jobs. On the Cuban sugar, the bags were five feet long, cumbersome and heavy. They were lifted on a wire pulley from the wagon up to the warehouse-loading bay, which could be six or more floors up. The bottom row of bags were standing on end leaning against each other which was known as the Jack, after which the bags would be lifted horizontally and laid across the top. We used to stack them three over the Jack, the top ones took a bit of lifting. These two handled warehouse upright trucks were about five feet high with the thick axle at the bottom with two heavy cast iron wheels also a steel plate which the bags rested on they must have weighed about sixty five pounds. Pushing them with a bag on was heavy going but still easier than stacking them. After an hour or so, someone would mention the football on the previous Saturday, after which the shouted conversation would go on for hours. Joe and I weren't interested in football in those days.

Friday night we made our way home on the overhead railway knackered as usual. Joe said to me: "I suppose they'll all be lookin' forward to the match, I hate it when they get started on that fuckin' football on a Monday mornin".

I said: "So do I."

Monday came and miserable faces everywhere. We all trundled into the warehouse, the fellers grabbed the trucks and Joe piped up in a loud voice.

"Anyone see the match?"

Everyone started talking at once. I looked in exasperation as Joe lifted his shoulders, spreading his palms out to the sides grinning from ear to ear, he'd started them off on the football two hours earlier.

There was a very big burly guy called Al. he always used Mondays to tell of his weekend exploits which were usually about fights he'd got into in the pubs.

"I left this fella for dead; I left that fella for dead." He was a big strong man, he had a party trick which was to grab hold of two fifty six pound warehouse weights which were square solid iron blocks with the handle set deep into the block. He would grab two in one hand and swinging his arm back propel them across the warehouse floor. He was always challenging someone to do it, especially me. I knew I couldn't do it, I'd already had a try on the quiet, and my hands weren't big enough to span the handles.

I had an idea. I said: "Could you push two of these warehouse trucks to arms length above your head?" he looked blankly at me. I placed the trucks back to back with about twelve inches between them, I looked down and grabbed at the axles pulling them up to shoulder height at the same time swinging them over so that the handles swung downwards. I then started to press them to arms length thinking of them as a pair of sixty five pound dumbbells. I pushed them about ten times and then thrust them forward and downwards on to the floor. That did the trick; I'd left him for dead.

Eventually we heard of a job in a private warehouse, which was supposed to be better. We got the job and on the first morning we were stacking cases of tinned fruit. These stacks were high, but Joe was putting them three cases higher, I said: "Why are you doing that."

He laughed and said: "I'd like to see the poor sods who have to get them down!" He was six foot four inches tall and a bit of a joker – in the nicest possible way. When we went into a Dockers canteen, some times he'd sit right down in his seat and say in a loud voice: "Oh well we'd better get going." As people looked over, he'd slowly unravel himself until he stood upright stretching his arms above his head. He was tall, but not as tall as he imagined! Even in pubs, he put his empty glass high up on the picture rail.

"I'd like to see the barmaid who collects that!"

We were working with an Irishman who had ten kids and two layabouts who sat all day behind the stacks drinking the juice out of the cans of fruit, while we did the work. Three weeks before Christmas the foreman said: "Right you three are finished tonight so pick up your money."

I said: "Look here we've done all the work while those two sat around, I'm not so bothered but this guy's got ten kids and Christmas is in a couple of weeks."

He said: "Mind your own business and get your gear," So I put my coat on and put my tea can under my jacket, and as I passed the office door, which was at the top of a steep set of stairs, the foreman shouted: "Hey you, stop there! What's under your Jacket!"

I said: "You mind your own business, I don't work here anymore." He grabbed my coat and pulled me round towards the office door and tried to drag me inside, so I gave him an upper cut right on the chin and he hurtled down the stairs. He was lying at the bottom, so I pulled my can out of my coat and shoved it under his nose: "That's what I had under my coat you snidy bastard," And Joe and I jumped on the overhead railway train. A few days later, we heard he'd died of a heart attack, but we heard no more, and cared no more.

A guy called Stan Waters opened a café on the dock road for the Dockers obviously because they were the main source of trade. There was plenty to go at with Liverpool's nine miles of docks plus all the streets of warehouses branching off the dock road. Stan Waters eventually opened more Stan Waters café's. They became a household name and the Stan waters nudger was a long crusty roll with various fillings, like bacon etc that was very popular. Joe and I used to frequent these places as we moved to different warehouses, however when we were at the North end of the dock road the most popular café was called the 'Griffin' so we went in there.

A very smart young girl who was busy going up and down the stairs immediately took my eye. I tried to attract her attention but she was apparently too busy. She was to tell me later that when she saw me walk in for my mug of tea at the counter, she thought – I bet he thinks he's somebody – and decided to pay me no attention. The factor was, I was dressed a bit different and had a different accent. I also wore a gold chronometer watch that my Mother (god help her) had bought me for my twenty-first birthday. I'd only been in Liverpool a couple of months and so I found everything a bit different from London.

I was suffering from an ulcer, which the warehouse job wasn't helping. In fact, just at that time I had been sent to a large warehouse, which was a massive high ceilinged room. In the centre of the floor was a stack of bags of cottonseed. This stack was about fifteen feet high and was a massive block about sixty feet by sixty feet. I had to stand on the top with another guy and a crane would lift a bundle of bags off a wagon and drop them on to the centre of the pile. We then had to place the bags into a certain pattern as we built up the stack. We used a hand and hook to lift the heavy bags. The other guy was experienced and I followed his instructions. As we sunk our hooks into each end of the bags he'd say: "Over ere' eh la, over ere eh la", in rapid succession. Each time he said it we lifted another bag dragging and carrying them to the positions. This was fast and strenuous and played havoc with my ulcer. The only thing that would give me any relief was a glass of milk, so the next time we went to the Griffin in our lunch break I managed to get the attention of the smart and pretty young girl. I'd now discovered she was serving the foremen and the bosses upstairs. They actually had tables with vinyl cloths. I asked her if she could get me a mug of milk. This she did – when I tasted it, I realised it was half water. I called her over and asked: "Why have you put water in it? This is no good to me," she said: "That's all there is." They actually watered down the milk before putting it in the tea. I couldn't understand the logic, presuming you'd need to put more in making your tea colder and weaker. Of course now a days most of the population use watered down milk paying the same price as whole milk. It turned out I chatted the girl up and managed to make a date with her.

We arranged to meet under Lewis's statue in the city centre; she lived miles away north in Bootle, whilst I lived in the south end of Liverpool in Dingle. On the first date she was an hour late, and each time I met her it was the same, one time it was 2 hours after the arranged time. What I couldn't understand was why I was still there when she came; I think I was fascinated by the manner of her speech and no nonsense attitude apart from the fact that she was obviously physically attractive. I think they call it love! Her name was Ellen.

On our first date, I think we went to the pictures. I walked her down to the pier head to catch her bus, as we walked into a large open square at the pier head we passed some green painted huts on the left hand side, as we passed a passage way between the huts. I manoeuvred Ellen into the passageway and put my arm around her waist bending forward to kiss her. She pushed me away with all her force saying: "What do you think you're doing?"

"I want to give you a goodnight kiss," I said.

"How dare you?" she said: "I hardly know you." Setting off with a good pace for the bus with me trailing after her apologising. I think there were about three dates before I was rewarded with a peck on the cheek.

Eventually we got married and raised three fine boys and a beautiful daughter. Unfortunately, the nightlife with its stresses, strains and temptations is not really conducive to an ideal married life. However, our marriage did survive for nearly thirty years and our kids were fully grown by then.

One day I bumped into Joe again and he told me he had a job in Speke in a concrete factory earning £15 a week for seven days. This was quite good money and he got me an interview. I turned up in my suit, at the site, which was a large open field with massive concrete blocks everywhere. A group of men were huddled around an extra large block working on it in a heavy downpour. I sloshed through the mud and spoke to the foreman. He said: "Have you got any old clothes? It's a dirty job you know."

I said: "Of course I have."

"Ok start in the morning."

The next day the field was solid ice I slipped and slid to the foreman. He said: "Ok, start on the units."

A fellow came over to me whose nose was black with cold, he also wore a black beret, he said: "You've just touched for the worst job in the place." And it was! We had to handle twenty-four tons of concrete a day with shovels to make our bonus. These units were about fifteen feet long and rested on three eighteen-inch walls. The first job on arrival was to scrape the bits of concrete off from the previous day, after which you had to dip a rag into a drum of oil and spread it over them to stop the concrete sticking. Oil doesn't freeze like water, but it gets intensely cold and when you plunge your hand in, it sticks to your hand, freezing it, rather in the same way that boiling milk sticks to your mouth when you mistakenly drink it. After that, a heavy vibrator motor had to be attached by a wraparound chain. There were twenty-four units and a dumper would deposit the concrete at the end and we would have to pick up a shovel full and step over the intervening walls, toing and froing until the unit was full, after which the vibrator was removed and the massive iron frame had to be lifted on handles to the next unit. The high stepping whilst carrying the shovel was great for the abdominals!

We had to make about a dozen smaller blocks after the initial twenty-four units to get our bonus. One day the foreman asked me if I'd like some overtime.

I said: "Yes".

He said: "There's five ton of sand over there – throw it into that high sider before you go." Every shovel full had to be thrown up five or six feet onto the wagon. I managed to do it in an hour. I'd started at 4.30pm, having finished our bonus work half an hour early. I finished it by 5.30pm.

The foreman came over and said: "That's good – you're on half an hour's overtime." – what a minge bag he was!

I acquired a Raleigh moped, top speed fifteen miles per hour downhill with the wind behind it. I used to leave home at 6am to drive the ten miles to Speke; I had to be there at 7am to help the crane driver lift our work from the previous day. I had to slide my hands off the ends of the handlebars on the bike; they were too cold to open the fingers. If any of the stones broke we got no bonus, although that was nothing to do with us. Although I didn't have a pick on me, I still lost a stone during the year I did that job.

When we got married, Ellen moved into my Mum's little terraced house in Hawkstone Street in Liverpool 8 where I lived. It was a very nice quiet little street with mostly rather mature neighbours. My mother had bought me a radiogramme which was a veneered plywood box with a lid on which held a radio and a turntable set into the top. These were very popular and my Mother put herself into hock for six shillings a week for it. The first record I bought was Joseph Locke singing *'Goodbye'* from *'White Horse Inn'*. I was still in the army at the time.

I also became a great fan of Frankie Laine, Tennessee Ernie, Joni James, Jeri Southern and Dean Martin. I used to open the front door and the window of the house when I played my records so that the neighbours could get the benefit, the main one being the *'Wheel Of Fortune'* by Kay Starr. They never complained and were always nice to me and nowadays I wince at the thought of what they probably really thought.

I'd heard a record on AFN (American Forces Network), which was different to anything I'd ever heard. It had a sort of metallic echoy guitar sound and a strident different voice. I got a friend who regularly did the transatlantic run to bring me back a copy from America, which he did. I invited my pals from the gym to come to the house for a makeshift party so I could play them the record. It was Elvis Presley's *'Heartbreak Hotel'*.

Within a year Ellen and I had two children, Rowland and Tony, there was only eleven months between them. There were only two downstairs rooms apart from the little kitchen and we occupied the front room. At night, we would put the table in the corner and pile the furniture on top so that we could pull out the put u up bed.

Freda my sister was getting fed up living in Paris and wrote to ask my mum if she could come and stay with her two kids. I told mum it wasn't an option there was no room. She agreed with me and wrote to Freda telling her she could stay till she found somewhere else. Needless to say, Freda arrived with her two kids Maureen and Steven who'd been born in Paris. Now it was crowded and inevitably within a short time, tempers got frayed.

Freda, Mum, Maureen and Steve

Things were brought to a head when Ellen and I were having an argument. Freda tried to break it up and got between us. I told her to keep out of it and she hit me on the head with something, I gave her a push and Ellen went for me. I held my hand to my head and said: "She didn't have to hit me with a bottle.'

Ellen yelled: "With a bottle!" and went for Freda. I intervened and explained it was only a little medicine bottle, after which we all calmed down.

Next morning I set out to find somewhere else to live, it was very difficult, there wasn't much around, however I got the *Liverpool Echo* and answered an ad. for an apartment in Carlingford Street off Parliament Street which was mainly in the coloured area. The flat was at the top of a four story Victorian house with eight steps up to the front door. I went in and had a look around. I climbed the stairs to the top of the house where there were two attic rooms; one was quite large and contained a double bed, nothing else. The other was quite tiny and was filled apart from two feet down one side by the water tank for the whole house. I asked the landlord where the kitchen was. He said it was in the cellar. He took me down the narrow steep staircase to the cellar where I saw pools of water on the concrete floor. There was an old electric cooker, which had only two burners working. It was thirty shillings a week and I was so desperate I decided to take it. When Ellen came to have a look, she asked the Landlord where she could keep the pram. Tony being a baby at the time. He said she would have to keep it in the cellar and he would help her when she needed to take the pram out.

It was a nightmare – when Ellen went up to the shops she had to get his help up the cellar stairs and down the front steps and of course the reverse when she came back.

After three days, the landlord had had enough and made it a major problem, added to which when I wanted a cup of tea Ellen had to go down four storeys into the cellar and wait about twenty minutes for the kettle to boil on the electric hob. I bought a tiny portable electric ring, which was a single quarter inch spring, which would get hot after half an hour. I placed it on top of the tank in the spare room. I decided to cook a tin of beans on it. Eventually after what seemed like a lifetime, they started to heat up. The landlady smelled them and ranted on about us cooking in the room.

The only other furniture we had in the room besides the bed was a cheap table and chairs and my radiogramme with which I entertained the neighbourhood by playing *'The Magic Touch'*, by the Platters.

Ellen's dad Billy came to see how we were getting on and was horrified, not just by the conditions but the fact we were the only white people in the house, which wasn't a problem for me. He told us we could move in with them giving us their front room. I was relieved because I was worried about the thirty bob rent. We were in and out of that place in four days.

After a month at Ellen's parents house Billy found us a flat above a shop in Derby Road, Bootle. The shop owner was a very nice Indian man called Mugbul Ahmed. The flat was good; it had a decent sized living room bedroom and kitchen. The only problem was the smell of Indian cooking which pervaded the atmosphere. The smell was strange to us and we found it overpowering, also the décor of the flat was somewhat creepy with strange objects on the walls, which in our ignorance we thought were voodoo objects.

Then Billy found us a ground floor accommodation, which was in a sort of triangle between two corner shops. The living room came to a point at one end where someone had built a cupboard to try and square it off a bit. The kitchen was actually the yard with a corrugated iron roof with a wooden partition wall at one end and a door leading to the back entry. The floor was the backyard flagstones and sloped down fortunately because when it rained the rain poured down the whitewashed brick walls. The sink was carved out of a piece of red sandstone, which had been scooped out to give three inches depth. It had a single cold tap, no hot water.

One summer morning I set off to work in my tee shirt and jeans, Ellen stood at the door waving me off, all the Littlewoods Pools girls were passing on their way to work as I crossed the road on my bike, a real Jack the lad, I stood on the pedals making the turn into Millar's Bridge. My foot slipped off the pedal somersaulting me over. Embarrassed in front of the girls, I glared over towards Ellen just in time to see the front door slam. She told me when I got home later that when she slammed the door; she collapsed on the floor with her back resting against the woodwork, absolutely helpless with laughing. She couldn't get up for ten minutes.

Our address at that time was 27 Irlam Road. It's now long gone but I'll never forget it because that's where my lovely daughter Diane was born.

From there, the council moved us to a maisonette from where we got an exchange to a small-attached house in Litherland. This house in Poulson Drive had a small twelve-foot garden at the front and a fifteen-foot garden at the back. The day we moved in, some kids were playing out front with a ball, the ball bounced in to the little patch of beaten earth, which was our garden. One of the kids ran in to retrieve it and my son Tony who was about eight years old at the time ran out of the front door yelling.

"Get off our land."

Fatso had managed to get himself a job working for Rediffusion. They were a firm that installed radio speakers into houses for a weekly rental. These radios were served by a central mast which covered a wide area mainly at the North end of Liverpool, they had three local radio stations, radio Merseyside, as well as the BBC Light Programme and the BBC Home Service.

Following Fatso's advice I went along had an interview and got the job. The job was installing these radio transmitters, which entailed bringing the supply cable to the house nailing it to the walls and installing quite a complicated switch on the wall by the radio. Soon after I arrived, they started tying up a TV cable alongside the sound cable. They were waiting to supply televisions in the same way. When the licence came through, the job changed somewhat. We'd been working in pairs with a handcart and long ladders on it, the senior or more experienced one of the pair would walk alongside the handcart and the other one would grab hold of the end of the ladder and push it, it was quite heavy because it also carried the toolboxes, cable etc. The foreman used to come around on his pushbike and check on us. I remember him arriving one day just as the lady of the house was making us a cup of tea. She offered him a cup and he removed his cap and sat down at the table. He took a sip of his tea and jerked away from it as it had burned his mouth. Realising this the lady said: "I'm sorry, I'll put some more milk in it."

"No its alright, I'll fan it with my cap."

I can still see him hunched in the chair, his hair parted in the middle, shirt buttoned to the top and his legs stuck out each side of the chair with his bicycle clips round his ankles, chin down eyes up holding the cap in his hand waving it side to side over his cup of tea. Very humble.

One thing that made the job so popular was the number of young women you came into contact with. Every house you worked on made you a cup of tea and a lot of chatting up took place.

We had one guy in particular who was a fanatical womaniser. He always wore a black duffel coat and as he walked along his eyes would be shooting from side to side taking everything in. We nicknamed him 'The Snake.'

One day I was walking along the top of a backyard wall and saw a young housewife hanging up her washing. The snake was in the next yard and I whispered down to him, "Nice bird in here."

He grabbed a ladder saying, "Where, where? Let her see my face, let her see my face." You'll gather from that he was extremely vain. He wasn't a bad looking chap but he did think he was god's gift to women.

One day he and I were working on the roof of Oriel railway station in Bootle, this was quite high, about thirty feet. The snake was carrying the ladder on his shoulder; I was bending down getting something from the toolbox. He had his back to me and turned as I stood up whacking me on the back of the head with the ladder. I yelled "Ow! That's your lot" and charged at him, he dropped the ladder and I grabbed him saying "I've had enough, you're going off this roof."

He dropped to his knees saying, "Please Roy, please don't, I'm sorry," he was serious and I let go and started laughing. He then realised I'd been joking and he said.

"You know what I was thinking Roy? If he pushes me over, I'll cover my face with both hands so at least I'd be a handsome cripple."

Now things were changing, vans were bought and the Rediffusion cable television supply business got under way. Some of us were designated to start putting up aerials in areas which the cable didn't reach. After a while, I got fed up and saw an advertisement in the *Liverpool Echo* for an aerial rigger. I went to the man's house, which was near the city about three miles from where I lived. He explained the job and said he'd pay me fifteen quid a week, a third more than I'd been getting.

I said: "that's good."

He said: "I believe in giving a good crack of the whip, start Monday."

Monday morning, I cycled to his house and he got the van out. We got to the first house, a two-story house with a very wide chimney; it was about eight feet by six feet. I got the ladders out. placed them against the wall and got the band wire out of the van.. The band wire goes round the chimney and supports the aerial. I said: "where's the cat ladder?"

He said: "Cat ladder? We haven't time for that nonsense, we've got a lot to do."

I started up the ladder while he was fiddling with something in the back of the van. I said: "Are you coming up?"

He said: "No I'm doing the aerial, you fit the band wire."

I had to scramble up the roof and grab the chimney. I thought how the hell am I going to get that wire around this chimney on my own. It was so wide, corner pieces had to be placed on each corner for the wire to be hooked on to. Somehow or other, I climbed on to the chimney, dangling the wire almost like a lasso, bending over each corner trying to hook the corner into position. I couldn't kneel because the chimney pots were in the way. Somehow I managed it and said: "Okay are you coming up now?"

He said: "No way – I never go on a roof, I'll pass it up to you." I had to ease my way back to the ladder. He climbed the three bottom steps and stretched his arms upwards holding the aerial in his hands. I had to reach down and pull it up; I managed to fit it and climbed down. He said: "You've been up there twenty minutes, that's no good, we've got to do eight to ten of these a day." At Rediffusion, we always had two men on the roof and did about two a day if there were no complications. What I didn't realise was that this guy took on jobs other fitters turned down.

When I saw the next job, I nearly died. It was in a street off Scotland road where there was a row of three story houses with very long steep roofs. I had to climb the ladder and throw a rope over the roof along side the chimney, then I went to the back of the building and did the same throwing the end of the rope along the other side of the chimney. I now had a rope around the chimney and was able to use it to pull myself up the roof. He had to climb to the top of the ladder and stretch the aerial to me as I stretched down for it. I fitted it and said: "Okay, how do I get down," the roof being too steep to slide down. He said: "No problem."

He stopped four lads who were walking past and got them to stand on the ladder. He said: "Okay you can slide down now," which I did, hitting the ladder with both feet so that the top of the ladder shot away from the roof for three feet before returning. This became the regular format on the steep roofs.

I had a week of hairy jobs – every one was a problem. Each morning I had to meet him at his house at eight o'clock. After the second weekend, I turned up Monday morning and he came to the door. He said: "I'm not well, come back tomorrow."

The next morning his wife came to the door. This happened each morning all week. On the Saturday morning, he came to the door himself. He said: "We're not working today."

I said: "That's okay but can I have my wages for this week?"

He said: "What dya think I am, you ave'nt worked all week, I don't pay people who don't work."

I said: "Well how are you feelin' now?"

He said: "I'm okay now."

"Well touch for that," and gave him a right-hander.

It was a horrible couple of weeks and I really wished I'd never met him in fact I felt I could have given him a hiding. Though that's not my style.

My London tailored Edwardian suit, Hawstone Street, Liverpool, 1954.

~ 7 ~
Out and About ~ ('Teds' ~ Back to the Circus and on to The Door)

EXHAUSTED AS I was, I still had to train three nights a week and went out to Mary Kates pub on a Saturday night with the lads from the gym Denny and George Rowan, Danny Regan, Fatso, Jimmy Clinton and Bob Hickson. Sometimes we'd go from there to the Locarno dance hall or the Grafton next door. There were often fights mainly in the Grafton. One would start at one end, and chairs would be swung overhead and it would spread round the room like a Mexican wave. They'd refuse you on the door if your trousers were less than 16 inches at the bottom or if your jacket was too long. They used a ruler to measure the distance between your jacket and the floor. This was to try and control the Teddy boy era. I remember four of us leaving a pub and walking towards the dance hall, one of us started to sing a pop song, not loudly, two policemen approached. One, a sergeant with a nightstick he would use to tap the end on the pavement to call for help.

They stopped in front of us and the sergeant yelled: "Shut up!"

The lad said: "I was only singing quietly." He shoved the nightstick under the lad's chin, screaming: "I said shut up!" We knew better than to make a fuss, they'd shove you in the back of the hurry up wagon and lock you up for the night as soon as look at you. When the Bill Haley rock n' roll film came to Liverpool, the kids were jiving in the aisles and ripping out seats. It was a great time for exciting music and the Teds took some controlling.

One Saturday night in 1954 Johnny Penn (Fatso) my mate from the gym and I decided to go the Locarno, it was a popular place particularly on a Saturday night. I was smartly attired in my London tailored Edwardian suit and Fatso was wearing blazer and flannels. The doormen were checking the trousers, and the jackets. When it came to our turn, he said.

"You're alright, but he can't come in."

I said: "Why not? He's not a Ted."

He just kept shaking his head, I'm sure it was the width of Fatso's shoulders that put him off. There was a policeman standing with the doorman saying nothing, he stepped forward saying, "Go on, you heard what he said: you're not on." I looked at him and realised I knew him although I hadn't seen him for ten years.

I said: "All right Carl, what's the score?" He just walked back to his original position not acknowledging me, just shaking his head. We eventually went next door to the Grafton, which wasn't so fussy. The policeman was Carl Daley who worked in the back of the market with me as well as being a boyhood friend.

Although the doormen were so strict at the Locarno and the Grafton rooms next door, both on West Derby Road they were the most popular dance halls in Liverpool, mainly because they were the largest. Others like Reeces and the Harlequin were just as popular but they were smaller and attracted a more up market clientele being just a bit older.

It was on a visit to the Locarno that I got talking to a smart evening suited guy on the door who it turned out was the manager. I'd actually seen him before in Vic's Gym. We became friends and always kept in touch, his name was George Armstrong.

A few years later, George became a general manager for a chap who had Bingo Halls. George approached me one day and told me his boss Roy Miller wanted to sell one of his places and told George if he was interested he would give him a choice of three he was selling. George wanted me to have a look at them with him with the possibility that I might get involved. I was very busy and heavily committed at the time but said I'd go with him.

George was struggling a bit financially and his car was a bit of an old banger. He picked me up in it and off we went. Unfortunately, it had no passenger seat so I had to sit in the rear seat with the open space in front of me. George hadn't been well briefed on the locations of these three places and we finished up driving miles around Lancashire, the Wirral and Cheshire trying to locate them. Because we spent a lot of time on winding country roads and I was permanently leaning forward supporting myself with one hand on the back of Georges seat I started to feel queasy. It took about eight hours to find the places and I was knackered when he dropped me back home. Anyway, George opted for a place in Birkenhead. His boss gave him what turned out to be a good opportunity and as time went on George became an entrepreneur owning several places. He used to be a proficient amateur boxer and was also a very good showman. He worked for me at one time managing the Executive Club in Seel Street.

Later on George got involved in a murder inquiry. Initially he was charged and sentenced, but was released after a complicated appeal – he wrote a book about it called *'Truth on the Ropes'*.

Fatso and I took Ellen into town one night to see the queers in the Old Royal pub. There was one called Sadie who liked to give a song and was a bit of a hard case and the hardest of them all who they called the Queen, Johnny Linus, he called himself 'Mother Superior' or 'Madame Fontaine', but the person we wanted to see was Gloria. She had long black hair and make-up and was extremely beautiful. He wore a black leather coat and used to sit there brushing his hair. The place was packed and I fought my way to the toilet. All the urinals were occupied so I had to pee in a lavatory already occupied by two others. One left and the other finished and was shaking his dick, and he kept on shaking it! I looked up and he was staring straight at me whilst shaking away. I said: "you dirty bastard" and shoved him against the wall. I stormed out furious to where Fatso and Ellen were stood in the passageway. A fellow shouted across them to his pal, using really strong language. This was unusual. People did swear a lot, but did it quietly always respecting female company. So, I turned round and asked him to keep it down. He said: "Who the fuck do you think you are?"

I said: "Listen, this is my wife here, not one of your old slags, so just keep it down."

He threw a punch and I caught him nicely on the chin, and down he went.

Somebody said: "Stand back, Billy'll kill him."

As soon as Billy's chin got up to three feet off the floor, I sideswiped him and he went into the wall. We then left and were walking along Lime Street when I heard running footsteps behind me. I turned my head and received a punch right between my eyes. I saw stars and pennies scattered all over the pavement. (The dodge was to clutch a screwed-up handkerchief in the clenched fist and insert pennies between the upper fingers, making a knuckle-duster.

I got a job as a lifeguard – attendant in Garston baths in south Liverpool; this was just before I got married. In fact, I got Ellen a job there with me for a while. The kids all called me Tony, because of a passing resemblance to Tony Curtis.

It was a great job for me, giving me a chance to get plenty of swimming and diving in. The most difficult part of the job was getting the kids out of the pool when we were closing. I'd have to go to the cubicles to get an item of clothing and dangle it over the water threatening to throw it in if they didn't get out. I never did but it worked. However, on one occasion two yobbos who were about nineteen years old just wouldn't get out of the pool, giving me the 'V' sign and swearing insults at me. I got the high-pressure hose out, after 10 minutes of this treatment with a powerful ice cold jet, much colder than the heated pool, it did the trick. They got dressed in their lockers very slowly. I appealed to them to get a move on, being the only member of staff in the building and with all the other customers long gone. One of them sat down on the seat in the cubicle and said: "I'm not moving, we'll stay here all fuckin' night", whereupon I grabbed him and dragged him out. His pal joined in and I had no choice but to thump both of them and throw them out. It was an episode that I'm not proud of!

Roy poses with a Ladies Fashion contestant at the 1956 Mr. Adonis contest.

The following summer 1956, I entered a Mr Adonis physique competition in New Brighton. They had the contest and judging in the bathing pool and the final in the local theatre where it was televised. It was the first physique competition on British TV and ran weekly in the summer for about five or six years, becoming known as the *Holiday Town Parade.* McDonald Hobley presented it with Joe Loss and his band. It became a popular event and all the winners of the serious competitions eventually became involved. Two other local lads, Jim McCullock and Vic Burdett were also competing. They were to become well known gym owners on Merseyside.

The time I entered a girl called Joan Hunt (Miss Britain 1951) who was involved with *Health and Strength* magazine was on the panel of judges. She came to tell me that the other judges had picked me and she'd said: "You can't give it to him", Bill Parkinson is in it and he's just won Mr Britain. She told me they picked me because I looked more like Mr Adonis, but, as she said: they don't understand physiques. The reason she explained to me, was that no one knew the outcome until the TV show in the evening. In the afternoon, a short list of six was decided. Some of the photographers called me over for a publicity shot and she stopped them saying "this is the man you want" pointing at Bill Parkinson and she felt I should know why. I would have been mortified if Id been chosen in front of Mr Britain, I certainly had no illusions about my physique, I was happy just to be in the final six.

One Saturday in Mary Kate's, we were sat in the snug where we could hear the latest Elvis, Billy Eckstine and Sarah Vaughan. I wore a new jacket that I'd had made London-style with a soft shoulder line so it would lie on the trapezius. There was a big guy called Bull Hogan who was cock of the walk in there. Apparently, he sometimes worked as an enforcer. As he squeezed past my chair, he stopped behind me and lifted the ends of my jacket shoulders saying: "What's this? What's this?"

I don't know how I did it, but I sprung out of my chair thrusting with my legs and punched him over my head because he was behind me. I caught him on the chin and he hit the deck. Well, the pub was up in arms. The women were screaming and kicking my shins and clawing at me shouting: "Get him outside Bull! Get him outside!"

I saw a look on his face, and thought he doesn't want this anymore than I do but we went outside and the whole pub emptied into the street. He took his jacket off and rushed at me straight into my fist (a bit like Tommy Nolan did). I can't remember the logistics, but I made a mess of his face knocking him down more than once, and he never touched me. The next day I realised I'd lost my watch and went to the pub to see if it had been found. When I walked in the bar, Bull was there with some of his mates. I thought this is it, what happens now? Bull pointed at me, he was sporting two black eyes, and said: "See that man there, I'm the only man in town who'd take his coat off to him." So, he turned the situation around making himself the hero and doing my reputation a lot of good! I'm sure when I stole it on him in the pub, it put him off his stride and hit his confidence for the moment. Fortunately for me!

Spending my formative years and reaching my adulthood mainly in the South of England ... coming to Liverpool I realise now must have been a bit of a culture shock for me. This was because of the Teddy boy environment I found myself in. I was mixing with a pretty tough crowd a lot of whom were not too concerned about the niceties of life. Having said that, it didn't really apply to the friends I'd made in the Gym who were my main associates.

Our favourite drinking place was Mary Kate's pub because people went for the music and atmosphere. One night in there, a girl across the room was giving me the eye, she was quite nice looking but I'd not been married long and wasn't interested in anyone else.

Alongside the pub was a narrow entry between it and the terraced houses it was quite usual for fella's leaving the pub to have a pee in the entry. The entry was quite well lit by a lamp post on the pavement close by. I came out of the pub at closing time and as I walked past the entry, I heard a noise and saw a girl holding her skirt up to her waist and standing with her bare legs astride, having a pee. I was shocked, this was not a usual type of behaviour. It was the girl who'd come on to me in the pub.

One thing I'd notice when I'd take a girl home in Liverpool the little terraced houses were always very well done out, nice furniture carpets etc. a lot of pride went into the homes.

In London the difference was marked, the houses of the same type were always very stark. The girls themselves went to great lengths over their appearance. They'd spend all their money on clothes. In Liverpool, the houses seemed to get first priority. I'm not saying Liverpool girls weren't smart but they didn't have the same access to fashion as the Londoners. Indeed, when I started to put on beauty contests later I was struck by the fact that the most beautiful girls came from the Northwest area.

*　　　*　　　*

In the summer of 1957, Jackie Lambert (Tarzan Jnr) contacted me and asked me to do the summer season in the aqua show for Prince Cox's Circus, which I did. I was introduced to a new team of divers. The leading diver was Mike Samson, he was from Poland originally with a very good physique, and he gave the impression that he wasn't weight trained, but certainly looked like he could have been, then there was an experienced diver called Jackie Stewart, tough and fit. Then a smaller guy from Ireland called Richard Poole (later on known as Ricky Pool) he was straight from the bogs, with a little Norman Wisdom jacket and curly hair which rose a foot above his head on the opposite side to the parting, like me he was new to the game and had been practicing all winter at Mathew St baths in London.

I got him on the weights and took him for a haircut and he was transformed in a couple of weeks. His physique improved rapidly. All the ladder work and swimming had a lot to do with it.

One day we were visited by the contestants in the *Holiday Town Parade*, and who should be with them on the judging panel but Reg Park. That was a great afternoon. Within two years, Ricky Poole had his own trampoline act and I saw him on TV at the London Palladium. I remember I broke the arch of my foot in a dive and I went home to Liverpool for a few days, I took Ellen to the pictures one evening. I had long hair Tarzan style which was unusual at the time. As we walked down the aisle to our seats, a voice called out: "Get your haircut," and another: "Yeah, you fuckin' poof, get your hair cut."

As Ellen sat down, I threw my Mac, which I was carrying in my fist, onto her lap and strode back up the aisle where two blokes aged about thirty sat in the back seat laughing. I leant into the seats and punched each of them in the mouth, before returning to my seat. Very bad behaviour, but the people in the audience were glad.

One of the bonuses in the aqua show was that we got into the local Queens Theatre free on a Saturday night. I remember going to see on stage Jimmy Young who was still making hit parade records, the warm up act was a young blond guy in a light blue suit and shirt, I thought he must have just got out of the merchant navy. He tap-danced, played instruments

Roy, Mike Samson and Jack Lambert

Mike Samson, Ricky Poole, Roy and Jackie Stewart, 1957

and sang and he was really good, his name was Roy Castle. Some of the girls invited Jimmy Young to come to the pool for a swim on the Sunday. He didn't turn up, and someone said it was because he wore a wig. Well maybe so.

Two or three of the girls in the show joined in the diving activity as partners in the dual dives. I did a dual dive with a girl called Spot (real name Lillian Griffiths). She would stand behind me on the board and I would reach back under her armpits and press her to arms' length. I'd then dive off and halfway down we'd divide into two swallow dives. Very straight forward.

Johnny McGrath and Kish

Unfortunately, one day on hitting the water I felt something strike my head. I climbed out and reached back in a theatrical way to help Spot as she arrived at the poolside. As she surfaced, I

A nervous attempt by Spot's stand-in

Water Phantasy Accident

RHYL GIRL INJURED

Twenty-one-year-old Miss Lilian Griffiths, of Meldrum House, Brynhedydd Road, Rhyl, a member of Prince's Water Phantasy at the Rhyl Open Air Swimming Pool, was injured during a performance of the water show on Monday. She was taken to the Royal Alexandra Hospital where eleven stitches had to be inserted in a head wound which she had sustained, but was able to return home later the same evening.

She was taking part in a tricky javelin dive from a diving board with another member of the high diving team, Roy Adams, when she dived too far out and hit her head on the bottom of the swimming pool. As a result of her injury she will not be able to appear in the show for some time.

Roy Adams also received a cut on the head which had to have three stitches, but he told the 'Journal' that this injury was purely a coincidence. "I think I must have hit something floating on the water" he said.

thought she's got a white bathing cap on which she didn't start with. The white surface of her head then filled with blood and I realised I was looking at her skull. Her scalp was rolled back like a carpet to the rear of her head. In that pool twelve feet out from under the diving board there was a rapid slope from the deep area to a depth of only five feet where there was an actual ridge in the concrete. Spot had hit this with her head! I picked her up and hurriedly carried her around the pool to the first aid area. By the time I got there, I was covered from head to foot with her blood and some of my own where I'd struck something on the water surface. The spectators' seats came right down to the poolside so they had a good view of all this. Spot didn't join the divers for the rest of the season, but she was back in the formation team within two weeks! The girl who stood in for Spot had some difficulty with that dive after the accident; she couldn't help cutting in to avoid the underwater shelf.

Part of the show was a high wire act called the Gunter Bergmann troupe. Gunter, the leading light of the act used to ride a bike on the high

Gunter Bergmann

Ricky Poole does a planche at the Aqua Show, 1957, supported by me.

wire, which stretched the full length of the pool twenty feet up. He also used to skip with a rope on the wire!

He was a tough German gypsy, a real womaniser who not only frightened all the girls in the show but also all the shop assistants in the town.

In the act with him was a very stout Nordic type girl who doubled as his sleeping partner and a young Frenchman called Pierre. Our young Irish diver became very pally with them and eventually they offered him accommodation in their bus. Richard went for it because it was cheaper than his digs and we were only paid peanuts.

It was okay for a while and then Pierre got jealous and Gunter gave Richard a sleeping bag and a groundsheet and told him he'd have to sleep outside. The weather wasn't bad and Richard put up with it for about a week. However one evening we went to the pictures and the chip shop afterwards and parted company. We went to our digs and Richard to the bus. Next morning Richard appeared at the pool dressing room where we more or less lived in the daytime. He was very upset, ranting and raving. I asked him what was wrong. He said: "when I got into my sleeping bag I felt something slipping around my socks. (He used to sleep half dressed) I got out of the bag and turned it out only to find that Pierre had shit in it."

I said: "What did you do?"

"Jeysus, what could I do? I had to put up with it, I'd nowhere else to sleep."

I got myself a part time job at the fairground on Saturday nights and all day Sunday. I was on the dodgem cars. When I asked about the wages, the guy said.

"We only pay ten shillings a day, you have to busk the rest."

When I asked him what he meant he explained that when you stood on the rear part of the all round bumper, you would lean forward and ask for the shilling fee. If he gave you a larger coin or a note, you'd count the change in your palm in front of him and then turn your hand over dropping the change into his palm. He'd frantically shove it into his pocket while trying to control the car. You'd have put your thumb over a coin or two holding them back as you turned your hand over. I have to say that as much as I hated it, I did do it but I'd only ever take one or two coins. The other fellow would palm as much as eight out of ten coins sometimes but I just couldn't go that far. It was Hobson's choice – do it or no wages, and I was already on a starvation diet!

With fairground men, 1957

I'd worked on the dodgems before when I was about fifteen in Felixstowe. I remember Freddie Mills arriving one day in a brown suit, he decided to have a go and I had the thrill of talking to him, he was preparing for his fight with Bruce Woodcock. This fairground was enclosed with high walls and when we arrived just after the war my father was in charge of it. It was used by the Admiralty for storage purposes. Just after it opened to the public, before I worked there, my pal and I were skylarking in the crooked house. We hid in a dark corner, I had a handful of pieces of string and as girls were passing along the dim passage I'd stretch my hand above their head, stroking the string gently across their forehead at the same time making a wailing sound, the girls would give a little scream and run out laughing.

Then on one occasion a girl came through and I played my little trick and she gave a little scream, unfortunately her boyfriend who was a mature man was following behind. He was a sailor in uniform; he came back up the passageway where I stood. He struck a light with his lighter holding it to my face at the same time giving me an almighty punch to my stomach. That was the end of that game; I was about thirteen years old at the time.

I palled up with a fellow called Dave Bowdidge who was a rough and ready type. I'd now got a part time job on a dart stall. All the stalls were linked by a passageway along the back. Dave took me there one night and broke into the passageway. He started pocketing cigarettes off the back of the shooting gallery. I wasn't interested in any of that and grabbed an air gun but he wouldn't let me have it so that was that. We never got caught and that was the end of my criminal career.

*   *   *

At the end of the season I went home to Liverpool and back to working at Lucas's factory. In 1957 Fatso and I went to London to see the Mr Universe contest, after the show we were in the theatre bar when a guy approached me and introduced himself as a talent scout. He said he was there with a film producer called Brian Desmond Hurst, he said the producer wanted to meet me. He said: "that's him by the bar with Lon of London."

Still at Rhyl, still half-starved

Now I knew who Lon of London was, he was a photographer who specialised in male physique shots. On his photos the men were either nude or in posing pouches. It was pretty obvious which market he focused on. I mentioned this to the talent scout, who said: "look this man is John Ford's nephew and a well-known producer in his own right. He produced *'The Red Beret'* and other high profile films. I can't remember the names. Well I went over and met Brian D Hurst he was a big man who looked down at me with I thought, bulging eyes, and said: "I'm very pleased to meet you, you're a good looking young man. Would you be interested in some screen tests?"

I said: "Look I want you to know, before you say anything else, I want nothing to do with queers."

He smiled and said: "I'd be lying if I said I wouldn't like to go to bed with you, but I am seriously interested in you from a professional point of view. Are you going to the Mr Universe dance tonight?"

I said: "Yes."

He said: "I'll send the Bentley to pick you up."

I said: "No, I'm with my pal John, we'll make our own way there."

We met up that night at the dance, I remember people getting Ron Lacy, the Amateur Mr Universe winner to show his impressive calves by pulling up his trouser leg. Hurst made arrangements for me to go to London for tests and I insisted John went with me.

A few nights before going to London for my screen tests, I went out on the town with Fatso and Danny Regan. We decided to visit a well-known pub on the dock road. The place was busy and we were soaking up the atmosphere, and Danny, who was only about 16 at the time, started talking to a group of girls.

He pointed me out, and said: "Our mate's going to London next week for a screen test," and the word went around the pub. Eventually we left and were walking up a street, which had an archway half way up. As we approached the archway we heard whooping and yelling and looked round to see the street packed with a gang running towards us. We looked to the front and carried on walking. Suddenly I was struck on the head by a beer bottle. The next thing they were all over me with bottles, fists and feet. I was being dragged this way and that and I thought, they'll keep hitting me till I go down, so I let myself sink to the ground, and they all started kicking which was probably worse. A group of older people came up the street and started to shout at them and they took off, saying: "That'll screen test you, you fuckin' Bastard."

I was lucky because I'd held my hands over my face and although the backs of my fingers were split open, my face was okay and I made it to London.

The leader of this crowd was called Barney and he worked on a hot dog barrow in Lime St. These barrows were operated mainly by Hungarian refugees who came over during the Hungarian uprising and they ran a closed shop, big money changed hands for sites for these barrows and intruders weren't tolerated! (More about this later.) Without my knowledge, Barney got a visit from Peter Hont, an ex-Army mate of mine, and swore it wasn't him who attacked me, but his brother. Not much family loyalty there!

Hurst lived in Grosvenor Place near Marble Arch, John and I turned up and rang the bell. A skinny bloke with a posher than posh accent said: "Yes, who are you?" Looking us up and down. John was carrying an old canvas holdall with a handle of hairy string, which held our joint belongings, underpants, socks and shaving gear. All we had was what we stood up in, tired old blazers and flannel trousers.

I said: "Mr Hurst's expecting us."

He said: "Wait!" went away and came back and said in a surprised tone: "He said you could come in."

We walked into a sumptuous lounge dominated by four armchairs with very high backs. He said: "Mr Hurst wants to see you", and took me to his bedroom. He was lying in bed; I stood at the foot of the bed.

He said: "Take your shirt off and let me see if you're as beautiful as I remember."

I felt like legging it out of there, but I was overawed by the situation and took my shirt off.

He then asked me to send John up, which I did. John came down looking flustered; he said: "He tried to kiss me." Eventually Hurst came down and told me he wanted to take me to a nightclub, he said they'd sort me out with something to wear, but he said they'd never let John in, so I refused to go. After he'd gone John and I decided to have a snoop around, we looked in his bedroom, and noticed a curtained off area, I pulled the curtain back, only to see a bed with a bloody great Irish Wolfhound lying on it with James the servant. The dog barked and growled and James said: "It's all right darling, calm down." The dog was actually named Darling.

We made some lame excuse about looking for our room and got out of there. The next morning Hurst sent for me again, I said to James: "Where is he?"

He pointed to a door and I went in. He was in the bathroom and conducted the interview whilst sitting on the lavatory grunting between sentences. The next morning I went to the door to bring in the milk and chatted to Janet Munro the next-door neighbour, she'd just signed a contract for eight films with Disney.

After the weekend, John went home, he needed to get back to work. Hurst took me for photographic tests, and that evening we went to a well-known bar called the Grenadier. With us was a famous film cameraman named Bob Krasker and a Norwegian 'starlet' with Brian called Christian. Brian ordered Black Velvets, which were cocktails of champagne, and Guinness; it was eight pounds a round! I spoke to Brian Hurst and he made a show of me, booming.

"This is more than Roy gets in a week to keep a family!"

The next day, Brian took me to the 'Q School of Acting and Elocution', where people like Vivien Leigh, Tony Wright, Diana Dors, Tony Britten and later Sean Connery went. Madame de Leon was the Principal of the Q School and she interviewed me. She said: "I can make you the new beefcake boy of British film. We will teach you how to act and how to speak and project yourself generally."

Mr Hurst said: "Right, find accommodation, which I will pay for. I'll also pay for the Q School for your time here. As far as your family is concerned, you will need to find part time work in order to make enough money to keep them."

I told them I couldn't risk my family in that way, so he advised me to go to my local council for a grant, which I did. Mr Hurst wrote to them saying he'd seen me performing and could guarantee my future.

Now, this was Bootle Corporation we were talking about. They wrote a nice letter to me saying that they thought it would cost too much and therefore wouldn't be able to recommend a grant to enable me to go to the Q School. So ended my hopes of a film career. Funnily enough, it never really bothered me. I had trained myself years before never to expect too much. Nothing is ever as good as you think it is going to be, but on the other hand, nothing is as bad as you think it'll be. Developing this philosophy has been the only way I could cope with some of the situations I've found myself in, in the past. That's not to say that it always works out. One thing I've found is that my joy of anticipation is somewhat diminished. When I think about it now, one of the most overriding feelings in the nightclub business was a general feeling of unease. When you were working, you could never completely relax – something could blow at any time.

We used to go to a sophisticated little club after work called the Pink Parrot. Norman took me there initially, they had a wonderful cook called Nadja, and her hamburgers were really special. One night she cooked me a fillet steak, and it was the first real steak I'd had in my life, steak had always been beyond my means. The Pink Parrot had a restaurant and a glass dance floor, the doorman was called Pat McKenna with his mate Charlie, and they had a sophisticated clientele and did well on tips. At that time there were very few clubs and the average age group was between thirty and sixty. It wasn't until the Cavern and the Iron Door came along that the kids had somewhere to go.

*　　　*　　　*

Starting at the Harlequin, with John Lloyd, Alan Hewitt, and unknown.

Ellen got a part time job in a dance hall in Church St Liverpool, called the Harlequin. One night the manager said he was desperate for a doorman. Ellen said: "My husband's a big fellow." So I went to see him and got the job. Nightlife was jumping in the 50s, although at that time there were no proper nightclubs. For excitement we used to go as Teds to the coloured quarter, which was the Parliament St area, to the shebeens, which were more like drinking dens. Fatso and I would go in quite often and be the only whites in there, but never encountered a problem. These places had great music, great atmosphere and the only thing they lacked (most of them) was a license! That's where I first heard Nellie Lutcher, Billy Holiday and Brook Benton etc. I remember one place we'd go in, when we were leaving, a massive black guy used to encounter us outside the door, he was known as Shadow, he'd hold out some packets of cigarettes and say "You want to buy some of these?" We'd say "Oh yes please" and buy a packet. Neither of us smoked, but we wanted to keep him happy!

When I started on the Harlequin there was John Lloyd who was forty-five years old, good at his job, but pushing on a bit and big George Dolce who was six foot four and twenty stone with a twenty inch neck. Big George was more the diplomat a gentle giant. On a couple of the nights there was Dick Sharples who delivered bread in the daytime. He was a good man to have in your corner, being extremely handy with his not inconsiderable nut! I fell into the job with ease. My four years in the guards had taught me a lot, on a twenty-four hour guard duty, you would spend eight hours standing alert on one spot, two hours on and four off. You weren't allowed to leave the guardroom during the twenty-four hours.

It's always the case when a gang of fellas approach, one will come to the front and do the talking. When refusing someone I'd always be prepared to talk rather than have to fight, of course. Unfortunately sometimes the conversation would turn and start getting aggressive, I'd still try to reason until the moment when he said something particularly bad making it clear he was going to kick off calling me something personal. When that happened my tactic was to step in close and give him an uppercut on the chin.

It always worked. Sometimes you'd come up with something else.

One time a fellow was giving me a lot of grief and I responded by saying: "Tell your crowd to back off and I'll take on any two of you". He gave me a scornful look and said:

"You – you cant fight, – you've never had a fight in your life! I can tell by your face – you haven't got a mark on you." Sticking my chin out I said: "Yeah – that's because I'm good!"

His chin dropped, he turned his head nodding up the street and they all took off.

A show of confidence even if it's not felt can be a good deterrent.

The place was very busy and was very well run by the manager Alan Hewitt, who managed to keep an up market clientele. The main problem was that it was getting so popular we had to close the concertina iron gates at 8.15pm, and the mob outside were almost baying to get in. That situation is always a bit difficult because you get regulars coming in late and people leaving early, so the gates can't be shut absolutely! One night a seventeen stone prostitute grabbed my jacket whilst I reasoned with someone else and dragged me outside and commenced clawing at me and kicking at my groin, she also threw a few digs and her language was choice! I didn't know what to do, not wishing to give her a punch or manhandle her in front of the crowd. John Lloyd suddenly rushed in and gave her two good digs right in the belly. That did the trick. It really shut her up! Anyway, we could only muster three doormen on the busy nights because we needed someone upstairs in the ballroom also.

Alan Hewitt said: "I can't find another doorman."

I said: "I know someone who'll do the trick if I can get him." When I was still in London I'd seen a photo of our British wrestling hero, amateur heavyweight champion Ken Richmond, who it was generally supposed was undefeatable. The photo was in a copy of the Health and Strength magazine under the heading – Ken Richmond defeated! There was a photo of him looking down at the victor Tony Buck of Bootle. I couldn't believe my eyes. Tony was to tell me later that they fought four times each winning twice. Well, I knew that Tony trained at a gym in Crosby and I went to see him. Tony was in this large shed like gym owned by Vic Burdett called the Crosby Weightlifting and Wrestling Club. A lone figure was pushing a very heavy bar off stands above his head, repping it. It was well over 200lbs.

I introduced myself, and he looked at me very suspiciously. I said: "I wondered if you'd like to try a doorman's job."

He said: "What's that?"

I said: "You stand at the entrance to the dance hall, be polite to everyone but don't let the dodgy ones in. It pays £1 a night." So, he agreed to give it a try.

On the Saturday night, he came breezing in wearing a three-piece suit with a waistcoat, very smart, a big camel overcoat and a nice collar and tie around his nineteen and a half-inch neck. He had cropped red hair and a neat red beard. A very impressive man! He said: "Hi, where's the managers office?"

I said: "It's upstairs."

He came back down five minutes later without his overcoat on, and said: "He wants to see you.'

So up I went, Alan said: "This fellow that you've brought – he wants twenty-five bob a night, what'll I do?" I said: "Well I'd give him it, we need him, nobody'll take him on." He said: "But they'll all want it."

So I said: "Well don't tell them."

Tony Buck

So he took him on, I was a bit miffed because he'd just gone ahead and asked for a rise completely disregarding me. I was glad to have him on board although I was still only on £1 a night! I was there for over six years before leaving to go to the Basement Club. I don't know where I got the energy from but I was doing three or four nights a week, up at 6am, and shovelling concrete all day long. On Friday night, you could guarantee you'd have a fight. I couldn't understand how some fellers who really looked nothing could be so aggressive picking on doormen twice their size; some of them obviously were genuine hard cases, but not the majority. Eventually I realised what it was, they'd go to Yates Wine Lodge and get tanked up on small whites. Glasses of white plonk; which sent them off their heads. Realising where the courage came from made the job easier to handle.

By 7.30 pm the place would be packed. It was freezing cold standing there on the door as you can imagine. In summer it would be okay if the wind off the Mersey wasn't blowing but in the winter it could be cold. I took to wearing my demob pyjama bottoms under my trousers until one Sunday night when I used to sign people up for the Sunday club, I realised that, when sitting down at the little table at the end of the passageway with my legs crossed, a good two inches of striped pyjamas were showing around my ankles and a piece of white pyjama chord was poking out of my flies – that was before zip flies came in.

We were very strict on dress policy. No pumps or jeans were allowed and if men weren't in a suit with a tie and a decent pair of shoes they weren't coming in. Girls would have to look smart too and the rough ones we'd turn away also. People came to the Harlequin in couples or alone or in groups but always looking to meet someone of the opposite sex. The routine was pretty simple. The girls would get in early and stand around the edges in groups. Most of the men would try to get in after 10pm when the pubs shut or as late as they could and walk around the floor weighing up the girls. When they found one they fancied they would ask her up onto the floor for a dance. Only a few of the men had cars then and those who did would swing the keys around their fingers as they cruised the floor, showing off their worth.

Tony Buck meanwhile was looking for training partners to batter down at the gym. Wally Booth and myself started to do a bit with Tony who introduced us to the elementary stuff. But to give him a workout we had to round up half a dozen handy characters, none of them less than fifteen stone. Tony would take us on one after another, you could only last a few minutes with him before flaking out. Tony however didn't rest and we'd have to go on with him time after time.

I was getting a lot less sleep than the others because of my sheer number of late nights and day time work, and felt it particularly on a Sunday morning when we'd start with a four mile run over the sand hills before wrestling. Still it helped Tony get some workouts and it certainly did us a lot of good. Swelling the ears somewhat!

Meanwhile over a period of time, I'd got some new men for the Harlequin. There was a pal from the gym called Eddie McDonough, who had done a fair amount of boxing before taking up weight training. He was very strong with terrific genetics physique wise. He made a good doorman, being very laid back and hard to upset.

After training for years, he decided to go on the competition trail and won major physique competitions, in Europe and in this country becoming 'Mr Britain' twice.

Also from our gym came Billy Austin and Tony Fitzgibbon, both fine physical specimens. Tony Fitz had a handsome face, which appeared to be cut out of granite!

Other gym members I can think of who became doormen were Harry Williams, Denny Rowan, Bob Hickson, Jimmy Clinton, Danny Regan, Alex Pinnington and Terry Philips who was another of the more exceptional physiques from our gym, who like Eddy started quite late on the competition circuit going on to win major competitions including his height class in the Mr Universe, four times, overall Mr. Europe twice and Height Class Mr. Europe four times plus three World titles. I think I started the trend of using body builders as doormen.

I'd refused entrance to a guy who'd walked away. I was standing by the cash desk as a couple walked up the passage towards me. As they drew alongside, a figure that had followed crouched closely behind suddenly jumped out and whacked me. Once again, I saw bright flashes and pennies all over the deck. He turned and legged it. Eddie McDonough went after him. Eddie didn't catch him, so he won the argument.

Eddie drawled in his slow way of speaking: "Well the good thing is Roy, it shows you can take a punch!"

Mr Hewitt started to do Bingo in the ballroom on a Friday night. The band, Leon Sait and his Orchestra, would go for their break to the Post Office pub round the corner and the Bingo would be quickly set up. I had to stand next to him and hand him the balls, which spun around in a Perspex case. I hated doing it, for one thing I was on my own and the crowd were not a bunch of old ladies. If a wag called something out, Hewitt would look at them and stop the machine, cocking his thumb towards me saying: "Dya fancy your chance with him? Do you? Is that what you want? Well, just watch it!" I used to think, my God, he thinks I'm King Kong! You never know who's in the crowd and he's issuing challenges for me.

Oil Painting by Roy

One night Dick Sharples was refusing a real townie, obviously a hard case. The geezer wasn't having any. He made a move and Dick had to head butt him.

He was lying on the floor, he grabbed hold of a nearby chair and started to pull himself up, only to slide down again. Eddie Mac said: "This lad's hurt here, it looks like his leg." So we sat him on a chair and sent for an ambulance. He continued to have a go verbally, calling us for everything in real choice language. What annoyed me was that he focused on Eddie calling him all the 'effing c's and so on. I said: "Hey, he's the one who's helped you, don't pick on him, he's a nice guy." He turned to me saying something like "Listen you fucking prick, he's a twat of the first order!" I was so furious I pushed him off the chair. Just then the ambulance men arrived and carried him out on their shoulders, yelling and screaming abuse at us as he went, threatening all kinds. Dick had stood on the guy's toes as he butted him, causing his leg to break when he fell backwards. We didn't realise his leg was broken – he was a hard man!

Roy with Tony Fitz, Harlequin, 1959

Another occasion that stands out was when we'd refused a bloke because of his bad attitude, I think – because he was quite presentable looking. He was about six feet tall, with a stocky build and a nice grey suit. He kept insisting that I went outside with him, finally I felt I had no choice. He squared up to me with his back to Burtons the Tailor's window. When we kicked off I hit him on the jaw with a straight right sending him backwards through the window head first. He was lying with his head inside the shop. His neck had glass below and above. One large pointed shard of glass was immediately above his throat. This was quarter of an inch thick plate glass and very heavy – I was afraid it was going to drop any minute. Eddie and I gingerly lifted him out. It was a dodgy moment. Eddie said the guy's feet left the floor when he flew backwards as I hit him. After we freed him, he simply got up and went off into the night.

Eventually Tony Buck went off to Perth to the Empire Games. I ran him down to Lime St Station to set him on his way. He certainly looked the part with his blazer sporting the union jack and his white trilby hat. He came back with the gold medal – the first one according to the press won

Derek Cassidy

by a British heavyweight for 50 years! Tony himself is not sure this is correct. He feels sure that Ken Richmond, who won bronze at the Olympics, must have had wins in the Empire Games.

A couple of salesmen started to come to the gym. Norman Paterson and Derek Cassidy, I got pally with them and particularly Norman, a really charismatic character. He'd been in the R.A.F at the latter end of the war and had a rather posh accent. He didn't stick the gym for long; he couldn't stand the smell. I was tickled by this and told him. I loved walking into the gym to the familiar smell of pumps and sweaty training gear. I can't remember anyone owning a tracksuit, so some of the sweaters did get a bit ripe!

There was a forty-ish overweight character in the gym known as 'fat Eric'. His claim to fame was that he'd appeared in a film, part of which was shot on Liverpool docks. His part was to step out of a cocky watchman's hut and say, "Tea up lads!" He became a film fanatic, a part of which made him dub different members of the gym with film stars' names. The slightest resemblance would do. Fatso was Marlon Brando – I was Rory Calhoun. We had Charlton Heston, James Cagney, Ernest Borgnine, etc.

When a new member joined, Eric would introduce himself. He'd roll up the short sleeve of his voluminous shirt, bend his arm to show his bicep, sticking his armpit under the poor sod's nose saying: "I'm Eric – the Baron, – the Baron of B.O.!" – and he wasn't kidding!

Derek was more serious about his training and is to this day.

I remember Derek was as hard up as I was, but he always looked smart in a suit and tie. On closer inspection I noticed that the collars of his shirts were always frayed and I mentioned a hole in the sole of my shoe. He said: "I always use cardboard from Weetabix packets in mine!" A few years later, he got a job on a ship working on deck and worked his passage to Canada, where he took jobs washing up in restaurants etc. I didn't hear from him for a few years. When I did he had three restaurants of his own. Norman took me to a club called the Basement in Mount Pleasant Liverpool. It was a cellar club, very atmospheric. He introduced me to the owner Yankel Feather who was a droll wit, with lots of character. He ran the place with his sisters Nell and Sarah. His customers were mostly people from the local theatres and also a lot of Spanish seamen, mainly officers.

Roy (Olympic Cut), age 17

I used to go to Horne Bros in Liverpool for a haircut. They had a proper gentleman's barbers in the basement, (not like the Mad Russians in Gildart St, which was a tiny little barbers shop where you stood in hair up to your ankles. He used to specialise in the Tony Curtis cut with a D A at the back and a centre quiff over your forehead. He asked me if I had a photograph he could use, the only one I had was taken when I was 17 years old. He stuck in on the wall to advertise what he called the Olympic cut. After he'd cut the hair, he would plaster it with, I think sugar and water and comb it into the style. It set like concrete and looked great – until you washed your hair! – There was a pub also on the corner of Gildart Street called 'The Dart'. In the early 50s it attracted a rough crowd. Sometimes Fatso and I would call in there for a bit of atmosphere before going to the Grafton. It was later on that we started going to Mary Kates on Scotland Road. Fights were frequent in 'The Dart'.

I remember one particular barmaid. It was said that if someone bought a drink with a pound note, she would wave it above her head before putting it in the till, thereby pinpointing a potential target with a few bob, ripe for mugging!). Well, the barber in Horne Bros told me one day that he'd started to receive letters from all over the country asking for locks of the Beatles hair (a pop magazine had shown a picture of him cutting their hair) he didn't understand what the fuss was about. Neither did I, although I'd heard their name once before when I called to see Wally Booth who did the door at the Cavern, the street was packed end to end.

I said: "What's going on?"

He said: "Ah the Beatles are on, it's always packed when they're on!"

I became a regular at the Basement and one night Yankel offered me a job on the door. I had to think hard about this because he wanted me to work every night, and I was still doing a full time job and three nights at the Harlequin, where I was now getting about £1.50 a night.

He said: "I'll give you £3 a night", which was good money. It made me the best paid doorman in town so I did six nights and remained at the Harlequin on a Sunday, which I enjoyed, and it gave me a change of scene.

The first night I arrived to start work at the Basement Club, it was pouring with rain. I went down the passageway between the buildings and into the yard. There were a few steps down to the entrance door, which was locked. A couple of minutes later a tall, handsome and refined looking bloke appeared. His name was John Chase – he was working as a part time barman. Daytime, he was at Liverpool Art College. John was wearing a long tweed overcoat and a small tweed Trilby, both of which he had borrowed off his father, and carrying an umbrella, which I was able to share 'til Yankel, arrived. John and I hit it off right away. He ran the little bar with one of Yankel's sisters, Nellie. I, of course, manned the door. Yankel's other sister, Sarah, ran the food counter and looked after the record player, which was at the rear of the counter. Yankel had painted the brick walls in sort of geometric, almost Moroccan-style shapes. He'd used

Yankel and Joan, 1961

oddments of furniture, including a couple of old sofas, and all in all the place had a great atmosphere with a mixed clientele; artists, pop groups, university professors, comedians – a sort of upmarket hippie place. My job was to keep up the standard of clientele. The lavatories were in the back yard, so I was constantly opening the door, not just to people arriving, but also to use the lavatories. This was a good way of building a rapport with the customers, helping me further in dealing with people.

One night, John came to me and said: "What's a snowball?" I said: "Its Advocaat and lemonade", so he rushed over and served it to the customer.

She said: "Where's the bubbles?" John said in his lovely plummy voice.

"Oh, you want bubbles!" He took the drink round to the rear of the till, stuck a straw in it and blew into it until it frothed right up. He plonked the glass down in front of the girl and said: "There you are my dear – bubbles!" That was the way he served Snowballs after that!

I gave him a lift home one night in my little Morris 1000 van. His twelve-year-old brother Paul opened the door of their very nice house in Allerton. His mother was in the kitchen hanging nappies on to a pull down drying rail with one hand and nursing a baby on the other arm. The baby was John's son, Mark, born when John was eighteen years old! John's mum, Eve, was a beautiful woman – she was the youngest of seven sisters and four brothers! One of her sisters was Jessie Mathews, who was Britain's most prolific musical comedy dancer and singer of the 1930s and 1940s. She was Fred Astaire's first choice as a partner in his first film. Jessie was too committed with shows and films in this country to accept, so he had to settle for Ginger Rogers! I then met John's dad, George, and his twin brothers Newton and Hugh.

George became one of my favourite people. He had lots of style, always used a cigarette holder and was a perfect gentleman. He was a member of the Chelsea Arts Club in London, which I visited as his guest on more than one occasion. I met some wonderful people there, mainly from the art world of course!

As John's brother Paul got a bit older, he started weight training and then wrestling, becoming a competent wrestler. He worked as a doorman later on while still in his teens, showing plenty of bottle when dealing with trouble.

I learnt a lot from Yankel in the way that he handled people, I'd been on the door six years before this so had fairly considerable experience, but because of the type of person he was, avant garde in the extreme, he showed me a new slant on things. One night he said to me: "I want you to start charging everyone who comes in, no walkovers". I said: "OK, no problem". Well the first person to come in was Brian Epstein who'd recently launched the Beatles. We had a little counter about four foot long, which I stood alongside after I opened the door. Yankel sat on a cushion on a little bench seat three foot behind the counter. He wore a little pork pie hat and a cardigan and always sat with one leg curled under him.

I said: "That's half a crown please Brian?" Yankel was staring straight ahead. Brian looked at him and said "Yank," in a drawn out voice, "me?" Yankel turned his head to the right lifting his chin and stared at the wall. When he heard the half crown hit the counter he turned back to the front. His whole attitude said: "If you can't pay me half a crown what sort of friend are you?" Brian went chunnering away into the club. Yankel made me aware of race, he'd say "Look at him he's a Persian, or an Arab." Or "Look at that girl isn't she beautiful, doesn't she look Jewish?" and I'd say: "No – she hasn't got a bloody big nose!" Which was the only thing I knew about Jews. In the army we knew nothing about what anybody was or cared! In fact, in the guards, in training the N.C.Os would look for a fault, like bandy legs, big nose, ears, spotty skin etc and focus on it, "You big eared prat, you bandy legged bastard" etc. It was all part of the humiliation process and we just accepted it. Nobody took it seriously. That's why I've been amazed in recent times when the guards tried to encourage blacks to join. They didn't last long because they saw it as racism when the format was used against them, "You black B" etc, so they got thousands in compensation for being racially harassed, but we all were! The army has had to dumb it down now, and has lost a lot of its hard edge. This is not the fault of the black lads; it's the politically correct crew who are responsible for setting them apart and creating this mindset!

As I say, I was still quite naive and one night I had trouble with a gang at the door of the Basement. It was a hard door because it was in a back yard basement with six steps down to the door. I was on my own and in the event of trouble had to get them up the steps. There was a narrow passageway between buildings which led into the yard, and on this occasion it was getting a bit rough, Yankel yelled out: "Sarah shut the door at the end of the passage and call the police" – (there was no door). They thought they'd be trapped in the yard and ran out, but the ringleader turned at the top of the steps, and shouted "Eichman had it right, Eichman had it right" and legged it.

I turned and grinned at Yankel "Yank he thinks we're bleedin' Jews!"

Yankel stiffened up and stuck his chin out "And so, what's wrong with that?" I'd been there a couple of months and didn't realise that someone called Yankel was Jewish! I was there probably another couple of months before I realised that he was homosexual.

Not long after I started working at the basement, I answered the door to an odd looking character in leathers and an all around fringe. I could see there were three or four of them similarly clad ranged up the steps. I knocked them back mainly because of his attitude, I said: "Sorry, fellas – not tonight" The front guy retorted: "But I'm a member! I usually come in with Arthur Ballard, come on George…" and they started to push past me. Yankel spoke out from behind me saying: "I don't know what you are a member of? You might be a Member of Parliament but you are not a member of the Basement!"

Whereupon I shut the door. The front two were John Lennon and George Harrison, with Paul McCartney close behind them. Ringo was on the yard.

Not long before I started at the Basement, Yankel started opening at lunchtime and in the afternoons. This was mainly at the behest of his sister Sarah who enjoyed the characters and the general scene at the time. There was a chap called Arthur Ballard, a Robert Redford look-alike who was head of art at the nearby college; he'd been a sometime boxer and was a wonderful artist having exhibited in London galleries. He'd bring some of the students in with him, including a lad called John Lennon. There was an old wreck of a piano which had half of the keys missing. People would occasionally mess about with it. One day there was the most horrendous racket from it and Yankel went through to see what was causing the noise. It was John Lennon making the row – he was unknown at the time – and Yank told him to pack it in; he gave Yankel a mouthful, whereupon he told the young Lennon to get out. As he left muttering abuse he twirled around a bunch of keys catching one of Yankel's own paintings which was on the wall making a score mark along it.

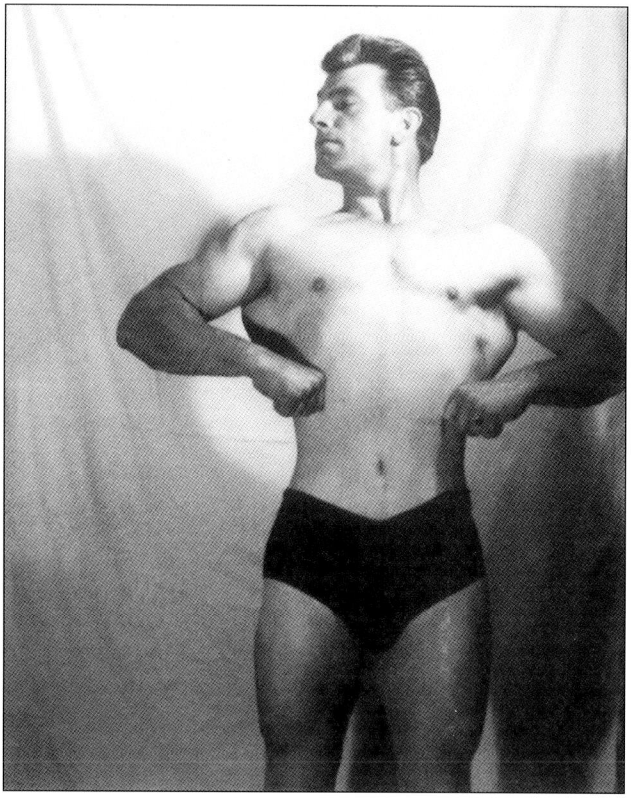

Tony Fitz

That was the reason Yankel was so against letting him in, even though he knew Brian Epstein well and knew that Lennon's band were his protégés. They'd just had some success with *'Love Me Do'*.

This was just before they hit the big time, when they were still relative unknowns. We didn't know it at the time but within a few months they would be on their way to becoming the most famous pop band ever who would be able to get into any club in the world – even clubs in Liverpool – tho' not the Basement!

Because of the strictness on the doors in those days, it was always a worry that certain of my mates might turn up, (always a doorman's problem) particularly if they'd been on the ale. The main one – who always managed to find me – was my old Army pal, Joe Lees, who was harmless, but could be lacking in some of the social graces, when he was 'pissed'. I opened the door one night and there he was baring his teeth in a big grin, his endless arms stretched out sideways, giving his customary roar of greeting. Yankel was sat in his normal position behind the counter, leg tucked under him. I introduced him to Joe, who always did an exaggerated handshake, with his elbow stuck outwards and upwards, pumping your hand up and down. He used his other hand to remove Yankel's little pork pie hat, slapping him on the head saying "Oh, what a luvly 'ead of skin." I was embarrassed, but Yankel was fascinated, Joe reached over and took Yank's hand and led him to the one-armed bandit (fruit-machine). I'll always remember the incongruous sight from behind, of big Joe with his long legs and size 14 shoes, hand in hand with Yankel – who was tiny in comparison – being taken to play the fruit machine. In all his experience, Yankel had never been treated quite like that. That was the thing with Joe – you never knew what he'd do next.

A girl used to come in regularly who worked in the Cavern. Yankel pointed her out, as he did everybody, and said: "There's a smart girl, always well turned out, not pretty but a nice girl".

One night she came over to us, she said: "Guess what? Brian Epstein's signed me up, he said I've not to let anyone hear me sing". Within a few weeks, her first hit record was in the charts, *'Anyone Who Had A Heart'* and she was Cilla Black.

Two young lads came into the gym one night, it was their first visit, I went into the changing rooms and they were passing around some rude pictures. I said: "Hey pack it in, we come here to train which is what you should be concentrating on."

They were suitably contrite, and were as it turned out nice lads. Well, one night one of them came into the Basement Club with Cilla, they became an item and came in regularly.

He was Bobby Willis who Cilla married.

(Nearly thirty years after this event, Sheilagh and I went to London with Tony West, her boss at his entertainment agency. Bob Carrol Gees, who was with Tony's agency was doing a T.V. show with Cilla called *Surprise! Surprise!* Tony went up to the projection room where he spoke to Bobby Willis. Bobby said: "You'll never guess who's in the audience – Roy Adams" Tony said: "I know I brought him!" I was amazed that he recognised me and even knew my name after thirty years!)

Jimmy Tarbuck used to come in a lot, he'd tell me a joke and I'd tell him one, at that time a lot of his jokes were based on Liverpool Dockers nicknames, for example, Fellow with a hunch back they called 'the angry cat' and another who used to cast off the ropes on the ships, they called him 'the lenient judge' because he used to say "Let that guy go" and "Let that guy go". There was an endless list of them. Jimmy obviously forged ahead with his career, and is now a celebrity.

Yankel is now a very successful artist having had exhibitions in Cornwall and London. He's received glowing endorsements from eminent people in the art world.

One night, a guy called Ritchie Dodd brought a couple of pals to the gym, one of them was a very bulky guy, on the heavy side, but not what I would describe as fat. His friends knew him as Fat Harold. Harold told me he wanted to lose some weight and I started to help him with his training. His weight eventually dropped to thirteen and a half stone from seventeen stone and he was delighted. As time went on, people started to refer to him as 'Aitch.' 'H' was, and is, a hard man. He had his own gang of followers and nobody messed with 'H.' in a one-to-one fight, he always gave his opponent the first dig and invariably won.

One night at the Harlequin, Tony Fitz and I were doing the door on our own. The band Leon Sait and his musicians used to stop for half an hour break.

A lot of the mostly male customers would get a pass out ticket from us and go round the corner to the Post Office Pub opposite the famous Bluecoat Chambers for a drink. On this particular night two of our customers, (little bespectacled guys who I'd describe as office types) headed out of the door on their way to the pub. Across the street was a group of guys who I'd seen around town.

One of them had a cat by the tail and was swinging it around his head. One of the office types went over to him saying: "Ah-please don't do that to the cat."

"Oh, I'm awful sorry." was the reply, at the same time flinging the cat into the gutter. It so happened that it was a dead cat. Some of the group grabbed the two and shoved them in a doorway where they took turns in giving them a punch or a head-butt. The cat swinging guy didn't take part. This was directly across the street from us.

I said: "Come on Tony," – we charged across the street and got in the way of the mob, shepherding the two office types across the street and into the dance hall. We then turned to face the mob. The spokesman was the smallest, little broken-nosed John Dalton.

He said: "What the fuck do you think you're doin'?" I said: "Protecting our customers."

As they grouped together menacing us prior to having a go, a figure suddenly appeared spreading his arms out in front of us, shouting: "Roy's a mate! Roy's a mate!" They immediately backed off and moved away, probably relieved, Tony Fitz was no pussy.

The figure turned back and shook my hand saying: "Alright der Roy?"

The figure was the indomitable 'Aitch'.

There was a shop in London Road called Olly's. It was next door to the Odeon Cinema and was a very popular men's clothing shop. I called in one day just to look around. It was a very small shop and was crowded out with some of the well known townies. They were busy trying things on, and two shop assistants were flapping around, trying to make a sale whilst keeping an eye on things. I walked out followed by Harold Hughes. 'H' joined me as I walked along Lime Street. In mid conversation he suddenly grabbed his coat collar, tweaking it in my direction, saying: "What d'ye think of the overcoat?" I said: "Yea, – it's great, what did that cost?" He smiled , raised his eyebrows and looked at me as if to say, – "Are you stupid?", and I realised he'd taken it on a permanent loan.

'H' formed his own football team, which almost always won their games. Apparently the opposition were scared to win in case they got a good hiding! In the event of 'Aitch's team losing a game and some retribution taking place, if anyone suffered a bad injury such as a broken leg, 'Aitch's boys would take the injured feller and show him where there was a broken paving stone. This compassionate act would enable the lad to claim compensation from the Council for tripping over the paving.

I was attending a committal proceeding in court one day and the opposition had asked 'H' to sit in the public benches with a few of their cohorts. This was to intimidate me into changing my evidence, which I didn't. As I stepped down from the witness box and walked down the aisle, 'H' looked at me and I raised my hand saying "Hi."

He smiled back and said: "Hiya Roy." – Not what he was supposed to do! Tony Bucks' brother Peter had a run-in with him on one occasion. Peter, like Tony, was a good, strong wrestler. When 'H' threw a punch, Peter went for his legs and swept him high above his head, as he brought him down for the smash, Peter told me:

"I couldn't believe it – he actually butted me on the way down!"

That was Harold, who, I'm glad to say is still going strong.

~ 8 ~
First Club

A LITTLE CELLAR in a yard behind Slater Street opened as a coffee club. We went in to have a look. There was a guitarist strumming in a corner and a couple of old sofas to sit on. A window to the tiny kitchen had been cut in the wall with a little counter over which a girl was selling coffee. It was a shilling a cup! Four times the price a café would charge, but we thought it was great because it opened late when the pubs shut. All we did was stand around and drink the coffee – there was no food! We went back the next weekend and it was absolutely packed with blokes. Not a female to be seen. The guitarist had gone and strains of a record player could just about be heard. A rash of similar places opened, each improving on the last one. Licenses were applied for, and the City centre started to have a nightlife.

As these cellar coffee clubs started to proliferate probably the most popular was the 'Jacaranda' in Slater Street. They had a coffee bar on the ground floor and a steel band used to play in the cellar. Alan Williams and his wife Beryl opened it. Beryl was a Chinese girl who was always there. The Steel band was called the 'Lord Woodbine' band, and sometimes the 'Silver Beatles', or the 'Quarrymen', (John Lennon's Group) depending when it was, would come in and accompany the stripper – when they put one on.

Another popular coffee club was the 'Pack of Cards', on Mount Pleasant, run by Neil English, a longhaired extrovert character, who later moved on to the Unicorn beneath the Cabaret Club in Duke Street and then the 'Odd Spot' in Bold Street, – they had decided to open a Disco at the rear of the 'Odd Spot' Casino called the 'Spot it to me'. Neil English ran it successfully for several years; – until he fell out with the owners. He approached me and I got involved with him in a club. For me it wasn't a good move.

There was also the 'El Cabala' in Bold Street, which was a beautiful coffee bar with a grand entrance and luxurious interior. I used to go there sometimes in the morning and have a coffee when I was on the afternoon shift at Lucas's factory. I remember Mike and Bernie Winters having a tremendous barney in there on one occasion. Lucy Claytons model agency was a few doors away also on Bold Street. Someone had approached me to do some pictures for the agency. They were for Coca Cola, and the photos were taken in the 'El Cabala' and also in their coffee bar in Southport. I took two days off work to do them. Everyone treated me like a star; they didn't know I worked in a factory. I was paid £17.00 a day – £34.00 – which equalled three weeks work in the factory!

One night Fatso and I decided to try the 'Jacaranda'. We went in, there were no other customers' being a little early. We paid Beryl two bob each and went down to the cellar. There was a painting by Stuart Sutcliffe (one of the original Beatles), which was blocking the fireplace. The cellar was very bare and the band had not yet arrived. The two of us were just standing there speculating how it was going to be with the band when two policemen came down the stairs with an Alsatian guard dog and told us to leave. Beryl was at the top of the stairs and she shoved our money back at us mumbling something about us not being members. There was no booze anyway so membership didn't apply. I realised the problem immediately. There were two guys stood behind Beryl. I recognised them as two who'd pushed past me on the Harlequin door demanding to see Mr Hewitt the manager when I refused them. They'd told me that I was a nobody and they would prove it. Mr Hewitt took me to one side, he said they were the nephews of the owner of the Harlequin, and asked me to let them in. I told him he was the boss and could let in who he liked, but if he let them in, I would go out and not come back! I realised it put him in a very difficult position, but I considered that if a couple of smart arses like them could upstage me in that way I'd have no authority on the door. I was after all the head doorman. He refused them. Getting Beryl to call the police by saying we were trouble was their revenge. It made no difference to us, next time we went there straight from the Harlequin after work. Being doormen they dare'nt refuse us. On our next visit the place was busy and Tommy Hartley who was a broad shouldered ex boxer was the doorman. We got friendly with him and eventually we were to share many ups and downs.

Norman Paterson said one day "Why don't we open a club Roy, you've got the experience, you could run it?"

With my good pal, Norman Paterson, 1962

My first reaction was that I thought we'd 'missed the boat'. It was 1962 and to me the area seemed saturated with clubs. There was the 'Blue Angel' in Seel Street, the 'Pink Parrot' in Duke Street as was the Cabaret Club. 'The Cabin' in Fleet Street was a successful club also. There were also a lot of drinking clubs in Liverpool's South End, which were mainly coloured clubs.

The 'Pink Parrot' was the most sophisticated club in town in the late 50's early 60's.When you walked into what had been a large terraced house, it had a mature feel to it – upstairs was the Casino, (before gambling was officially legalised). When you turned left from the hall, you were in a room with a glass dance floor with lights underneath, (the first one in town), the dance floor was central and you would cross it to the bar on the left, or to the dining area on the right. The dance floor was usually crowded with drinkers, – it was only twelve foot square. Late on, the diners would dance on it. The centre of the floor between the dining tables, which were positioned around the walls, had been taken out and below could be seen the drinkers in the basement bar. The door policy was very strict, as it was in most of the clubs at that time. In fact, non-regulars always found it daunting, approaching the doormen, who were usually very brusque in their attitude. There were very few clubs so they could afford to be fussy.

I had been thinking along Norman's lines – so he easily talked me into it.

I'd looked at a couple of premises with Yankel but he'd decided against expanding his operation. So, Norman and I went out and had a look. We decided on a house in Seel St, which had been used as a place for bottling medicines, we decided to put a little restaurant with a bar and kitchen on the ground floor and we had three bedrooms upstairs which we knocked into one L shaped room with a bar at one end and a dance floor in the corner of the L.

I spent every spare minute labouring, knocking walls out for iron girders etc and painting symbols on the walls. A fellow Norman introduced me to, said: "I can give you some work for some daytime money", because I was still working the Basement of a night. He showed me a furniture van filled to the roof with 56lb bags of spuds. He said: "Take them and flog them around the flats in Kirkby and I'll pay you £10 a week. When it's empty, bring it back and I'll fill it up again!" Now the trouble with most of the tenement flats in Kirkby is that they have a big courtyard around them, so you can't park close. So I'd pull up, unlock the shutters at the back of the van, take out two bags of spuds and carry them across the yard and up the stairs often to the third floor. That was 1 cwt at a time. They'd say: "Not this week" and I'd cart them back unlock and lock the shutter and go to the next one. Fortunately, my two eldest boys Rowland and Tony were able to help me on a Saturday, which made life easier. The £10 was my contribution to the club. By the time we'd got it open there were 2 extra partners, we needed them for the funds. They were Tommy Barton and John Turnbull. Tommy actually owned his own gym. He was broad shouldered and good looking. He was also something of an entrepreneur when I met him, doing contracting jobs on premises. John Turnbull was a manager for a central heating firm and being on a good salary was one of the elite being a member of Liverpool's famous Racquets Club housed in Parliament Street. John and Norman were keen golfers; Tommy and I were more into weight training, swimming etc. We called it the Chequers Club and now it was all down to me! It had taken eighteen months to do the work. It was now June 1964.

I started a new policy with the Chequers. I opened up to a wider crowd – greeting people with a smile when they approached the door, I was still fussy on who I let in, but because of the welcoming attitude there was less aggravation. I'd refuse people, explaining why: dress not suitable – no tie – too drunk, and, last resort: non-member. It gave the place a more relaxed atmosphere. I started a policy later on, when I took on doormen, of saying to them: "I don't care if the worst bum in the world, who you'd never let in – under any circumstances – turns up at the door. Just remember, he's paying us a compliment, he wants to come in our place and help pay the wages – and refuse him with that in mind"! I've found it makes a difference.

The place was a success and very soon, I was able to give my partners a few bob each week. Not a fortune, but a good bit more than I'd been able to earn before. We started off with me doing the door and stocking the bars, cooking burgers in the kitchen etc. My partners obviously decided that was the best way!

Eventually we employed a cook, Nadja, (stolen from the Pink Parrot) who was a Yugoslav and a great cook, plus a doorman to help me at the weekends – Wally Booth, who was now at the forefront of amateur wrestling, holding several British titles. Later, Terry Phillips and Tony Buck were to work at the Chequers Club – and Alan Webster, an amusing and popular personality.

When I opened the Chequers, we charged one and sixpence for a half pint of bitter (the price in a pub was under a shilling a pint). We sold Tetley's Bitter at that time. One day a beer salesman came in singing the praises of Double Diamond bitter. I'd not heard of it before and I was easily convinced that it was something special. So much so that I charged two shillings a glass for it! It was the dearest bitter in the City! At that time, most clubs had an entrance fee for non-members of five shillings; girls were let in for free. I'd decided that every non-member would pay. When girls arrived for the first time, they'd say "What's it like in here?"

I'd say, "Well, the bitter's two shillings a glass." They'd look at each other, say: "Oh – it must be good", and start to walk past me.

I'd say, "Five bob each please ladies."

"What! You charge women?"

I'd say "Look, I think women are as good as men anytime and should be treated with equality and respect. People who let women in for free are just using them to entice men in. For me, a woman's money is as good as a man's."

"You're right, three please." – They would go in happily.

One of the main reasons I charged them was, if I didn't and the club was quiet, they'd turn around and leave. Once they'd paid, being female, they would stay and wait until it got busy! If it was really quiet, I'd go in, buy them a couple of drinks, and chat awhile until more people came in. It worked wonders. Surprisingly, at the time there was no such thing as draught lager, only bottles. Pubs generally didn't sell any lager. Hotel bars and posh little cocktail bars sold bottles of Carlsberg. As the clubs started to take off, cheaper brands like Skol and Carling came in and eventually the draught lager, which was to have a terrific impact.

I was stood at the bar one Tuesday night in the Chequers and the place was empty. I said to the barmaid: "If I can't get next Tuesday busy then I'll have to close." I'd already closed on Mondays and really didn't want to lose another night. We'd started putting Country and Western groups on at the weekend, which were really popular. I went to see the three most popular bands we used. I said: "What do you do on a Tuesday?"

"We rehearse, there's no work about."

I said: "Ok, I'll pay you twenty-five bob a man to play for me, you can share the equipment!" There was The Hillsiders, who had actually appeared in America at the Grand Ole' Opry, The Ranchers and The Miller Brothers. There were five Hillsiders, costing me six and a half quid, the four Ranchers, costing me £5 and the two Miller Brothers, two and half quid – three for the price of one! I got five hundred tickets printed, advertising 'Tuesday night at the Chequers, a Country and Western Jamboree' with the three bands all playing. I gave all the tickets out at the weekend and the following Tuesday it was packed! The Chequers was the place to go on a Tuesday and continued to be for years. These particular bands were excellent entertainment. Kenny Johnson, the lead singer of the Hillsiders, had a great voice and personality. They were all good musicians – drums, guitars and electric guitars – those three bands were all different and a night out with them was a great pleasure. Each week I gave out fewer tickets so I could charge people, gradually phasing the tickets out. It was now 1965 and the Beatles were wowing them all, beat groups were at their zenith. However, the country and western bands were equally popular – apart from anything else, they had to be able to ***sing*** and ***play*** their instruments. It was a peak time for them also. They had to be good to get work in Liverpool because country music had been popular in Liverpool since the early 1920s, so the punters knew what it was all about! One night I booked a band called The Blue Mountain Boys and they really had some talent. They'd lost a leading light in their band, a singing guitarist named Tony Allen. He'd left the band in 1963 and teamed up with an attractive female singer called Rikki. They went over to Jersey where they had a slot in the Opera House, then on to Germany from where they travelled extensively with a German agency, eventually travelling and performing in such places as Nashville, getting to know people like George Jones, Don Gibson, Chet Atkins etc.

I got to know Tony and Rikki a few years later, in fact Rikki told me when they first met Don Gibson they were booked on the same bill. The club manager told them they were to follow on straight after him. He said when you hear *'Oh Lonesome Me'*, that's his last number, be prepared to follow straight on. Rikki was standing in the dressing room enjoying a glass of Canadian Club and Coke in her bra and slip ready to put her dress on when she heard *'Oh Lonesome Me'*. He'd opened with his closing number and was so hopelessly drunk couldn't continue. Rikki hopped on to the side of the stage in her bra with one leg in and one out of her dress. Needless to say the show went down a storm. Tony, Rikki and I became good friends. Their son Ethan Allen is now a recording artist with great talent.

The Blue Mountain Boys when they came to Chequers had two exceptional singers, Johnny Paul and Patsy Foley. Johnny Paul's voice was very different. He did his own interpretation of songs, which I particularly liked. In those days, he was hard up, having a gang of kids to keep. I took him to one side one night and asked him if he could wear something other than the old check lumber jacket he always had on. He said: "This is it Roy!"

An eye for the girls

WHEN Tricia O'Donell became the Most Wanted Girl in the World, she was not the first Miss Pyramid to achieve international acclaim. Only the year before Jenny Macadam started on the beauty queen trail, as Miss Pyramid. She quickly became Miss West Coast, and is now Miss United Kingdom.

The man with the eye for the girls, who started them on the road to fame, is Roy Adams, owner of the Pyramid Club.

Spotting beauty queens is only one of Roy's achievements. He started out life as a body builder and, among other things has been a wrestler, a member of a high diving act and a stunt man.

Having settled down to the quieter life of a club owner, Mr. Adams has made the Pyramid one of Liverpool's best clubs.

The man who supplied our fruit machines, Tony Stannard, had brought in some of his old suits and asked me to flog them for him at £5 each, so I told Johnny to pick a couple out, which he did. I found it difficult to reconcile his day job with singing – he worked in a mortuary! He told me one day that one of the guys he worked with was a nutter. He said sometimes when a corpse was brought in, this fellow would pull out a knife and frenziedly stab it in the chest, screaming "fuck off! – fuck off!" - with every stab.

No wonder Johnny was a drinker and unreliable! Patsy Foley on the other hand still sings to this day and is tremendously popular.

A massive guy called Billy Nevis was now managing the group; his brother Bunter was the main man in the band. Billy became a great friend and was always there to help if there was any trouble. He unfortunately died a few years ago.

Sometime after Tommy left the Jacaranda they got a new doorman who'd come up from Cardiff, his name was Fred Waldron. He was and is a giant of a man. Six foot four and big and broad – a bit like one of the new breed of body builders except big Fred didn't lift weights.

He became a high profile figure in the seventies and eighties doing door work and some personal protection work for people like Derek Hatton the notorious militant councillor.

I was involved in a place in Colwyn Bay, which was having trouble with a local gang. I took big Fred there with me one night. We did a tour of the of the various bars in the area asking questions about these trouble makers and the gang didn't re-appear – the word had soon got out about Big Fred! Fred moved on and taking advantage of his very good baritone voice became a cabaret singer using the stage name of Carl Fredericks. I booked him on several occasions very successfully.

Another big man who I had to send up to Colwyn Bay when we first opened was Barry McLelland. He was a real giant, being six feet eight inches tall. His appearance was all that was needed to keep order. Big Barry liked to gamble, he liked to play cards and he actually worked for me for a short time as a blackjack croupier at the Chequers. He had enormous hands and couldn't help cheating when he dealt. I saw him doing it a couple of times and was amazed at how obvious he was. I gave him something else to do before he got us into trouble.

One night in the Chequers early days I was doing the door on my own. A group of lads turned up wanting to come in. I turned them down and one of them stepped forward and started to give me earache. He started to slag me off, telling me what he was going to do to me. I'd half closed the door when they approached and was standing with one shoulder sticking out. He was standing on the top step while he ranted at me. I shot my right arm out and grabbed him by the collar. I dragged him inside, slamming the door with my foot.

I grabbed his other collar with my left hand and gave him half a dozen good shakes, rattling his head against the wall each time.

I let go of him and said: "O.K., big time, – now's your chance." His face puckered and he blurted, "I'm sorry!" I opened the door and shoved him out saying to his mates: "Here's your leader – he's all yours."

When we'd been running the Chequers for 4 or 5 weeks, I'd accumulated a little cash for the bank. It was only a very small amount, but I put it into the old vanity case, which Ellen had given me to put the float in when taking the cash home at night. In the late 50s, the vanity case was an essential fashion accessory for the girls. It was a small oval box about six inches deep made of cardboard and covered in plastic animal skin, like snakeskin. We were living in a small council semi in Litherland, Liverpool, and one morning there was a ran tan at the front door. It was eight clock in the morning and the next-door neighbour was standing on the doorstep holding the vanity case. She said: "Is this yours, only my little boy picked it up in the road. I told him – 'Don't be playing with that dirty old thing' – but he said: 'But mam, it's full of money' – so I guessed it was yours!"

Roy with Big Fred, 1976

I'd put it on the ground while I locked up my old Morris 1000 van and forgot to pick it up! The vanity case probably had about £25 in it, all in change, so I decided to bank it. Ellen and I sat at the kitchen table counting all the pennies into twelve's, the shillings into twenties etc. We screwed each stack of coins up in newspaper wrapping it tight, as we'd seen the gasman do when he emptied the meter. I put it all in a small canvas kit bag, which was about 2ft long.

Norman had opened a bank account at the Nat West in Chapel Street. This was a very impressive building, with massive 15ft high bronze doors with large lion head handles. Inside it had a vast main room, a good sixty yards long, with a counter each side running the full length of the room; marble pillars supported the ornate ceiling high above. I walked in wearing a T-shirt and jeans, carrying the ridiculous canvas bag, which I now realised, looked nothing like a bank cash bag. I stood in a little queue with men in office suits. When I got to the counter, I handed the cashier the bag saying 'Chequers Club'. He looked at me putting his hand in the bag and pulling out bits of newspaper and flinging them round the counter, saying:

"What's this? What's this?"

I said: "It's the takings."

He said: "Did Mr Patterson give you a paying-in book?"

I said: "No."

He picked up the bag and tipped it out on to the counter, spreading the neat little bundles of coppers around. He was tut-tutting away so I shot my arm out and started to drag the coins towards me saying: "Forget it, I'll go somewhere else!"

He said: "No, no Mr Adams, we'll sort it out." Which he did, but boy was I embarrassed with all those smart office types waiting in the queue. However, as time went on and the business picked up, whenever I went to the bank he always made a point of greeting me politely even when he was attending another customer. When I look back, I'm surprised to think I was so naïve at thirty-two years of age!

*　　　*　　　*

Norman and Vera Paterson, Roy and Ellen Adams, John and Audrey Turnbull, 1966

One night, a guy called Richie Dodd called in. He was a friend from Vic's Gym. He said: "I like this place Roy, do you mind if I bring some business friends in for a drink?"

I said: "Of course not." About a week later, he turned up with eleven friends, several of whom I recognised as faces I'd had to keep out of the Harlequin – being brainwashed in this way, I decided I couldn't let them in! I said: "I'm sorry fella's, there's too many of you" (I always had a policy anyway for not having large male parties as when they've had a few drinks they always get boisterous, and if there's only one or two on the door, you can have problems). One of the group, John Dalton, was short with a broken nose. He shouted: "What dya mean it's only a fuckin' rubba!", whereupon he hit me over the eye with a knuckleduster. I stood my ground and smiled bravely at Doddy … "Come on Richie, there's no need for this."

He said: "You said we'd be alright and now you're knocking us back." Of course, he was right, but I had to stand on. The entrance hall was narrow and there was a small square table against the wall and I stood in the space between the table and the wall. Because I was at the nearside of the table, it created a four feet passageway between them and myself. So, in order to kick off, one of them had to face me on his own, and while they were mentally deciding who was going to do it, the police arrived and saved the day. Their leader was called Phil Glennon and he had a very large following and was very respected by them all. He didn't engage in the argument and more or less stood quietly to one side. It was a nothing situation, but it was my first encounter with Glennon's mob as they were known at the time.

I was obviously concerned about when they would come back to prove a point. Phil was to tell me a couple of years later that he liked the way I handled the situation and wasn't looking for revenge. Unfortunately, I was to fall foul of them later on and to experience consequent problems. Glennon's gang were the main gang in the City, but there were also families who it wasn't wise to upset. Generally, most of them didn't basically set out for trouble. The main problem was if you upset one member of the family, you had the lot to deal with! Unfortunately, there's always a loose cannon in any family, so violent incidents were not uncommon. There was also the Molloys. The Molloys were, and are, a boxing family. Jimmy Molloy Snr., famous as an amateur British Middleweight champion, his brother Tommy was also the Professional British Champion.

Good reasons for not upsetting them.

Meanwhile at Chequers I got involved in an incident with a guy who was ripping a radio out of a car. Someone called the police and the guy was arrested. He was friendly with some of Phil Glennon's boys and an intimidation process started in order to frighten off the witnesses. I was being phoned with threats at all hours, a real over-reaction to the theft of a radio! It did make life uncomfortable, because I lived out of town and drove home late at night and I took to carrying a shotgun. Eventually the situation boiled over. Tommy Hartley had finished his spot of singing and left the club with Brenda his wife. Next thing, there's a ran tan on the door and Brenda is screaming: "Roy, a gang is beating Tommy up." I looked around and the doorman who was with me had disappeared; I looked quickly for a weapon. There wasn't one, so I ran out into the street. When they saw me they legged it, expecting me to have support. When they saw I was on my own, they started back. Tommy was lying in the road with a stream of blood pouring from his head into the gutter. He wasn't moving and I thought, my God, they've killed him! They came charging at me wielding iron bars, tyre levers etc. I turned and ran into the club, slamming the door behind me, as the bars were thrown – hitting the door and fanlight. We found eight iron bars inside the fanlight when we replaced the glass. The ambulance came for Tommy followed by the police. One guy in the club who used to do a bit of wrestling with us remarked: "I'd respect you Roy if you had a mark on you." Of course, neither he nor his pals who were with him had joined in. I felt terrible about the whole thing, knowing I'd ran and left Tommy out there, although they'd finished with him. I'd never turned my back before, though I know I had no choice. If they did that to him what would they have done to me?

When we arrived at St George's Hall for the court case, there must have been at least 100 blokes on the steps. Talk about running the gauntlet. They were yelling at Tommy: "What are you going to do, you know what it means?"

Tommy just shouted "I'm gonna make sure he goes down."

As it happens, the guy Tommy had named got off because in court Tommy'd said: "Yes, I think that's him." Not a positive ID! Prior to this case also, we'd had to suffer six months of threats and intimidation. But that's the club business.

A smooth character called John Capper came into Chequers one night with a girl called Diane. He wore a fawn overcoat which he informed me was Vicuna and had cost him £1,200. This was 1965, so in today's terms that's £12,000! He was very quietly spoken

Left to right, seated: Eddie Murphy, Marty Battle, Richie Dodd, Phil Glennon, Jobo Jones; standing: unknown, Tommy McArdle, Joey Murray (Photo: Courtesy of Richie Dodd)

and quite refined. The girl Diane wore a white Macintosh and sported an enormous knuckle-duster ring on her right hand.

He said: "You know by law you can have two gaming machines in your club."

I said: "Yes – we've got two."

He said: "I bet you didn't know one can be manually operated!"

What he had was a gaming table he called the 'Golden Five', which he called incorrectly a 'boulle table'.

I said I would try it out. It was a success and helped the club a lot. I didn't realise he'd tried a dozen others before me. When I said yes, they all said yes and he's always thanked me for getting him started in Liverpool.

Ellen and Roy Adams with Doreen and Tommy Barton, 1971

Above: The outside of the Chequers Club, circa. 1963, before it opens

Opposite, top: Inside the Chequers Club circa. 1964

Opposite, bottom: The outside of the former Chequers Club building in 2002

CUBA
CUBA
ISM

Tony Buck, Joe Phillips, Big Barry, Roy, unknown and Jimmy Tierney.

Some well known faces at the Lincolns Motors Party

Paul Kelly, Roy and Eddie Walker and Frank McGowan at Gatsby's, 1975

Richie Harper with Roy at Shorrocks Hill

Roy with Pat McMullen

~ 9 ~
Jokers & Tricksters

JUST OUTSIDE THE town centre in the Edge Lane district was the Joker's Club. The owner was a black guy who everyone addressed as Joker. His club was open around the clock – in fact, one of the national newspapers had a headline one-day saying 'Britain's only twenty-four hour club – why is it allowed? Read all about it in the next issue.' The article didn't appear. The general opinion was that so many police officers used the place it would cause a scandal. So it was stifled.

One night, a member of another Liverpool family was refused entrance, so he rounded up three or four of his family and approached the doorman with a sawn-off shotgun. Joker appeared at the doorway demanding to know what they were at. They produced the gun saying "If you don't let us in we'll shoot you, this gun is loaded", so saying, the guy with the gun opened the breach by pressing the ends down, whereupon the cartridges fell out onto the ground. Joker, who was a man in his 60s, who didn't care a toss, produced a pistol from his pocket saying: "Look, I've got a gun and I'll shoot the lot of you if you don't get lost!" He then walked inside and they scrabbled around for their dropped cartridges. Just before they'd arrived, a Norwegian seaman had been thrown out. He looked around outside and noted a tree which grew close to the building with a branch stretching across the roof. He decided to climb the tree and drop onto the flat roof and find a way back in, which he proceeded to do.

When the other guys reloaded their gun they started shouting threats and fired a shot in the air which so startled the Norwegian that he fell out of the tree, landing on the gunman and his brother, flattening them both. When the other brother rushed over to retrieve the gun, he legged it thinking they were after him. Needless to say, they also got out of there as fast as they could!

Joker's wife, Nellie, virtually ran the place and worked around the clock. Everyone knew her. When Joker died, he left no will and no indication where his savings were. Nellie was left with nothing. Apparently the police did find the remains of bags of money, which had been destroyed by rats in the cellar. I believe people still go and dig up the ground hoping to find the money!

One night in the Chequers club I was doing my usual mine host having a drink with a customer, it turned out that he was from London and was a colleague of John Capper who had introduced our first gaming table. We had now installed a roulette table as well as a legalite table. I was bemoaning the fact that the roulette table was costing us money. He explained to me that roulette was usually installed in a Casino, more as an attraction than a money making prospect. He said they usually worked out its worth on an annual percentage basis, say four percent per annum. You had to view it that way because of all the weeks you lost money. He then told me that he had a system where he could guarantee a gambler winning at roulette though it would be of no help to the casino. He got a piece of paper and showed me the system, which he said had been worked out by a million pound computer. He told me he would normally charge fifty pounds for the system but I was such a nice guy I could have it for nothing.

It was a fairly simple system based on structuring the amounts you bet. The main problem was the betting limit on the table, which was generally five pounds. Because of this, you would buy half a crown chips e.g. two shillings and sixpence. They worked out that ten pounds in half crown chips were necessary to cover all contingencies, so Ellen and I decided to give it a whirl. Because you only bet on evens the best you could do was double your stake.

The usual thing was to stick to one side, black or white. If you were on black and had a long run on white your stake would climb very quickly to reach the five pound limit, so that was why two of us played so we would be responsible for half each of the stake of ten pounds. You knew as long as you kept betting the black would come up eventually and give you your money back plus ten half crowns profit. Of course, if you could play on a no limit table with five-pound chips, you'd win fifty pound each time. Sometimes three spins of the wheel would give you your profit but more often it took a good few more spins and you'd be worrying about the limit.

It was actually working well for Ellen and I. We'd go for a gamble before going to the club or after dining out, we'd aim to play four games, which would make five pounds. (fifty pounds in today's terms) feeling confident, we decided to try it at the Odd Spot in Bold Street.

I strolled up to the cash desk and asked for ten pounds in half crown chips. She handed over ten pounds worth of five shilling chips explaining they didn't do half crowns, so we started playing praying we'd have some early luck, we didn't – in fact we very quickly reached the limit with a lot of our own money at stake. I had to dig deep to buy more chips from the croupier to bet the required amount… It was difficult because we'd got used to the half crown bet and I completely lost my way. We eventually walked out sixty pounds out of pocket, which at that time represented all we made in a week at the club. It was really a blessing in disguise because the club was getting busier and required my full attention and that little gambling lesson was enough to discourage me.

A few years later on trips to London, I used to be a regular at the Playboy Club and loved to gamble in the casino. I'd get forty pounds worth of chips and no more at the time, it was enough to give you the enjoyment of a gamble without being silly. Sometimes I'd come out on top. If I didn't, it didn't matter. The food and drink was free in the casino.

Tommy (Tacker) Comerford was a big guy who engaged in various unlawful activities from time to time. He was a popular figure with a personality. Tacker was famously involved in what was, at the time, Liverpool's biggest ever robbery. This was at the Bank of England in Water Street in 1969, when they broke into the main safe using a thermal lance, getting away with something in the region of a quarter of a million. My pal Norman Paterson had opened a club called Tracy's in Stanley Street. He was standing outside one afternoon talking to Tacker who had stopped his car to say hello. Norman was bemoaning the fact that his business was bad. Tacker said: "There's only two club owners I know who are straight, that's you and Roy Adams, just come with me for a minute."

He led Norman to his car and said: "Open the boot." Norman did so. The boot was packed with bundles of fivers. Tacker said: "There's thirty grand in there – take five for yourself." Norman gasped and managed to choke a "no thanks". Tacker said: "I can't believe you."

Norman said: "You know that sales job you have. You're a good salesman, I've watched you work. Well, if you were to go and buy me a pair of brass cufflinks out of your wages, I'd wear them with pride!"

That was typical of Norman.

On another occasion, one of his people had been attacked in his club and a deputation came to see him to stop him testifying, threatening him.

Norman said: "I've got a bigger gang than you lot, they all wear blue and they're called the police!"

One of them said: "Yer norra grass are ya?" He replied in his best voice: "I will be the biggest grass you've ever known if you bother me or my staff again." They had no answer to that!

Tacker grinned, got in his car and drove off. It was a few years later and I was stood at the bar of my club, Gatsby's, where I was experimenting with a promotion, which was a topless barmaid. When I walked through to this bar, it was packed, they were all standing around the bar ten deep, gawping at the barmaid. Nobody was buying a drink, a very loud posh voice boomed behind me, "I want to speak to the manager, this is a disgrace!" I turned around to see the beaming face of Tommy Comerford. He'd just got out of the nick! I remember the guy who used the thermal lance. He used to come into Chequers. I called him Farley Granger after the film star, as he was a good-looking man. He called himself Brian – God knows what his name was!

One day Tacker and Richie Dodd were driving along Princess Boulevard Liverpool where there were several churches of different denominations, they noticed that one of the churches had the doors open so, out of curiosity parked the car and went to have a look, they were looking at the wonderful ceiling when they heard a noise from the darker far end of the church. They walked over to have a look and here were two characters rolling up sheets of lead which they'd stripped from the roof, each roll must have weighed a hundred-weight, they'd also collected copper pipe which they were cutting up, Doddy said: "I'm police Sergeant Dodd and this is Inspector Comerford," where-upon Tacker said: "I can see what's being going on. This is very serious stealing from church premises. I should arrest you both now, however you can't replace the stuff and I'm feeling a bit benevolent, I'm trying to raise money for a police charity so if you take that stuff out to my car and pack it in the boot and the back seat I'll say no more about it." This they did and Doddy and Tacker drove off with the loot!

There's a club called the Cabin still going strong in Liverpool. It had a matriarch called Mrs Windsor (she always got the formal title). She was a horror on the door, never indulging in social graces, being a woman she got away with murder. Tacker told me one night he called there for a drink with some of Phil Glennon's boys and she refused them – now they weren't used to being refused anywhere, so one of them said: "Let's drag her outside and see what's she's got to say." Tacker was able to intervene and calm them down. Although, having been refused by Mrs Windsor myself in her terse, abrupt manner, verging on the insulting, it would not have surprised me if someone, sometime, blew their top with her!

When I started work in the first club I was still living in Litherland in Poulson Drive. One day I was waiting at the bus stop on this council estate when a very elegant and good-looking girl appeared. She looked like a Parisian fashion model, even wearing a small hat. I thought what the hell is she doing here. She appeared again a few days later at the same bus stop. Several months later after I opened the Chequers, a well-known popular guy called Vince McCaffery came into the club and who should be with him but the same girl. Vince introduced me and left me talking to her at the bar. She told me she was from Canada and she was a physiotherapist. I didn't know what that was but I was impressed. She was very nicely spoken with a transatlantic drawl. I found out later she was quite a character and made it up as she went along. Her name was Pat Duncan and she lived on the Litherland estate where we lived. It turned out a couple of years later that her father worked for us at the Sands club in Ainsdale looking after the gardens.

Vince, Pat and Marcus

Vince eventually married Pat and they had a son called Marcus. She was a girl with a great deal about her; both men and women took to her because of her personality. Vince was also a very handsome man and very well liked though a real playboy. They were to split up eventually which was a shame because they were a great couple. Vince had done a little boxing and he had twin brothers Brian and Mike who were also into boxing. Brian became a successful boxer (more about him later). Vince's son Marcus went into the army as a professional soldier and became Army heavy weight boxing champion. Vince worked for a firm in Manchester selling vending machines. He came to me one day saying there was a vending machine that could produce three hundred meals a day. He said: "Why don't we open a café which has half a dozen machines with a real variety of food? It would be the first automatic serve yourself café." I thought it was a good idea and set about looking for premises. I found a site in Stanley Street and started work on it whilst applying for planning permission. Vince proposed that his brother Brian who had recently retired from boxing come up from London and run it. Well time passed, the place was nearly ready and no sign of the machines. Vince paid one of his visits and I tackled him about it. I said: "You haven't got these machines yet have you?"

He said: "A bit of a hiccup there Roy, might take a bit of time."

I told him we didn't have time and got to work altering the premises. I put in a proper kitchen, new counter tops and opened it as a proper café. Brian ran it with his wife and after a short time we came to an agreement and he and his wife took it over completely.

That was 1970 and it only closed down in 2002. Brian and his wife ran it the whole time.

Brian McCaffrey with Big Barry behind him.

Vince continued to live in Manchester, he was a real high flier with several well known girl friends, but eventually married again this time to celebrity Lyn Paul, one of the New Seekers. She was a great girl and they seemed happy for a while. Vince came back to Liverpool and got involved in a club called the Chauffeurs. One day he announced to Lyn that he was going to Spain for a weeks holiday, she asked him who was going to look after the club and he told her he would get someone in. "No need," she said, "I'll look after it, I can do the banking and I'll keep a record of everything." So off Vince went not realising that Lyn knew he was taking a girl. When he arrived home there was no sign of her, she had taken the takings and his books and done a runner. He came to see me and told me she'd phoned him, that she knew about the girl and if he wanted his books back he'd have to buy her a car. He went off to the South of England where she'd arranged dinner at a country hotel. They had a romantic meal and finished up holding hands. Lyn went to the ladies room and never came back. She took the car and the books. That was the end of that.

Vince had said to me in the early days of the marriage: "Roy, when a couple are married and working isn't it usual for them to pool their earnings?"

"Well yes," I said: "Usually."

He said: "Well I put mine in but Lyn doesn't."

I said: "What are you earning?"

He said: "Two hundred a week," which wasn't bad.

I said: "And what's she earning?"

He said: "Three to four thousand a week.'

I said: "You can't expect her to hand that lot over."

He said: "I wouldn't mind but she's bought her parents a house and a car and her brother the same and gave me nothing."

I said: "She probably wants to see how things are going first." As it turned out, she was a good judge. Vince later married a page three girl who featured topless in the Sun Newspaper. She hit the headlines with 'Freddie Starr ate my Hamster' which featured a picture of Freddie holding a hamster in his mouth. I think it was one of Max Clifford's early stunts.

Vince's first wife Pat, was diagnosed with cancer and given a short time to live. Everyone was heartbroken. She refused to see anyone and arranged her own funeral.

The hymns the flowers the cars, everything, she was still very young, in her early forties.

Norman, Tommy Hartley and I were having a short break in Majorca, we'd never been before but Eric Armitage who was Normans friend had a yacht moored in the centre of the main harbour frontage. He pointed out a building across the road telling us there was a super nightclub there, which we should visit. We'd spent the day riding up and down the Island on three motor scooters, which we'd hired and decided that evening to visit the nightclub. On the ground floor, there was an entrance from the promenade road to a restaurant, which was part of the club. We dined there, made ourselves popular and were given passes to the nightclub, which had its entrance above, and to the rear of the prom. Inside it was like a theatre with high backed upholstered couch like seats around little tables. After a few drinks at the bar, we ventured into one of these seats and started to enjoy ourselves. A band came on stage and the night really got going. The place was now busy, the dance floor was crowded the singers a male and female were great and we had a good time.

Tommy Hartley still worked for us at the Chequers where he used to get up and give us a few songs with the trio. Norman was suddenly inspired to say to me: "Why don't we get Tommy up to give us a song?"

Tommy Hartley with Silas and my two youngest, Diane and Paul

I didn't think the bandleader would go for that and said so; undeterred Norman made his way down the isle to the stage where he called the bandleader over and started talking to him. I could see the man shaking his head and Norman holding his sleeve and trying to persuade him. Eventually Norman came back to the seat where we'd been joined by a couple we'd met on the beach. He said the bandleader had said he'd see what he could do. Tommy had borrowed a brown suit jacket off Tommy Barton, which he'd set off with a pair of Zoot style flannels and a pair of winkle picker long out of fashion shoes. This was his evening attire for the holiday. So we're all chatting and having a drink when the band leader suddenly announced: "We've been persuaded to let a customer give us a song, here he is, Tommy Hartley."

There was a smattering of half-hearted applause except from our table where we pushed Tommy to his feet. Tommy self-consciously made his way to the stage with a hurried shuffle. When he got to the steps that led to the stage, he had to turn his feet out sideways because of the length of the winkle pickers. He stood on stage looking distinctly uncomfortable and the bandleader handed him the microphone. The bandleader walked to one side with his hands by his side his palms spread outwards in resignation. As soon as Tommy gripped the mike his whole demeanour changed, he was suddenly in his element. He turned to the band leader, gave him instructions and raised his right arm giving the beat, turning to face the audience he went into his favourite song .... which he sang perfectly. Everyone had stopped talking after the first few bars and he sang to perfect silence from the audience who when he finished applauded loudly calling for more. Tommy went into another song, as he approached the end of the song the final words reaching a really high crescendo he then repeated the phrase approaching it in an even higher key. I thought he'll never reach this note, but he did to rapturous applause, he bounded back up the isle where we stood applauding and waiting. I said: "Tom you were in fantastic voice tonight."

He said: "To tell you the truth Roy, you couldn't have got a tanner between the cheeks of my arse when I sang that last note."

The club was called Tito's and as far as I know it's still going. I went a few years ago and they'd built a glass lift shaft on the frontage of the promenade, it also had a retracting ceiling and on balmy nights, you could look up at the stars.

A few years later, Norman was to get involved with Joe (piano) Henderson a top act in the 60s and 70s. Norman bought a bar from him and they were in Majorca for a meeting with the syndicato, which was the licensing committee. Joe being in show business was friendly with some of the underworld characters from London. They'd arranged for a night out with Joe at Tito's and Norman was invited along. They took a shine to Norman and his posh strident tones and personal charisma telling him never to put up with any grief from anyone. They were only a phone call away, of course that was never Norman's style but he appreciated the offer.

On another occasion Norman asked me if I fancied a trip to New York, there was a holiday offer of four days and nights for sixty pounds a couple hotel included. There were two people in New York who I thought I'd like to go and see. Ellen said she'd like to go so we went.

One of the people I wanted to look up was Irwin Brookes, a black guy who turned up at Vic's Gym one night in the 50s. He wore a skintight woollen tracksuit and had a great physique. He'd apparently competed in the Mr Canada competition and been placed tenth. It was hard to imagine anyone beating him He was living in a flat in Liverpool and working on the American Army base in Burton wood. I started doing a bit of training with him and we became quite pally. Sometimes after the workout, he would take me back to his house for a health drink. He'd mix two bottles of Guinness with Casilan protein powder four eggs and Complan also Glucose powder to sweeten it.

He invited me to meet a couple of friends of his who lived in Upper Parliament Street. The thing I noticed as I was climbing the stairs was the bathroom door was open and a tap was running into the bath. I went over to turn the tap off and saw the bath was full of bottles of beer, it was summer time and the water was cooling the beer, typically American. Irwin introduced me to his best friend who was called Jackson he was very impressive and a lot like a black Burt Lancaster. About once a month I used to have a party in my long suffering mothers little terraced house. Irwin and Jackson came along a couple of times, their whole demeanour was a lot more sophisticated than ours. They brought along gifts of cigarettes Brandy and scotch and really gave the night a lift. The first time we had one of these parties we bought a keg of bitter which cost five pounds for the men to drink and a bottle of cheap port which cost six shillings with two large bottles of lemonade so that the girls could have port and lemon. The lads would call in at the pub on the way for a half of bitter putting the glasses under their coats and bringing the glasses with them to the party. Everyone threw three or four shillings into the kitty for the booze. We were all there to enjoy the music and basic though it all was, we always had a good time.

Irwin left Liverpool on a nuclear submarine on which he was the chief engineer, we said our goodbyes, he said something like: "Its been good to know ya, we're not gonna meet again so this is really goodbye."

Fourteen years later I'm in our hotel room, found his number in the telephone directory, and rang him, I was amazed he answered and on the following day took us into the Bronx where he'd arranged a party. This was a no go area and we were made really welcome and felt quite relaxed although we were the only white people there.

Irwin introduced his pretty niece to Norman, she was a well-educated sophisticated New Yorker and they hit it off, her name was Myotte Coker.

At the Copa Cabana in New York. Foreground left, Norman and Myotte Coker, foreground right, Roy and Ellen.
The two blokes second from the far end were the nuisances.

The other person I wanted to look up was named Bobby Campbell; he'd been a butcher in Liverpool and also a doorman. Bobby was a real heavy weight with exceptionally broad shoulders with very short hair that looked like black velvet, he was a non-aggressive friendly type. He'd been on holiday with his wife in New York and liked it so he went there to live with his wife for a trial period. When we got there, I rang him and we agreed to meet at the Copa Cabana nightclub where Buddy Greco was appearing. Norman decided to bring Irwin's niece along and the four of us duly arrived at the club. They had a small reception bar with a stage in the corner. We sat down at a table and ordered a round of drinks. A trio appeared on stage with a young slim girl singer, they were a black trio and were terrific we decided to have another drink and enjoy the music before going into the club. We'd actually paid five dollars each to see the show and have a meal in the Copa, this was a special offer organised by the hotel where we were staying. Bobby had arranged to meet us in the reception bar for a drink before the show. He hadn't turned up when the time arrived for us to go into the room for our meal and I called for the bill. I gave a large note to the Chinese waiter. He came back with my change on a tray some notes and a large amount of silver, I picked the notes up and started to talk to Ellen, she nudged me looking past me. The waiter was still there, he was standing looking at the tray and then at me. Ellen muttered: "Don't be intimidated by him." I said: "No chance I've given him a good tip."

The waiter beckoned another Chinese waiter who came and stood along side him, the two of them glaring at me. I stood up and moved my chair so that my back was to them then sat down and carried on with my conversation. We then went inside for our meal. The people from the hotel had all been put on one table, there were about twelve of us. The waiter put some bottles of wine on the table which we helped ourselves to, the next thing Ellen, who was sitting next to me on an end seat said: "Sort this out, will you Roy?"

I saw the waiter and a man in a suit having a heated discussion, I asked them if everything was all right. The waiter said: "The wine goes with the meal and those two guys (nodding down the table) want brandy and a scotch." I said: "Well that's okay, just give it to them and charge extra." I handed him the money and forgot it. The set menu was handed out, there was a limited choice and we ordered. Next thing, there's another discussion between the waiter and his boss. I said: "What's up now?"

"The meals a set meal and one of these arseholes wants steak and the other wants lobster."

I said: "If you can do it that's not a problem we'll pay the difference. When the meals came, the steak was on a bare plate, no trimmings no veg, the same with the lobster. Ellen begged me to say nothing. She said: "I'm frightened in here Roy, I want to get out."

I have to say the place was intimidating; it was like a theatre with tables. Stood around the walls at the back were men in bow ties and black suits, and others were moving around the place, in bow ties and red velvet jackets who were referred to us as the captains.

We watched the show, (the wonderful impressionist Frank Gorshon, who played the Riddler in the first Batman film, followed by Buddy Greco) which was great and then, left. As we walked through the reception bar, I saw Bobby Campbell standing at the bar. We went over and joined him, he was standing with a little scouser who I recognised, he greeted me with the usual: "Hi'ya Roy, still doing the door?"

Bobby now had longer Beatle style hair and he was obviously well thought of, he raised his hand saying: "I'll get you all a drink." The aforementioned Chinese waiter came running over, belting off to get the drinks. I told Bobby of our experience with him and he said: "Ah the general rule in here is tips is fifty percent of the bill," which made me feel as though I had been stingy.

Bobby was working at a club called Dangerfields. He was on about four hundred pounds a week – this was 1969 so it was a good screw. He said he would give it another four years and then he was coming home to open a business. I said: "What's it like working the door in New York?"

He said: "When I got started and the customers got stroppy I gave them a crack and they'd leg it up the road. Not like Liverpool, if you gave someone a crack in Liverpool that's the start of your problems and they never go away. Anyway the boss took me to one side and said if you get problems you pick up that phone on the wall and place it down again. After that, that's what I did, two little men in suits would speak to them, and they'd be gone. New York is heavily Mafia controlled."

Bobby was promoted to Maitre D, then manager and I understand he eventually became a partner. His wife's sister was married to a real hard Liverpool doorman called Jimmy Penn; he'd worked for me at Gatsby's in Victoria Street. He told me that Bobby had done really well; he'd bought a beautiful house, which was used in the film *Godfather 2*. The film company paid him 80,000 dollars with two first class tickets to anywhere in the world whilst they were filming.

Bobby chose Kirkby in Liverpool!

Bobby died a few years ago – they brought his body back home and the burial service was in Scotland Road. It was strange to hear his American son in law reading the eulogy in Liverpool's Scotland Road.

Roy with Fatso (Johnny Penn)

CHEQUERS CLUB
One of
70/
RPOOL
09 2917
"There is a
o of livin at Che
THE SHAKESPEARE SHOW BAR
207 4667
No Membership Required
ALL NEXT WEEK
30th October
RAY FELL
6th November
Visit LIVERP
Mr Pickwicks
FRASER ST. off London Rd.
051-207 4605
OVER 30s NIGHTS
Mondays & Thursdays
DANCE/CABARET
SPECTACULAR
Tuesday to Saturday
PEZ ESPADA
2 TEMPLE STREET
051-263 9580
CITY OF CHANGE & CHOICE
PYRAMID CLUB
TEMPLE STREET,
LIVERPOOL 2
Tel: 236 7682/8941
BARS — T.V. LOUNGE
DANCE
MEMBERS NOTICE
WISPA
H ROAD, LITHERLAND
051-928 8771
30s NIGHTS
onday & Thursday
TRY & WESTERN
very Wednesday
OP OF THE POPS
ery Tues., Fri. and Sat.
Leighton Court
COUNTRY CLUB
NESTON WIRRAL
Tel 336 1426/1734
THE BROADWAY CLUB
TRY
THE OTHER PLACE
27 STANLEY
The Four Winds
HANOVER ST. LIVERPOOL
709 895
BOBBINS
GARSTON—Tel: 427 5320
STAG NIGHTS
Thursday
DISCO
Friday
CABARET
Saturday & Sunday
NOW!
STADIUM TO CLOSE
L'S PREMIER NITE SPOT
WOOKY HOLLOW
ROAD, LIVERPOOL 6. 051-263 2796
Forthcoming Attractions
BERNARD MANNING
DEL SHANNON
ROCKIN' BERRIES
SID LITTLE and EDDIE LARG
TOMMY COOPER
LINSONS
LITHERLAND 051-928 7442
£40,000 facelift for wooky
back of the moon
Proprietors :
R. J. ADAMS, T. C. BARTON
TOAD HALL COUNTRY CLUB
SHORE ROAD, AINSDALE
SOUTHPORT
Tel. 77563
THE STRAND CLUB
STRAND ROAD/LITHERLAND ROAD
922 3842—Telephone—922 3842
Wednesday, Thursday, Friday,
Saturday and Sunday

Squires Restaurant Club
60a ALLERTON ROAD . WOOLTON . 428 5163
physical
perfect ?
If you want to present a new
on the beaches this summ
now is the time to start shapin
body with a visit to
A&B HEALTH STU
for gents and ladies
17 TEMPLE STREET
Sauna, Sunray, Weights, Wrestling & Boxin
Physique Moulding Courses for
Men and Women
Monday to Friday 10 a.m. to
Cabaret
step on it go to
FRASER STREET,
LIVERPOOL
RUSSELLS
Watch this col
THE WORLD'S MOST FAMOUS CLUB
LIVERPOOL'S OWN
Cavern
OPEN
Thur, Fri, Sat, Sun, Mon.
from 8 p.m. to 2 a.m.
Continues its policy of promoting
and encouraging the best in
popular sounds
'HEAVY ROCK' – PROGRESSIVE BEAT
THE
RUMFORDS
COACH
HOUSE
LICENSED TILL 2 am
THREE FLOORS
THREE BARS
UGLYS
disco
Duke Street, Liverpool 1.
Bucks Place
(Members Only)
HEALTH CLUB
FOR
PROFESSIONAL
GENTLEMEN
RD SQUARE, LIVERPOOL 2
STRAND
Samantha's
Playground
DAVIES STREET off Dale
LIVERPOOL
Telephone:s MAGhull 5570
AINtree 6527
ROCKY
SEDDON
38 LIVERPOOL RO
LYDIATE
THE NAME?
CHELSEA
REACH
WHERE?
PROMENADE,
First Class Restaurant
Statue is multi coloured, says
the Rev. Donald May.
HOME of the MERSEY BEAT
THE
CAVERN
SPECIAL BREW
Sole Management
John Seddon
051·920 5234

EXECUTIVE CLUB
INVITATION
Ecsta
HOME of the MERSEY BEAT
THE CAVERN CLUB
LIVERP
WRYDAIT Ltd.
CASINOS
W. GRIMWOOD.
A. M. McGOWAN.
D. CHAND.
Kingsway Club
ABC TELEVISION 19 56
Please Admit Contestant in A.B.C.
"Holiday Town" Competition to
New Brighton Tower Theatre,
Saturday, 28th July, 1956
THE CAVERN
LIVERPOOL
HOME OF THE MERSEY BEAT
featuring
FREDERICKS
ENTERTAINER
Tickets £15
for 7.30pm
would like to introduce you to the new
'SANDS CLUB'
SHORE ROAD, AINSDALE
lavishly fitted out in Victoria
Music, Dinin
IRON DOOR
jazz club
GARY SPIERS
INTERNATIONAL
EVERY ASPECT OF SECURITY UNDERTAKEN
0585-136948
PROPRIETOR:
ROY ADAMS
Introducing you to the
EXECUTIVE CLUB
122 DUKE STREET
LIVERPOOL, L1 5AG
Your Host Manager:—
PETER McKENNA.
SHORROCKS
HILL
COUNTRY CLUB
COMPLIMENTARY
ADMIT TWO.
LIFEBOAT LANE
FORMBY.

Terry Phillips

Eddie McDonough

~ 10 ~
Singers

TOMMY HARTLEY WAS working at the Chequers. One night he was late and I asked him where he'd been and he said: "Sorry Roy, I called in at the Blue Angel to ring you, but Freddy Starr was on the phone to Rory Storm so I had to wait for half an hour." The joke being that they both had terrible stammers! Rory Storm had a group called the Hurricanes and he was a popular attraction at the Cavern which had really come into its own with the advent of the Beatles who by now, 1964, were going great guns in America and elsewhere.

In the mid fifties, just before Elvis hit the scene, I remember going to the Odeon Cinema to see Bill Haley and the Comets live on stage, part of the promotion for the film *'Rock Around The Clock'*. Bill Haley's Comets were revolutionary, with sax' players dropping to their knees and others lying on their backs, thrashing their legs in the air whilst still playing their instruments. The audience got up and were dancing and jiving down the aisles. Cinemas were being wrecked up and down the country! Little Richard, Chuck Berry, Jerry Lee Lewis, Elvis etc; these were the real 'rock'n'rollers.

A colourful character in the 60's and even to the present day is P.J. Proby, who famously split his trousers on stage at the London Palladium. That little fiasco did damage his career. In the early days, he was friendly with Elvis Presley and used to play football with him, he also used to do demo tapes of songs for him, being able to sing like Elvis. In those days, he was up there with the best. The first record he had made was in a style associated with coloured singers. He called himself Jett Powers. He sent a record to a radio station which only played black music they played it and it was popular until they found out he wasn't one of their own! It did however draw attention to him – he had a great voice and his appearance at the London Palladium was his high spot. On that occasion, his big number was *'Somewhere'*. During one of the performances, his trousers split. This made the headlines at the time, but did make people wary of booking him. Later on, he had a hit with *'Hold Me'* and ballads like *'We Kiss In A Shadow.'* He landed a part in the musical Elvis, in which he was fantastic as the King. Unfortunately, in one of his many mad moments he fired a gun in the dressing room and was sacked. Some years later Bill Kenwright, the impresario, revived the show and put Jim (as we call him) in the lead. He complained to the dresser one night, saying he wanted a new costume. She said it wasn't on, so he took a razor blade to it and split it on stage. She then got a gold Elvis costume out and told him to wear it. He refused so Bill Kenwright insisted on it. He then got out his little blade and did it again. The costume split and Bill Kenwright strode onto the stage and frog-marched him out of the stage door in front of the queue saying: "You'll never work for me again." Jim said those famous words: "I'll be back!"

The first time he worked for me was at the Pyramid. I remember at the start of his opening number the electrics failed. We all stood in the dark; his mike was also off! He just carried on singing with his backing as if nothing had happened. He was great! He worked for me several times after that – I used to put him up at my house where he regaled me with wonderful stories about those early days. He came from the same part of the world as Jerry Lee Lewis (a great favourite) and in many ways was of a similar mindset. The last time I put him on was at the Kingsway in Southport in the late 1980s. I was amazed at

P. J. Proby getting cheeky!

the interest it generated, people travelled from all over Britain. Some of them walked around for hours before his appearance carrying various mementoes like old programmes and LPs, too treasured to be left at home. I put him up at the Dukes Folly Hotel in Southport, which was owned by my good friends Mike and Jill Peterson. Proby had been living in a council house up near Burnley for about twenty years and appearances were very rare. Jill said he was the most fastidious guest they'd ever had, keeping his room immaculate, making his own bed etc.

I had all the tables in the cabaret room booked for that occasion. When the time came for his performance, he used a backing tape, which for him was most unusual, he normally insisted on live backing. I gave him an introduction and announced him 'P J Proby!' He didn't arrive. I did it again, still no sign. After the third time, I went over to the dressing room door where he now stood. I said: "What's happening?"

He said: "Where's my fucking intro?"

I hotfooted it to the DJ and said: "What are you doing?"

He said: "I forgot to wind the tape back!"

He came on stage and started with *'Hold Me'*, shrugging off his white leather coat, which stuck, he had to swop the mike over to get it off! By now, he was really off his stride. Though he saw it through, it wasn't his best performance.

Looking in the *Liverpool Echo* one day at the club adverts. I saw the Kraal Club in New Brighton was advertising an appearance by Jackie Wilson. I couldn't believe it, one of America's top cabaret artists appearing in a tiny Merseyside club. I phoned the club and they confirmed it was the one and only Jackie Wilson. I'd been collecting his records for many years and had to go to see him. John Stanley who owned the club told me he was doing some agency business and he'd booked Jackie into a big cabaret venue. Part of the deal was an appearance at John's club! We went into the club cellar where he was performing. It was packed with people but so tiny that there were probably only about sixty people in the place. The big moment arrived when Jackie came out and started his first song with his customary leap in the air, cracking his head on one of the ceiling beams, which were very low. He didn't let it faze him and he performed wonderfully. After the show, I ***had*** to go and see him. John told me he was on the third floor in Twiggy's bar (Twiggy was a very large and lovely lady). Jackie and I had an immediate rapport and we drank and talked until four in the morning.

Jackie Wilson was surprised that I knew so much about him as he was not widely known in this country. I explained that I regularly went to second hand shops. One in

P. J. Proby pays a visit, 2001

particular was called Edwards in Kensington, Liverpool. Seamen would bring records in from abroad and they had a terrific variety. Brook Benton, Jeri Southern, Joni James were favourites as well as jazz vocalists like Sarah Vaughan, Dinah Washington, Joe Williams (Count Basie's vocalist), and Ella Fitzgerald who I think recorded more songs than anyone.

Actually sitting with Jackie Wilson in the bar in New Brighton was a high spot for me.

We arranged on his next trip he would base himself at West Tower, the mansion I now lived in, and tour from there. He went home to America and suffered a stroke – he was in a coma for eight years and then died. I often wonder whether the bump on the head in the Kraal Club had anything to do with it. His rendition of *'You'll Never Walk Alone'* is a great favourite, among others. His voice is different to anyone else I've ever heard!

Another famous club in the city centre was the 'She Club,' owned by Tony and Mike Coburn. Tony and I were training partners for a while at Vic's Gym several years before. He was a motorcycle cop at that time. The 'She Club' was in a cellar in Victoria Street, which is a main road to the Mersey Tunnel. They put a cabaret on there and it certainly had an atmosphere. It was full of streetwise townies and could be intimidating to strangers. I remember they had Vince Hill on one night. He sang one song and fled, saying to his agent: "Don't you ever, ever book me into a place like that again."

I went to see Johnny Nash, taking an LP for him to sign. He sang a song to a backing tape and also made a hurried exit. I was waiting for him as he came up the stairs into the street thrusting the LP at him for him to sign. He stared at me wild eyed and scribbled his name. When I think about it now, it was a pretty daunting crowd in there. I myself at that time had a Zapata moustache and was big and bulky. I was used to the nightclub scene and

Ann Halton, beauty contestant with Roy, who is showing off his Zapata moustache.

people, it's only when I look back I realise the perception of people who weren't used to it must have been so different. They also had a pretty ruthless bunch of doormen at the She club. People knew that they wouldn't be handled with kid gloves if they got out of order!

The She Club doormen became embroiled in a very nasty situation involving a serious fallout with some of the town's hard cases. It reached a peak when the doormen had a callout and went looking for the other parties. Some were dragged out of their beds in the middle of the night; one guy was dragged naked out of a wardrobe. People were badly beaten, one guy losing an eye. The court case was reported as the Chicago Trial. Two

Terry Philips helping to raise charity money at Shorrocks Hill Country Club', 1981

of the doormen actually went to jail for two years – it was a no win situation. Having said that, the place was atmospheric and I enjoyed calling in there for a drink seeing acts such as the Black Abbots with of course the hilarious Russ Abbot, and when I saw PJ Proby there he was the best I've ever seen him.

Terry Phillips set about opening a club in Tuebrook, Liverpool, with Frank Sharrock, who had worked as a joiner on the set of Cleopatra. Frank had good ideas and a flair for décor. He and Terry worked together on various ventures. This one they called the Wookey Hollow and it was an immediate hit, being a big star cabaret club in Liverpool. They featured many of the big names there, including Frankie Laine, Joseph Locke, Freddie Starr, Frank Ifield and Max Bygraves – they are just some that I saw. Terry also booked an American singer called Lovelace Watkins who virtually brought the roof down. He was such a seat filler that Terry was bringing him in for a week practically every month and was always getting a full house. Many years later, I was to book him at the Kingsway in Southport. He was supposed to return the following year, but sadly died. His obituary was in the Times newspaper – that's how I found out.

I remember having a drink with Joseph Locke after the show which was very good, although he did say to me: "Ah, the old voice is fucked now Roy" (I didn't think so). He was in the Irish Guards and one night he put on a special performance at the Royal Albert Hall for the Battalion – a great night!

When Frankie Laine was on, he finished his act with his hit *'The Kid's Last Fight'*. I remember a bunch of Glennon's boys were across from me and we joined in the chorus *'Come on kid, come on kid, and hit him with a left and a right'* grinning at each other and punching the air. It was great fun! Terry like myself worked hands on in the clubs and had

Rocky Seddon (with cigarette) at London's 'Talk Of The Town' with Paul and Barry Ryan and ladies

Rocky Graziano (Somebody Up There Likes Me), Tom Jones and Rocky Seddon

quite a few of them over the years, his wife Alice worked alongside him. At the time of writing he's in his 60's and still pumping iron!

Not far from the Wookey Hollow in the Tuebrook area of Liverpool was the New Montrose Club owned by Ernie McGrae – known by all as Ernie Mac.

Ernie headed a band called the Saturated Seven, which were obviously the club's resident performers. They were extremely popular and with Ernie's personality his club was successful. He opened the New Montrose after closing down the Montrose club which used to be just down the road.

Rocky Seddon was a guy I first met just after the Chequers opened he'd been touring the world with singing stars Paul and Barry Ryan as their road manager, he came bounding in one night leaving his car parked right outside. Someone came in and said: "Wow! Who's the car outside?" I went to have a look, it was an E Type Jaguar I had never seen one before and like everyone else, loved it. Rocky was friendly with a gym friend Jimmy Adanis and also one of my doormen Alan Webster. He became a regular and I got to know him quite well, he had a business card depicting a matchstick figure of the saint with a halo from the Leslie Charteris books. The only difference being, a pair of boxing gloves it was wearing with his name, Rocky Seddon. He was obviously a good self-publicist because he landed a job as a bodyguard to Tom Jones. Rocky had done a little boxing, which with his personality endeared him to Tom. He was only a little fellow and he became more of a companion and organiser than bodyguard. He sent me post cards from him and Tom from all over the world when they were on tour. One time he asked me to organise a party at West Tower, so that he could bring Tom along, the arrangement wasn't definite so I organised nothing. When Tom did eventually visit Liverpool, we went to the Wookey Hollow for a meal. The 'Wookey' had a wooden bridge in the center leading toward the stage front seats. We were sat at a table for four near to the bridge. It was early and the place was quiet. Half way through our meal, four fairly mature scouse girls came clattering with their high heels over the bridge; one of them looked at our table and said: "Ooh! Look der's Tom Jones."

Her friend said: "Ooh – look at his funny little nose – I don't like it, do you?"

"Ooh no I don't!" All of this in very loud voices. We felt embarrassed but Tom ignored it. He'd recently had a nose job; he did have quite a prominent nose before which I thought suited his macho personality.

Before meeting him, I expected him to be a brash sort of character but he was just the opposite, a real quiet gentleman. He and Rocky parted company after three years, and Rocky came back to Liverpool to get married. He was on first name terms with celebrities, like Frank Sinatra and Elvis Presley and there were show business stars amongst the wedding guests. His wife left him after eight years. He was suffering from severe arthritis and was on painkillers, he took an overdose and fell down the stairs.

His death was due to the tablets and not the fall. Poor Rocky.

* * *

Another great character that I became friendly with in the late 60's was called Carlo Marugliano, who was a born and bred Liverpudlian with a typical scouse humour. He was a keen weight-trainer with a good physique and he also had red hair, which tied in with his Italian name. Carlo did door work and was a well-known prankster – always up to something. He was a good handyman and came to work for me at West Tower, fixing cars, gardening, etc.

Outside Vic's Gym, aged 27, 1959

I took the family away on holiday, leaving Carlo to look after the house; I also gave him permission to use my Bentley Continental, which was my pride and joy. On returning from the holiday, he reported that everything had been fine. He'd done bits of work, exercised the dogs, etc. "Oh!" he said: – "I also used the Bentley a couple of times. I picked up a gorgeous girl in Liverpool and offered her a lift home, inviting her to my house (West Tower) for a coffee." – "I gave her the coffee and offered her a drink." – "She said she fancied a gin and orange, so I poured out the gin and opened a cupboard door, looking for the orange, – and a pile of ironing, tea towels, etc. fell onto my head." – "She gave me a funny look, but I laughed it off and we sat in the lounge." – She said: "I notice your car number plate has the initials R.A., – Yet you call yourself, Carlo, – why's that?" – "Flustered", I immediately replied – "Oh! I bought it off Rex 'Arrison!" He knew he'd blown it then. Rex Harrison, the film actor, had died a couple of years earlier.

Carlo's brother Vic was a well-known doorman who worked at the "SHE" club in Liverpool.

We split our partnerships up at the Chequers, which was up and running successfully. It was now 1967 and we'd started work on a semi-derelict building on the beach at Ainsdale near Southport. Norman and John stayed at the Chequers and Tommy Barton and I took over the new place, which I called Toad Hall, because it was in a preservation area for the Natterjack Toad. We did it out in Tudor style and called it a country club, it being out of town. I decided to make Monday night our special night and set about doing a promotion. Ellen got together with the chef Henry and produced a wonderful buffet with roast hams, roast beef, smoked salmon and a couple of pig's heads on display. I'd distributed five hundred tickets on previous weekends and everyone was geared up for it. Toad Hall is in a fairly isolated spot being on the beach at the bottom of the main road from Ainsdale Village. One hundred yards before Toad Hall there was a sharp dip in the road. About six o'clock in the evening I looked out of the window and it was raining quite heavily.

At seven thirty, Ellen and I went down to the bar and set up buckets of Moet Chandon on the bar in preparation for the customers. I'd offered free champagne from eight till nine to bring the punters in early. At about eight forty five, the doorbell rang and with relief, I ran to answer it. There was a lone middle-aged man on the step soaked to the skin. His Mercedes had gone in to the dip in the road which was full of water, he couldn't move it and no one could get past. His name was Joe Alcock and he became our first regular customer. Another first was a good loyal doorman called Eric Keller.

About forty people did eventually brave the elements and make it to the bar. We had to stay up all night with them because there was no way out. However, by morning, the water had retreated and taxis were able to approach. All I could think of was the waste of food. Not to be beaten, I did exactly the same promotion the following week and on the Monday, we had impenetrable fog – another disaster. Undaunted I repeated the exercise on the third week and we had a snow blizzard which started at ten o'clock by which time we had in sixty people. Again, we climbed the stairs just as the children got up for school. As it happened the people that did make it had a wonderful time and spread the word. The following Monday and every Monday after that for about ten years the place was packed. After the first four weeks I gave champagne to the ladies only and beer to the men, gradually fazing out the free drinks as the place took off. As it got busier I brought in a young fellow as Ellen's assistant, his name was Peter McKenna.

We introduced gaming there and it was a popular place. (In fact, Tommy still has it although I left it in 1971). Whilst at Toad Hall, the government decided to legalise and control gaming. Premises with gaming casinos were reduced from 4000 to 100 overnight! The Kingsway in Southport had run a successful nightclub and casino for years, but the Southport area was not a designated area, so both the Kingsway and Toad Hall missed out. The Kingsway put in an appeal and won, which meant that we also won being in the same area. Unfortunately for us, the new rules were not popular with the punters. We had to have a separate entrance out of sight of the club entrance. This meant that if a couple wanted to gamble, they had to go outside (and we were on the beach!) in winter and brave the elements to get to the other entrance! It spoilt a few hairdos!).

The Kingsway was owned by a father and son, George and John James, from Cardiff. They ran the most upmarket club for 30 miles around, featuring cabaret with Tom Jones, Sandy Shaw, Engelbert etc., and people like Sir Hugh Fraser and other high profile figures gambled there.

They were having some problems with some local villains and John said: "Leave it to me dad." He went to London and came back with Frankie Fraser. Well, 'Mad Frankie' sorted things out in quick time and gave some of his pals a shout. Southport became a regular haunt for them. Why not? It's a great place. There was a problem with fiddling by some of the croupiers, but it was quickly solved – one or two fingers had to be chopped off as a deterrent!

Now Frankie Fraser is one of the underworld's most notorious enforcers and in his autobiography 'Mad Frank', he writes about how he ran a racket of one-armed bandits that he used to ply across the country. He had machines in bars and clubs in Southport and recalls trouble at the Kings Head on the sea front. He had just installed his pinball and fruit machines in the basement there when "hooligans from Liverpool tried to smash them up." Incensed, Fraser, by his own account: "Did three of them with a big lump of lead outside the club."

It wasn't the only violent encounter he had in the town. Worse came at a club called the Horseshoe where Fraser was drinking with Eddie Richardson. An altercation broke out with Southport club owner Peter 'The Greek' Joannides and Richardson apparently smashed a glass in his face. The club bouncers then turned on the London men and chased them into the street. Richardson and Fraser were subsequently arrested and charged but the case was thrown out when Joannides, his face sporting fresh scars, had a change of heart and claimed not to be able to recognise his attacker. The collapse of the trial caused an outcry and George Brown, the deputy leader of the Labour Party, made a public statement and called on the Home Secretary Henry Brooke to hold a full investigation into police allegations about intimidation of witnesses. "This seems to be a case which needs to be looked into further," he said. But nothing was done. The row had been about allowing them to put in one-armed bandits into the club. In the end, Fraser says his company went on to gain the rights to put machines into more than 50 clubs dotted around the area.

Across the road, a couple of hundred yards from Toad Hall is The Sands. The Sands had a casino also prior to the gaming act. One night they had a visit from a very heavy London crew, it was the Richardson's, Charlie and Eddie. These were real tough cookies that finished up getting twenty-five and fifteen years respectively in what were known as the torture trials. A couple I know who were there on the night said they came in wearing long coats and hats, hands ominously in their pockets. However, I think they decided the place was no threat and just let it be.

Tommy and I became involved in the Sands for a while as well as Toad Hall nearby. Also I had opened up a club in Liverpool with a local businessman, Harry Waterman.

Harry Waterman owned a bottling works in Garston called H. King & Co. When we started with the Chequers club he agreed to supply the carpet for which we'd pay two

Harry Waterman stands on a step to speak to Roy and Larry Newport.

thousand pounds over a period of time, in return for supplying our beer and spirits, etc. He already had an interest as a partner in a bar in Dale Street, known as the Temple Bar. As we progressed and opened other places, some together, some individually, he continued to supply us. He'd decided he'd like to own a club, – after asking around he was told, "If you want a partner who can run a club, Roy Adams is your man!" He was to tell me this later. Eventually he approached me and asked me if I'd be interested in opening a club in Temple Street, in a couple of warehouses which had been a club. I had a look and went into it with him. He bought the property, for I believe, six thousand pounds. A small amount of money. He would receive a rent and we would jointly pay to refit it. This was a big project for me because of the sheer size of it. Somebody had previously made a start and gone bust. Prior to them it had been the Iron Door Club, home of the Searchers, in fact there was a massive painting of the Searchers head and shoulders, high up near the ceiling. When I refitted it I put a false ceiling at that end because I was doing it out in an Egyptian theme. I was actually working on the new club, which I called the Pyramid, at the same time as Toad Hall, 1966-67.

Harry had a business partner called Harry Isaacson, they were locally referred to as 'Wagon and Trailer'. However, Harry Waterman went ahead with deals on his own, after I got involved with him he bought Hartley's Jam factory in Aintree, dividing it up and selling the various parts, which included several rows of houses. He then moved to Ireland and the Isle of Man. Harry got involved with other people in other clubs and got a bit of a reputation as a backer. Some years later it used to irritate me when people used to describe him as my backer. The truth was that we went in fifty-fifty financially.

I had my work cut out travelling to Liverpool each day and most nights. We were getting regular gamblers at Toad Hall, including some of the London connection. It disturbed me having them in the place for obvious reasons. One of these guys was a very presentable looking fellow who I used to talk to. One thing I realised about him was that he was an extremely cold person – he really lacked warmth in his persona. I was told by one of his crowd that he had moved to Southport to be out of the way. He had fallen foul of a crowd down in London who had virtually crucified him, nailing his hands to a door and slicing up his back! They used an axe on him. This almost certainly accounted for his personality! I came home in the early hours from Liverpool one night and Ellen said in a worried tone: "I lent Eric Mason £75 tonight" (that was £750 in today's money!). I said: "That'll be the best £75 you've ever spent" – I was right, we never saw him again.

On Eric Mason's first visit, led by Davy Chand and Billy Grimwood, one of the guys was known as the doctor, he liked to play blackjack. As the dealer dealt him a card, he would pick it up with two fingers making it somersault twice in the air then catching it in the two fingers and return it to his hand! This was such a sharp move, it would terrify the croupier making her feel ill at ease. Another of the party was boxing champ Jimmy Molloy and three other London heavies. I suppose having a well-known boxer to show them round gave them some extra chutzpah. When they arrived at the door, the doorman (Alec Evans – a good doorman who was there for a few years) was spoken to by Davy – he said: "There's eight of us – we know Roy", whereupon Ellen stepped forward and interrupted saying: "You'll all have to pay five shillings each." These guys looked at each other in disbelief – in London they were treated like royalty. Davy said to me later: "We just paid up, we knew it was your club Roy, and she was your wife, though it was a bit embarrassing for me and Billie!"

As it happened I was friendly with Jimmy Molloy. He'd joined the A and B Gym – we had to get a punch bag for him as we concentrated more on wrestling.

Ellen certainly had courage, on another night she was walking around the club keeping an eye on things. She paused at one of the two blackjack tables where some of the London crowd were gambling. She watched for a while and sensed that something wasn't right. She felt sure that they were at it! Following her sixth sense, (she was notoriously perceptive) she called a male member of staff and went into the Gents washroom. She went straight to a lavatory cistern and lifted the lid. There was a pack of cards in the water. Ellen gathered them together and strode up to the table, she threw the soaking wet cards in the middle proclaiming, "This game's over!"

One night, two Pakistanis came in to play blackjack and won £800. This was a lot of money. A friend who was a regular, who knew the score, said to Ellen: "Don't play them again, you can't win!" I passed this message to Tommy at the Sands, but he shrugged it off saying, "They're what we need – some serious gamblers."

I said: "Tommy, I've been told they're at it – they're not playing here again." Unfortunately, I couldn't tell him where the tip had come from, so I understood his attitude. The following Sunday I was driving home from Liverpool at 3.00am and as I approached the Sands I could see it was all lit up. As I came around the traffic island by the Sands entrance, I saw Tommy stood outside.

I said: "What's going on?"

He said: "We've got those Pakis in."

I said: "Tommy, you're not playing them are you?"

He said: "Yes."

I said: "How much are we losing"

He said: "About £2,000."

I sped over to Toad Hall in my car and dragged Ellen out of bed. She came over and dealt one hand. They cashed in realising that she was too wide for them. Tommy had to give them a cheque for £2,000. With them was Billy Grimwood – he'd apparently been on the phone in the hall, saying "We won't be long now fella's, we'll meet you at the top roundabout." This in Tommy's hearing so he'd think there was a gang waiting. I spoke to him when I got there saying, "What's going on Bill?" He said: "Roy, honest to God they're dead straight – go and watch them. I have, they're doing nothing wrong." The banks opened at 10.00am. I arrived at two minutes past to stop the cheque – they beat me to it, they'd cashed it! I realised it was my fault, I should have told Tommy my source, after all he was my business partner.

Well, they went to a club on the Wirral called Leighton Court, owned by friend Eric Armitage, who I had warned. He lost £600. A few weeks later, I answered a knock on the door to six detectives.

They said: "We believe you lost money to two Pakistanis?"

I said: "Yes we did."

He opened an album full of different designs of playing cards. I pointed ours out and he showed me a petal missing off a flower on the design on the back. "That's an Ace," he said – two petals missing was a King etc. He said they'd been operating this scam all over the country. We had a couple of customers who were identical twins who I called Heckle and Jeckle. One of them worked as a croupier for quite a while and his wife also. It transpired that these guys had broken into the Sands and swapped the packs of cards in the storage area. That's how it was done! The next weekend I went to the Cabaret Club in Liverpool where Billy Grimwood was working in the casino. The head doorman was a mate of Phil Glennon's called Jobo Jones. He and the other doormen were surprised to see me on their territory. It wasn't long after we'd been at odds with each other. I said: "Where's Billy Grimwood?" Someone went to get him, he came down the stairs slowly, leaning forward, hand over hand on the banister, obviously wondering "What the hell's he doing here?"

"Hiya Roy, come on up." We sat down upstairs in the cabaret room, there was only us there.

He said: "What are you doin' here?"

I said: "I want to know where those Pakis are."

He said: "I don't blame you Roy; they ripped me off as well! I think they're in Nottingham."

I said: "Well I want to go after them."

He said: "Well I'll come with you, but I warn you I'll be going in strong."

I said: "That suits me, you can have a grand if I get the £2,000 back."

We arranged to meet the following Friday but he didn't show. I made another arrangement but he still didn't show! So I had to give it up, I had no way of finding these guys. I thought that was the end of the matter that Billy must have been so well paid that he didn't fancy having a go. But I couldn't have been more wrong. It turned out that a few weeks later the two gamblers decided to go to the Gorsey Cop in Childwall, which was now owned by George Downing. So, he went to his old mate Davy Chand and told him he'd heard about the scam and that they were having a go at George. So Davy goes to the Gorsey Club and puts pressure on the Pakistanis making them hand over all the money they had in their kitty, which was over two grand. Billy stood by not saying a word, sharing the proceeds afterwards. I'd put the idea into his head and he went ahead without me, at the same time preventing George Downing from being ripped off and putting some money Davy's way. He didn't even mention my involvement.

This gave them an idea. George Downing used to gamble heavily, his favourite casino being the Odd Spot in Liverpool's Bold Street. They managed to work some marked cards into the Odd Spot and showed George how to identify them. They gave him five grand and sent him to a big card game at the Odd Spot. George sat down with the five grand and played all night finishing up losing five and half grand! Billy and Davy weren't pleased; this was a great deal of money. Enough to buy a couple of decent houses at that time. What they hadn't understood was that George had to gamble. By taking advantage of the marked cards, he wouldn't have been gambling. He couldn't help himself; he actually enjoyed losing as much as winning!

Billy was well occupied with his London friends. One night he said to a pal of mine, Chuck, who had a reputation as a hard case: "How would you like to earn £100 a week?" Chuck said: "Oh I'd certainly like that." Billy said: "I'll introduce you to some people in London, they'll take you to a club or restaurant and point out some geezer – anyone will do. All you have to do is go over to him and chiv him. After that, you're on the books. A £100 per week." Chuck was a tough nut but not in that sort of activity and he told him so. Like most of the villains, socially Billy was good company and was generally popular and easy to get along with.

We closed down our Casino at Toad Hall, the punters didn't like the new rules and we found it impossible now to make it pay.

At that time, club memberships averaged out at about two pounds a year. Upmarket clubs like Toad Hall charged about a fiver. I had an idea. I said to Ellen I'm going to drop the membership fee to one and half quid and make members pay to come in. She said: "You can't do that – charge members, it's never happened, besides, what'll be the point of being a member?"

I said: "First of all with ninety per cent members it'll keep the police off our backs also members will pay only half a crown to come in, non members will pay double that at five bob."

The difference it made was surprising, it turned the profit round and soon other clubs followed suit. Life was certainly easier when we didn't have to worry about having an excess of non-members. It was many years later before late licenses were granted without having to be a club.

While Toad Hall had its problems – in tandem with them, the Pyramid in Liverpool also had its situations so there was never a dull moment.

There were some characters around town who were loners, they didn't knock around with a gang but still managed to get a reputation.

One tough guy who used to call into the Pyramid to have a drink with me was Billy Vaughn, who was naturally big and burly. He had a real soft side when it came to dogs. If he saw a dog chained up, it really used to get to him. He also enjoyed classical music. This was a side to his character which I was privileged to share.

A contrast to Billy was an equally hard man, Andy Shacklady from Kirkby. People dreaded Andy coming to their door, when he got drunk he was a major problem. If someone phoned the police during one of his kick offs, they would never send less than six busies to arrest him. I've seen him on the ground with half a dozen bobbies dancing round him trying to get the cuffs on him. When they finally managed it he'd still be kicking and struggling furiously – they were terrified of him.

One night I heard a bit of commotion at the Pyramid door and went to have a look. Joe Phillips was holding the large iron door, it was open about six inches. Andy Shack was banging at the door demanding Joe let him in. Joe was telling him he'd had too much drink and he couldn't do it. I told Joe: "Let me have a go".

Joe looked at me – "D'ye know who this is?"

I said: "Yes, let me have a go."

Joe stood back and I opened the door wide. He was one step up from the pavement but I was still a step higher.

I said: "Andy, you can't come in here tonight – don't spoil it for the future."

He looked blankly up at me and I placed a hand on the outside of each of his shoulders and turned him around gently, easing him onto the pavement. There was a bricked up window directly opposite the Pyramid door, with iron bars still in the window cavity. Andy went across and grabbed two iron bars and tried to pull them apart, at the same time roaring and growling, but he couldn't do it, the bars were extremely thick.

He gave up and reached under a parked car, lifting the front up and bouncing it up and down before heading off down the street.

I've never understood why he just accepted what I did. I can only think he saw me as a figure of authority.

On another occasion I got a phone call from my brother-in-law Billy Randles. He was running the Peacock club in Duke Street. He said: "Everyone's gone home but I've got a problem, Andy Shack is sitting on a chair in the middle of the room and won't budge."

I rushed over there with Joe and Larry Newport. The bar was on the first floor, we galloped up the stairs to where Billy was waiting. Joe went over to Andy and Larry went to follow him, I grabbed his arm and we went to the bar ten feet away.

Joe said: "Alright Andy?"

Andy said: "Who are you? Fuck off!"

I got some lagers in and called over "Drink Andy? Drink Joe?", giving them a glass each. We all downed our drinks and I said loudly to Larry: "What are we hanging round here for? It's all over, let's go to the Cabaret club for a drink. Come on Andy."

Andy stumbled down the stairs ahead of us and into the street, he continued across to Slater Street opposite, heading god knows where. We jumped in our cars and went home. Of course the Cabaret club was well closed by then.

Joe Philips at the Pyramid

Night Club Tug 'O' War Team Left to right, back row: unknown, Kevin Knight, Roy Adams, unknown, unknown; front row: Alan Webster, Alec McGowan, Brummie, Eddie Bean, John Steadman and Bob Larkin

~ 11 ~
Running the Gauntlet

THERE WAS A club in South Castle Street called the Black Rose and the doorman was Pat McMullen, when Pat got aggravation he used to get out in the street and fight them with his shirt off. He eventually opened up his own place called Cindy's in Victoria Street. With the chequered career he's had, his story would make a good movie!

Pat grew up in the Scotland Road area of Liverpool. An area that was very full of life in the raw. It was a close community, people stuck together through good and bad times. There was plenty of hard drinking and hard fighting and it also had its fair ration of villainy. By the time a lad was eighteen and got his calling up papers for his National Service, he'd be a streetwise city kid. Pat was a case in point.

Soon after he joined the army he was sent to Malaysia and in no time got himself into a bit of trouble in the barracks. They locked him in the guardroom but he broke out of there and into the Company Office where he pinched the payroll. He was sentenced to two years at a Court Martial, but the army wanted him to serve it in a civvy prison. They stuck him in Singapore's famous Changi jail notoriously one of the world's worst prisons. In no time at all, Pat managed to cause a riot in the Euro wing over the terrible food and horrendous conditions. After two months, they transferred him to Tang Lin Military prison in Singapore for another month and then to the troop ship Empire Halliday under army escort to Liverpool's Walton Jail to finish his sentence.

The next time he got banged up was some years later when he got twelve months for fighting in the Jacaranda, however he won his appeal against the courts findings and came out after wasting four months of his life in jail.

Pat got a flat in Upper Stanhope Street on the corner of Berkeley Street. The house was known locally as Joe the Watchmakers. Joe having the shop on the ground floor. The area generally was always referred to as the Parliament Street area or around Parly. It was very cosmopolitan. People from all nations lived there except maybe the Chinese who lived mainly around the Pitt Street and Nelson Street area known as China Town.

Two characters who lived in the house were Stanislow Weskalowski, a pole and Joe Ungi a Hungarian who years later became a Councillor in Manchester. They started a business in town, which was selling hot dogs. These fellows had come over to England in 1957 the time of the Hungarian uprising when the Russians invaded.

They built the first hot dog bikes themselves, as Pat said: he'd never seen a hot dog bike before except on the movies.

They opened an office in St Andrews gardens by the Bullring, an area where plenty of bad guys lived!

The prime site for a hotdog stand was at the corner of Skelhorne Street by the side entrance to Lime Street station, opposite the Crown pub. There was a beef burger bar on the right as you walked into Lime Street Station main entrance on Lime Street, in fact I remember a French body builder Robert Duranton who had competed against Steve Reeves in the Mr Universe in London and in 'La plus belle athlete du monde' Mr World in Cannes. He'd been wrestling at the Liverpool Stadium and decided to have a burger before catching his train. He bit into his burger and spat it out exploding: "What's this garbage?" There was murder and he practically wrecked the place.

I have to say, the only beef burgers you could buy at the time were absolutely dreadful. It was the early 70s before a guy opened a really nice quality burger bar in Stanley Street. Apparently, his father had given him a sum of money to start a business. It unfortunately failed but the burgers were great. Just like the American ones. His dad wasn't too pleased though!

I digress as usual. Back to the hot dog stands. Joe and Stan didn't finish work till the early hours, 1am, 2am. They knew Pat did door work. They got to know him through various coloured clubs he'd worked at where very often Pat was the only white man working on the doors.

They offered him a job keeping an eye on the hot dog bikes and sorting any problems. His main function however was to get the bags of takings safely back to 'Joe the watch-makers' in Berkeley Street. The other sites for the hot dog stands in the City Centre were by the Adelphi Hotel and the Empire Theatre, also by the Royal Court Theatre, Central Station and St George's Plateau.

At that time there were only two evening forms of entertainment for the general public on weekday nights – the pictures and the pubs, they both finished at 10.30 and there was nowhere else to go so people would get themselves a hotdog and coffee. There was a proper van by the Punch & Judy stand on St. George's Plateau which was always busy. There were some restaurants around which were not really frequented by the general working class public, except for the Chinese cafes mainly at the weekend when the dance halls were open and people would like to go for a Chinese meal afterwards.

The nightlife was in the Parliament street area, clubs like Fat Johnnies, Dutch Eddies. JJs, and Wilkies. However, this was really not an area where the main general public used to go.

George Wilkie got pulled in for a tax problem, they were attending a hearing and George pulled a gun shooting two of the officials, fortunately, no one died.

What amused Pat was the names of these coloured clubs in relation to the owners. Dutch Eddie Vandenburg called his club the Tudor. JJ Johnson called his the Mayfair Club. They loved these posh names. Of course, there was also the Somali Club and the Nigerian Club; these places reflected the long Afro history associated with Liverpool.

In the 1950s, this was the area for excitement. Scotland Road was dead once the pubs were closed as was Bootle and the City Centre. The Southend or Liverpool 8 as it was known was the place to be. Parallel to Scotland Road was Walton Hall Road where there was a dance hall called Swainsons, which stuck with traditional ballroom dancing even in the rock-'n'- roll era. Having said that – there was nothing poncy about Swainsons. Sometimes if a guy tried to cut in on an excuse-me dance the guy would remove his hand from his girls shoulder and transfer it in a straight line to the guys jaw. It was common to see guys dancing with bandages on their heads or fists, black eyes and plasters on the nose. These frequent punch ups gingered the night up a bit. A lot of these dance halls were above Burton tailor shops like the Harlequin in town and Blair Hall in Walton Road, another notorious place for fights, particularly in the Teddy boy era. Well known Ted's were Harold

Pat McMullen

Hughes and his gang, John Gillon, Georgie Singleton and the Glennon boys. They'd often go there to relieve their boredom.

The Teddy Boys did become a major problem in the 50's. Gangs of Teds would go on the rampage looking for fights. Dance halls were the main victims; it was difficult to control because all the young people dressed in the Ted fashion, male and female. The troublemakers would come into the dance in two's and three's and gang together once they were in. They'd be looking for trouble and more often than not there'd be other gangs in there. When it kicked off the bouncers would have no chance because of the numbers of people involved. That's why door staff who were capable and streetwise were so important, they'd know the main troublemakers and keep them out. Knives and knuckledusters were commonplace. Some would go further. I knew of at least four different guys who would carry a claw hammer, a formidable weapon. I remember escorting a well-known family member, out of the Chequers one night. He was bent forward, placing a bet on the gaming table and I could see the shape of the hammer under his suit. It was stuck down his belt at the back – in my club!

John Gillon's dad was a respected tough guy in Liverpool. He'd been a pretty successful boxer appearing at the stadium but his main popularity stemmed from his success as a street fighter. I vaguely remember him working on the door of the Clock, a pub in London Road in his later years. He and Joe Phillips (my sidekick at the Pyramid Club) used to have bare fistfights on the bombsites on a Sunday.

It ranked with pitch and toss, a gambling game with pennies, as a popular Sunday pastime.

I remember Joe saying to me after John had died.

"That Gillon was hard, me and him would fight for hours on the 'Oller' on a Sunday!"

People used to throw them money, that's probably why it went on so long, so they'd catch the ones leaving the pubs or having just got out of bed.

The club business was in the early stages of taking off in Liverpool. A couple of Greek clubs opened up in Princess Road, they sold lager which was only 5 per cent alcohol, the punters didn't really notice the difference, just being in these places gave them enough excitement. They got around the licensing laws by the low level of alcohol in the drinks, so licensing wasn't a problem – it was fisticuffs, which eventually got them closed down.

The shebeen's were still going. They were illegal drinking dens mainly run by black guys.

I walked in one by the Rialto picture house one night after I'd finished working on the door. It was a small terraced house packed with people. When I squeezed my way through to the kitchen, there was a guy stood behind a trestle table, which was covered in small cans of beer, which he was handing out at a shilling and sixpence each. (Sixpence in the off licence.) Music was blaring out and everyone was happy to be somewhere they shouldn't.

Where Pat lived at that time, Herman Street, by Upper Hill Street there was a tiny shebeen in one house called the Kit Kat club, it was unusual because it was run by two white guys and was very popular, it became one of Pat's haunts, he also used to go to his mum's house in Scotland Road for his tea before going to work down Parly. One day he was approached by a guy called Steve Holden who told him he was having trouble with a family from the Southend, he was working as a doorman at the Black Rose. He asked Pat if he'd come down and back him up. So Pat went down and introduced himself to the owner Harry Roberts, positioning himself at the entrance, nobody turned up, including Steve Holden.

Pat had a nice easy night and was given the job and that's how he came to work in the city clubs. His mother had a barrow in town selling fruit and flowers, she was popularly known as Dolly (Years later her sons opened a pub in Scotland Road which they named Dolly Hickeys after their mum.) She'd park her barrow outside a shop called the Piano Galleries. The owner was a nice man called Jeff Ginsberg. He'd call her in for a cup of tea and a chat. One day Pat called by and Jeff said: "Look, I've got all these one armed bandits in the coloured clubs, would you like a job emptying them for me in the afternoons when there's no-one there? If you do it, you can have half the profit." Pat couldn't see any downside to this deal and he went for it! Pat and Jeff Ginsberg had a good working partnership, which developed into a friendship. Jeff drove a Bentley and lived in Hunts Cross on the outskirts of town. One day they finished late and to finish off a good day Jeff suggested they go for a drink, so they drove into town and hit a few bars finally finishing up in a shebeen. Jeff started on Champagne and then on to his favourite drink, which was Anisette; Pat stayed with the beer. A smart fellow with a girl came along side and said to Jeff:

"What are you drinking?"

Jeff said: "Oh, no no! I wouldn't impose, this drink is too expensive."

The fellow said: "You've got it wrong, we're Police Officers and this is a raid, Your drinking illegally and you're nicked." Pat hadn't heard of this situation before. He thought it an incredible waste of Police time with all the violence and thieving going on in Liverpool 8. Of course, later on when Pat had his own bars, he knew all about it. He was a man of many talents, he'd given up the door work in the early 60s and went to work in the Stretton Club in Wood Street as a croupier, he'd worked as a croupier before in Nigeria so he was very experienced.

He didn't go to work until 10.30; he'd met a beautiful girl who he'd see before going to work. He would leave her at nine to go home to get changed for work. One night he'd just got in and there was a knock on the door, it was a guy from a detective agency. He asked Pat if he knew who he was. Pat said no. He said: – "I'm Allen" – "I've been tailing you for six months for the D.H.S. As far as I could see, you're not working. I'd watch you leave your young lady and be home by 9.30."

He didn't realise Pat went home to get changed into his suit in order to go croupiering.

Allen decided to start his own detective agency and offered Pat a job. He said he was impressed by Pat's clever manoeuvrings so Pat became a private eye. He went everywhere with Allen on all sorts of jobs. It was now the Allen detective agency and because Allen had all the contacts, there was plenty to do. They followed many types of people on many types of locations. Pat said: "I'd be on Southport beach wearing a souwester and a pair of wellies watching people do what I wanted to do!"

Allen said to Pat: "You know when I give the evidence to a guy, photo's etc., and proof that his girl is unfaithful. Nine times out of ten, they shove it in their pockets and don't take it any further. However if it's a woman she'll take it all the way – always."

When I opened the Chequers and had fallen foul of the Glennon boys, Pat used to come in and have a drink with me, giving me moral support, doing the door on my own on the weeknights I'd be glad to see him. We still meet up for a drink or meal to this day.

The Black Rose premises were taken over by Tony Buck, Terry Phillips and Wally Booth and renamed the Gauntlet.

After a year or so, the partnership split up and Tony became the sole proprietor. The place was heaving and they got a mixed bunch in there, including plenty of villains and plenty of headaches. Davy Chand and his brother Roy used to go there quite a lot. One night there was a dispute at the gaming table which was one of John Capper's Golden Fives which was now known as legalite. It finished with Tony having to take Roy Chand outside – it got to the point where Tony grabbed the front of his jacket and held him up against the wall. Now, both Chands were about 5' 10" and heavily built, streetwise and strong. Dave Chand jumped in and Tony grappled him in a similar fashion, whereupon Billy Grimwood jumped on his back and bit his ear. Tony was able to throw them aside but the rat pack were there all having a go! They were running into the club and grabbing bottles off the bar to hit him with. Tony was by now in the middle of the road like a bear at bay. He had blood running into his eyes from the bottle attacks, blinding him, plus his ear was hanging off and flapping against his chin. They were still wary of getting too close to him and Grimwood tore the chrome strip off the side of a car and was trying to poke his eyes out! One guy who bravely moved in was Phil Spitall – he was a fourteen stone, six foot two inches, ex-fighter. He was dancing around Tony and trying to land the odd punch. Because he was blinded by his own blood, Tony shot his hand out and grabbed the back of his neck, wrestler style, and pulled him down. They started shouting at Tony: "Fight like a man you coward", so Tony stood back and let him up – that was the end of that. He was surrounded by bodies when the police arrived. He was still on his feet. They couldn't beat him although at least twenty had had a go! The only help Tony had was from Sonny Phillips, Terry's brother. Sonny was the doorman at the Gauntlet and a very gutsy fighter. He gave a good account of himself but there were just too many!

I went to his house the next day to see Tony. He was looking a bit battered with his ear stitched up.

I said: "How are you feeling."

He said: "Okay, I'm only worried that I've lost my image as a sportsman!"

My painting of Tony Buck.
He was 11 times Northern Counties Heavyweight Champion; 4 times British Heavyweight Champion and 3 times British Light Heavyweight Champion (1957 to 1966); Gold Medallist Light Heavyweight, Commonwealth Games (Perth 1962);
and British representative in the Olympic Games, Tokyo, 1964; World Championships, Ohio, 1962;
and Manchester, 1965.

I got the word that some of these guys were worried in case they should bump into Tony in the street and I heard that some of them were actually carrying guns. A couple of days later Tony was back on the door, and a deputation turned up to see him. Tacker Commerford and Jobo Jones. They said: "What's the score now Tony?"

He said: "I've fought you your way, now I'll fight you mine – come to the gym and I'll take you on two at a time!"

They grinned and Jobo said: "We don't fight like that Tony; it's all or nothing with us! We fight with iron bars."

Tony said to me: "They're eating crow, wanting bygones to be bygones – what'll I do?"

I said: "Tony, you can't win with them. They'll ruin your business. Just cool it for now – you can always get revenge in the future."

So they came back into the club and spent a fortune. I think Tony decided it had turned out to be a business promotion! About a year after that I got a visit to the Pyramid Club by one Eddie Palmer, accompanied by a guy known as Yank Shannon, a broken nosed tough guy. Palmer had a bad reputation round town in general. One thing he liked to do was call at different clubs and borrow a fiver from the owner, or in pubs off the landlady or whoever. It was always a permanent loan, which was never paid back. People were too intimidated to ask for it! My tactic whenever he entered my place was to say "Hi Eddie, have you come to pay back that fiver?" Not that I'd ever lent him anything, but it saved him asking. Anyway, on this occasion he was obviously psyched up, he ordered two drinks and said: "We're going to see that Tony Buck. I'm going to have it off with him."

I laughed and said: "I wouldn't advise it." He then shadow boxed a bit and said: "Yank, tell him what I'm like, tell him about my straight left" demonstrating at the same time. They knocked back their drinks and left. I immediately phoned Tony and said: "Palmer's on his way down. He wants to fight you."

Tony said: "Okay, well I'm here." Palmer being a dangerous man, Tommy Hartley and I jumped in the car and followed on down to the club. The manager of the Pyramid at that time, Brian McCaffrey, followed on a little later. He was an ex-boxer who, in his bid for a British title, gave Johnny Cook his hardest fight. When we got there, they were face to face in the cobbled street outside the club Bucks Place. At that time, Tony was busy with a girlfriend, drinking quite a lot and not training, so he was overweight. He was wearing a thick sports jacket. Palmer was laying down rules: "If one goes down, the other lets him up" etc.

He said: "Take your jacket off Tony."

Tony said: "Let's get on with it." At this stage, Yank Shannon was probably bothered because Tommy, Brian and myself were now there.

He turned and said quietly: "He's tooled up you know." We searched Palmer and Tom found a butcher's fork with two eight-inch prongs down the back of his trousers between the cheeks of his backside, the obvious reason for wanting Tony to remove his jacket. Although Palmer was a big man, about 17 stone, heavily built and a capable boxer, he had been known to use a knife on occasions. He started to dance around Tony, picking him off Ali style. Tony was slipping and sliding on the cobbles. He'd taken a few blows to the face and was bleeding. He reached in and pulled Palmer down, immediately Palmer said: "Barley, barley – the rules Tony, you've got to let me up", which Tony did.

Tommy Hartley was getting worried.

He said: "I don't like this Roy."

I said: "He can't hurt him", shouting: "Tony, you'll have to box him."

Palmer was now six inches taller, up on his toes with confidence. Tony put up his dukes army style and started to box him, I saw Tony's enormous left fist connect, followed by his right and Palmer seemed to shrink before our eyes. Tony smelled blood and stepped in, his face four inches away. He brought his forehead forward, driven by the power of his nineteen and a half inch neck, and connected with a bone-shattering thud. Palmer hit the deck; he forced himself up onto his hands and knees, shaking his head from side to side. Tony started to walk away, hesitated and looked over his shoulder: "Have I licked you?" Palmer while still on his knees, now nodded his head and Tony went into his club and slammed the door. We went back to the car and Palmer came stumbling after us and said: "I had him beat Roy. Look – I broke my hand on him, otherwise I would have won."

I said: "You had no chance!"

Eddie spent the next couple of nights going round the clubs saying how he'd almost beaten Tony Buck. Tony told me later that after we'd left Palmer knocked on the club door and asked Tony if he could come in and clean himself up. Tony was taken aback and told me "I let him in for his cheek!" Credit where it's due, he did have the guts to fight him, and in fact, he was face to face with another formidable opponent two or three years later.

Dinah May competes in a Miss Pyramid Contest

~ 12 ~
A Day Out

THE VICTORIA SPORTING Club in Temple Court in Liverpool was owned by Tommy McArdle, nicknamed 'shake hands McArdle', or 'Tucker.' He was very friendly with the boxing fraternity; his club was more an afternoon club. He used to stand outside and people used to call by and chat to him. Any ex-fighter who walked past, Tommy used to call him over and give him a few bob. He was also friendly with a lot of the criminal fraternity and from time to time people would come up from London and meet with local heavies in his club.

In fact at one of these meetings my name was on the agenda. The London crowd were discussing starting protection in Liverpool, the nightlife in Liverpool being very vibrant at that time. They said they needed a high profile figure to work on and set up as an example. Somebody – I don't know who – suggested Roy Adams as probably the most well-known club owner.

I was tipped off, but not by McArdle. He used to sit in my car and tell me I was the son he wished he'd had, etc. If I'd known what he was a party to I would have had nothing to do with him.

Sometimes he'd come into the Pyramid with friends and order say ten burgers or ten steaks or whatever. I always made him welcome. Tommy's standard greeting was a hug and kiss on the cheek. Of course charging him for anything wasn't an option! If I called in his place he would reciprocate, but I never had the time. One day he said:

"A few of us are going to London to see Alan Rudkin fight for the World Lightweight title, would you and Tony fancy it?"

I said: "That sounds great, get us a couple of tickets." Three weeks passed and I'd heard nothing and there was only a couple of days to go, so I went to see him.

I said: "Did you get the tickets?" He gave me a blank look.

"You know, for the Alan Rudkin fight."

He said: "Oh – no problem, no problem. See you at Lime Street station Saturday morning." Tony and I were duly getting our tickets at the station ticket desk, who should come bounding up looking enormous in a bright, almost yellow suit but Eddie Palmer. "Hiya Roy, hi Tony, me uncle Tommy's on the train – I'll go and save your seats." We looked at each other thinking that's all we need – Eddie Palmer! We decided to try to get seats of our own, but we had no chance. As we walked up the platform, Eddie was halfway up the train with his head stuck out of the window beckoning to us. There was a set of six seats with a table on one side of the aisle and two on the other side. Tommy Mc and his wife Ruth, Tony and I and an ex-boxer, and a popular local singer called Gerry Devine sat round the big table and Eddie on the other side at the small table. The train started to fill up and a smart man, obviously a gentleman, sat opposite Eddie.

There was a lull in our conversation and Tommy spoke to the gentleman.

"Off to London are you sir? We're going down to see the big fight. How about you?"

"Oh it's just routine for me, I'm going on business."

Tommy said: "And what business are you in, if it's not a rude question. My name's Tommy McArdle by the way."

He said: "I'm in the confectionery business and my name's Jacobs." There was a pause and Tommy said: "Are you Jacobs of Cream Cracker fame?"

Mr Jacobs said: "Yes that's me" Now you could see Tommy's mind working and he said: "Oh an old colleague of mine is part of your organisation. He's an ex-fighter and his name is Dom Volante."

Mr Jacobs said: "Yes I know Dom Volante, he sweeps up in one of the factories."

So Tommy sits nodding and smiling, then he snapped at his wife

"Ruth get a pen and paper and write this down. Dear Dom, we are on a train travelling to London to see the Rudkin fight. We have just met your guvnor Mr Jacobs and have to say how lucky you are to be working for such a fine gentleman, your old pal Tommy McArdle."

He folded the note in half and handed it to Mr Jacobs "I wonder if you'd do me a favour Mr Jacobs and give this note to Dom Volante for me – it's okay, you can read it."

We had four ex-fighters with us and when the train arrived and we got off to head to the ticket collectors, one of them said: "Eddie, what happens now?" Eddie had told them not to buy tickets. He said: "Follow me through and do as I do" as he went through the barrier and the man said: "Ticket please", Eddie cocked his thumb behind him and walked through. The others followed doing the same. Ruth and Tommy had gone through first. When Tony and I handed in our tickets, the fellow said: "What about the others?"

We said: "What others? There's just us two!"

Tommy said: "Right, a couple of taxis now, we're going to the Waldorf Astoria for a wash and brush up."

In the Waldorf, he leads us into the washroom.

He said: "Get your shirts off. I'll get some nice clean towels." An attendant was stood behind a raised counter at the end of the room. Tommy said: "You – give us some towels."

The fellow said: "We don't have them, use the hand driers." Tommy said: "This is the Waldorf Astoria and you don't have any fuckin' towels!"

The fellow handed a well-used towel over, saying "This is all I've got, it's my own towel."

Tommy snatched it off him and brought it over to Tony and I and said: "You're in good shape Tony – you're in good shape Roy." We self-consciously gave a quick dab at our armpits and put our shirts back on. We certainly didn't need a wash. We then went into the lounge at Tommy's insistence and ordered scotch all round. Eddie said: "Can I have a pint of beer uncle Tommy?"

Tommy said: "Where d'ya think you are? This is the Waldorf Astoria, you'll have scotch the same as the rest of us!"

When we arrived at the ticket barrier at Wembley Stadium, Tommy said: "Right gather round, we're two briefs short here so we've got to work something." As he said it, Eddie vaulted over the turnstile and was gone. Mrs Rudkin then went in and Tommy tried to follow her. The man stopped him and Tommy said: "I'm with Mrs Rudkin, she's the

At the Astor Club, Mayfair ~ left to right: Tommy Mcardle, his wife Ruth, Roy , Eddie Palmer, Tony Buck and Gerry Devine

mother of the main attraction." The man wasn't having any, but one of the others sneaked in while he was talking. Alan Rudkin unfortunately lost the fight and Tommy said: "I'll take you to a pal's club and after we'll go to the Astor Club for dinner etc."

As we walked down the steps into the pal's club, we were greeted by a Tommy McArdle look-alike; they were like two Mantovanis hugging each other with a Mafia-style kiss! We were led to a table and two large jugs of beer were provided. The place was empty at first and then twenty blokes filled a long laid up table. They had been to the fight and supported the cockney lad. Tommy started to call over to them, giving them some mild banter, mild insults etc. When they started to return the insults, Tommy didn't like it. He stood up brandishing a full bottle of scotch, threatening to climb over the rail of the balcony we were on. Now these were twenty tasty looking boxing enthusiasts, so I sat Tommy down and said: "Let's go, we need to get to the Astor Club." The lager was fifteen bob a jug, which was expensive. Mantovani kept out of the way – in fact we never saw him again after we sat down. Palmer said: "I told you to let me settle the bill!" Of course, he wouldn't have paid anything and may have caused someone some pain, so I'd jumped in and paid it first.

We went to the Astor Club, which was the base for the Nash family. We settled down to a meal and drinks. The Club was packed; we enjoyed our meal and watched the cabaret. We're having a drink when a fight broke out on the far side of the room. McArdle jumps to his feet shouting "Lumber Eddie, lumber Roy, lumber fella's." They all jumped to their feet – I put my hand on Tony's shoulder. Jerry Devine also stayed seated. I said: "We're keeping out of it! The Nash lot will sort it out!" Tommy looked for a moment, and then sat down again followed by the others. Tony and I decided to leave and head for the station. Well, we seemed to walk miles to Euston; I don't think we had any money for a taxi. There wasn't a train till 6am so we had to hang around for five hours! We saw Tommy Mc walking disconsolately across the large open area in the station, his head drooping, shoulders hunched with his raincoat held in his fist. When they let us on the platform we sat around a bench seat. Eddie went walking up the platform and went onto a standing train. He proceeded to bring upholstered seat cushions out and lay them along the bench. He laid down and got comfortable. Tommy Mc was giving a running commentary on this: "What's he doing now – Jesus, he's taking the fuckin' cushions out of the train! Oh oh, here's the busies" – two railway police were walking up – "Look they're bollocking him now – they're making him put them back, God, now they're helping him!" Then he shouted, "He's not a bad lad, officers." Eventually, the train left with us on it – Eddie and the other lads spent half the journey dodging in and out of the lavatories, avoiding the ticket inspector. It was certainly a day to remember!

* * *

At the top end of Liverpool's Seel Street was the Blue Angel club, owned by Alan Williams, famously known as the man who gave the Beatles away, having been their manager in the early days. The Blue Angel in the early 60s was a great club, which attracted people from every walk of life. Sometimes I'd pop in there for a drink after work at the Harlequin. They did a beef curry with rice which I've still found unsurpassed. The Rolling Stones were in one night and got into an argument over football – I think they were supporting Fulham. One of them, Brian Jones I think, said he thought Liverpool were rubbish. A big mistake! I had to jump in and prevent them from a hiding, being in my doorman 'outfit' – bow tie and evening suit gave me the necessary panache to get away with it. If I hadn't, I think the Stones may have finished up less handsome!

Fatso told me one night he was in there and a girl was stood leaning on the post at the bottom of the stairs. She had the latest beehive hairdo. The hair was piled up high like a guardsman's bearskin and she'd had little flowers placed all over it. When the girls had their hair done like this, they couldn't comb it or wash it for weeks. A drunk appeared at the top of the stairs and lurched his way down using the banister for support. Suddenly, he started retching and then threw up all over the girl's head. There were bits of carrots and tomato hanging from the sweet flowers adorning her hair! I think she'd probably wash it after that!

There was a little blond guy who sang with a group called 'The Midnighters' every Monday night and I used to go especially to see him. He had a crew cut hairstyle and wore a T-shirt. I remember thinking how much local talent there was around. I thought it was a shame he won't get anywhere because he was a real entertainer. His name was Freddy Starr!

When the Chequers club opened, Freddy started coming in for a drink before going to work at the Blue Angel. He couldn't be serious for a minute and was very, very entertaining. One night, we were having a particularly slow start and I said: "Hey Freddy, how about getting up and giving us a song?' He said: "No Roy, I don't like..." I said: "Go on –

I'll give you a quid!" So, he got up and did half an hour singing like Elvis, his best impression. He must have done this for me half a dozen times. Little did I realise that within three years I wouldn't be able to afford him at two or three thousand pounds a night! Never mind a pound!

* * *

Alan Williams, the Blue Angel club owner used to go to the Odd Spot casino where he enjoyed the odd flutter. He became quite friendly with Billy Grimwood, Yank Shannon and some of their acquaintances; he brought them to the Blue Angel starting a down turn in its fortunes. A doorman who worked there at that time was Charlie Scott. He was something of a hard case who I'd met when I opened the Chequers. He'd started doing a little boxing as a youngster only having three fights in the ring, having butted the referee in the third one. He gave it up, not even going to a boxing club and started work at the Storyville Jazz Club in Temple Street, which with the advent of rock'n'roll became the Iron Door (the home of the Searchers) and later on was transformed by yours truly into the Pyramid Club for the next twenty years! Charlie was the youngest doorman in Liverpool at the Storyville, being only sixteen years old! He went from there to the Hope Hall Club in Hope Street, which was under the Hope Hall cinema, later on it became the Everyman Theatre.

When he was at the Storyville, he went to the Cavern one night where the doormen refused to let him in, because the Cavern, with its all-night sessions, was the direct opposition to the Storyville. Charlie went to the joke shop and bought a box of stink bombs. He took them the following night and said: "If you don't let me in, I'll stink the place out!" They wouldn't – so he did! He lobbed them into the doorways and down the stairs, clearing the place out. The doormen, Tommy McNally, Kevin Connolly, Wally Booth, Larry Newport and of course Paddy Delaney chased him, he legged it down the street and they couldn't catch him. He went back the next week and they were scared to hit him because of the stink bombs, which he threatened to use again, so they let him in.

Well, now Charlie was at the Blue Angel and some well-known London villains had been coming in for about a year with Billy Grimwood. Eric Mason was very friendly with Billy as were the Lambriano brothers. Larry Newport was also working the door with Charlie, but he left about this time to go to the Victoriana Club.

One night, Chris Lambriano told Charlie that they were expecting some friends for a meeting and not to charge them at the door. Charlie said: "How will I know which is them?" Chris said: "They'll be with a guy known as 'Tank' – you'll recognise him alright!" There were only two doormen on the door, Charlie and Jimmy Evans. When the doorbell rang, Charlie looked through the spy hole. There were three steps up to the door and a fellow who was standing on the pavement stared straight at him. This was Tank, who was as wide as he was high! With him were one of the Nash brothers, Reggie Kray, Dave Scott, Eric Mason and some hangers on. There was a sort of alcove by the window and they all sat down there.

Stood at the bar were some local hard cases – Bunner Dunne, Tommy McDonald and two others from Huyton (a real rough area). Bunner Dunne was not very tall and not a great fighter, but he was notoriously strong and would put his arms around an opponent and squeeze the life out of him. He walked over to one of the beer pumps and ripped it out,

Charlie Scott with Roy

beer squirting everywhere! Charlie said to Jimmy: "You'd better throw him out."

Jimmy said: "You're the little hard man, you throw him out!" Just then, Davy Chand came in. He was a big guy who could have a fight. Davy went over to Tommy Mc and said: "Look, you know the lads are on the door, do us a favour and throw him out."

With that, Tommy McDonald pulled out a gun and hit Davy over the head with it. Obviously not hard enough, because Davy butted him and the fight really started. Davy Chand, Jimmy Evans and Charlie against Bunner Dunne, Tommy Mc and the two from Huyton. Charlie told me it was the worst fight he'd ever experienced, it spilled out into Seel Street, ending up in Berry Street and outside the Masonic pub. Charlie was still fighting one of the Huyton lads when another ran over and kicked him. Jimmy Molloy arrived with some of the lads who saw this. In those days in a man-to-man, anyone who kicked in would have the crowd against him, so Jimmy Molloy knocked him out saying: "You dirty bastard, kicking a man when he's down." The fight got really heavy, ears and noses getting bitten off in the process. The police arrived and closed off Berry Street and Seel Street. They called in the fire brigade who were looking for bits of ears, noses etc The Kray lot never interfered, they just stood and watched.

Charlie told me that two enormous policemen arrived in Trilby hats, which made them look even bigger. One was detective inspector John Ralphson. He went over to the Kray crowd and said to Reggie Kray: "I want a word." They went into a telephone booth at the club and Ralphson produced a gun saying: "If you don't get out of town, I'll blow your head off!" He'd been issued with the firearm for a police security job that day – but they hadn't given him any bullets! Charlie said: "We didn't know what was going on, we'd always been pally with Bunner and Tommy Mc."

We arranged to meet at the Dart pub the next day for a straightener, though somehow I knew it wasn't going to happen. They told us they'd started the fight to impress the Krays that was why Bunner tore out the beer pump. They knew the Krays wanted to start protection and Bunner and co. wanted to be involved! Charlie actually became quite friendly with the Lambrianos, especially Chris, and Dave Scott. (Nowadays I believe Chris is a market gardener with no interest in the ways of the old days).

They actually paid Charlie a visit at the little prefab he was living in at that time. He wouldn't let them in at first because he thought he was being set up. That wasn't the case. They said: "We couldn't believe the goings on at the Blue Angel, what our lot said that night was that there'll never be a protection racket in Liverpool."

Charlie said: "How come."

Chris said: "How can you run a protection racket in a town where when you pull a gun on someone, they head butt you!" Of course, that was Davy Chand to Tommy McDonald.

Whilst on an earlier visit to Liverpool Reggie Kray and Co. went to the Cabaret club in Duke Street, while in there they spoke to Tacker Comerford. Tacker told them that this was their territory and they wouldn't put up with any out of towners trying to take over. His advice to them was that they should leave.

The next day six or seven of Tacker's crowd escorted them to Lime Street station and saw them on the London train.

*   *   *

Sometime after leaving the Blue Angel, Charlie went to work on the door of the Odd Spot in Bold Street. The Odd Spot had a casino, which catered for really high rollers, like George Downing. He'd put bets on sometimes amounting to thousands of pounds. Everywhere he went he was usually accompanied by some of Glennon's boys, being a big spender.

One night Jimmy Tarbuck turned up with a big guy. He said: "Hi Charlie, just me and my friend."

Charlie said: "You're alright but that scruffy bastard's not getting in looking like that!"

Jimmy said: "But this is Sean Connery!"

Charlie said: "I don't give a fuck who he is, he's not getting in!" So Sean had to go back to his hotel and change, after which he came back – no problem!

Some years later, there was a function at Russell's Club in Walsingham Square. Charlie was stood at the bar and who should be standing alongside him but Sean Connery. Charlie turned to him and said: "Hi Sean, you won't remember me," Sean said: "Oh, I remember you, – Charlie 'Fucking' Scott. I've only been knocked back twice in my life, both times by a scouser! The other time was when I called on Tom Jones in Las Vegas. His minder, Rocky Seddon, said: 'You can't come in, he's resting.' "

I said: "Tell him it's Sean – he'll be pleased to see me!"

Rocky said: "He told me not to disturb him and I won't." So I didn't get to see him!

Charlie had his own unique sense of humour, which has always been accompanied by his habit of swearing. I always had to tell him to keep it down, as I didn't allow it in the clubs. These days you'd get no one in if you barred swearing. His personal charisma does bring in a lot of people to his places. A couple of years ago, he was at a big charity function, which he helped to organise. Sitting at the same table was the Duke of Westminster. During the auction, the Duke made a generous bid for an item, paying £2,000 for it. Charlie said: "That was very good of you, very generous."

The Duke said: "When it's a children's charity, you can always call on me for support, I'll do anything for children."

Charlie said: "Anything?"

"Yes,' said the Duke: "Anything."

"Then why didn't you throw half of fuckin' Chester in with the two grand?"

On a more recent occasion he was invited to a function by a friend but said: "No, you'll only sit me next to some boring fucker and it'll drive me mad." He was assured that wouldn't be the case, but on the night he was sat between two elderly gentlemen, one of whom was David Sheppard, Bishop of Liverpool. After sitting for an hour, bored out of his teeth, Charlie turned to his companion and said: "I know you Dave, we've met before."

He said: "Really, have we?"

"Yes, you used to come into my bar, Le Bateau, in Duke Street."

"That's right, I did call in occasionally."

Charlie said: "I'm a neighbour of yours; I only live three doors away from your gaff. (Meaning the Anglican Cathedral). I live in Rodney Street."

"Oh," said the Bishop, "If I can do anything for you at anytime, let me know!" Charlie said: "Well there is something you can do for me as a matter of fact!" "Certainly, what's that?"

"Can you turn those fuckin' bells down on Sunday mornin' – I get no fuckin' sleep!" And that's Charlie!

The Blue Angel is still going, the door run by Alan Peterson who's been there for years. Charlie has several bars in Liverpool and they are all successful. Charlie has a real creative flair, which along with his personality makes his places popular.

~ 13 ~
Martial Men

WALLY BOOTH AND I had opened a gym called the A and B in Temple Street. We had a wrestling mat at one end and weights the other. There just wasn't anywhere in Liverpool for wrestlers to train. Crosby gym was out of town. A Scottish friend of Wally's called Finlay Buchanan turned up one day. He'd been backpacking around the country wrestling in different gyms. He didn't mind how far he had to travel, in fact it was after a visit to Istanbul where he went to gain wrestling knowledge from Turkish wrestlers, that he decided to visit Vic Burdett's Crosby gym in Liverpool so that he could meet up with Liverpool's Olympic wrestler and Commonwealth Gold medallist – Tony Buck. It was 1965 and he was on his way home to Scotland, but couldn't resist jumping ship at Liverpool.

He was a great wrestler, less than twelve stone, but when he wrestled someone like myself three and a half stone heavier, he could make himself feel like sixteen stone. You couldn't move him until he was ready, and then he moved you! Finlay stuck around and married a Liverpool girl and came to work on the doors. He liked New Years Eve off, so he could go to Scotland and have a binge with his dad!

When the Chequers first opened I was stood on the door having a confrontation with some characters and Tony Buck called round for a drink. He stood with me, and the next

Wrestling Wally Booth

thing we were joined by a young fellow who I'd seen around. He stepped in front of Tony and me and half crouching started swaying from side to side like a preying mantis and said: "Okay, who's first, come on." They all calmed down except one who was a very thickset guy with cropped hair.

Roy, Tony Buck and Terry O'Neill, 1980

Tony said: "Why don't you just leave it?"

This idiot said: "Who are you – you fuckin' asshole?"

Tony clapped a hand on the outside of each of this guy's shoulders and swept him upwards and backwards. He landed on a car bonnet six feet away. Tony only seemed to move his arms. I was very impressed.

The young guy who'd joined us was called Terry O'Neill. He was only sixteen at the time and had padded himself out with sweaters to look bigger. A few years later, Terry was to turn up at the A and B gym with a half-Maori friend of his called Gary Spiers. They called in to watch us doing a bit on the mat. Wrestling that is! Gary was a huge, bear-like man, his bare toes which were always on display a good one and a half inches wide.

Terry met Gary in 1970 whilst in Japan; both of them loved karate and had worked in the physical security business. They became friends and when Gary decided to leave Japan, Terry encouraged him to come to England. He came to Liverpool and it became his base. At six foot and two hundred and forty pounds he was ideally suited for the 'bouncing' profession. As well as karate, he did wrestling and judo and was an ex-rugby player. He'd left Japan with a Sandan Black Belt from Master Gogen Yamaguchi (the Cat). More about Gary later.

Terry O'Neill meanwhile was working various doors around the city and gaining a reputation as a man to be respected. Terry was interested in all types of man-to-man combat. He was also an ardent physical culturist developing his physique in line with his abilities.

In Karate he was to gain an impressive record in the world of fighting arts – including a Masters Degree (6th Dan Black Belt).

He was:
Seven times British Karate Champion (Form)
Four times British Karate Champion (Fighting)
Five times European Team Champion (Fighting)
Thirteen times British Team Champion (Fighting)
South African Games Gold Medallist (Fighting)

In preparation for the Miss World Contest, Miss Israel, Dana Feller, is accompanied by karate expert Dennis Martin on her jogging session through London.
Photo Courtesy of The Press Association

Gary Spiers (courtesy of Fighting Arts International)

One door he worked on for some time was in a club called the Downbeat, (later called the Victoriana) he was joined on the door by Jimmy Parry among others. It was his first time in charge of a door.

Another impressive guy I met through Terry was Dennis Martin, who had been involved in many forms of personal combat since taking up karate over thirty-five years ago. After about four years' training, he started work at the Blue Angel in 1969. He'd trained at the Red Triangle where Terry also trained. He'd started to go for nights out at the Cavern, where Terry was doorman as well as Larry Newport and of course Paddy Delaney.

In conversation about karate, Dennis says Terry explained that what they were doing in training was karatedo, a sport version of combat. This made him aware of the difference between sport and real fighting. He was more influenced by Terry than anyone else, because he was actually doing it night after night in the city centre. He says: "I just adapted what worked for me from traditional training and also picked up a few tricks of the trade from other guys on the doors. I worked with several wrestlers and learnt from the grappling aspect, which was lacking in karate. If it worked, use it! Plus tricks of the trade you learned from other doormen – how to assess people, calm them down etc. Later on, I came to develop this more into a less traditionally based system applying it to bodyguard, door work and personal self-protection. I went into close protection/VIP protection and spent about sixteen years working on the teams. I also ran a team preventing drugs in a very large rave club. Terry and I used to grapple sometimes for fun in the foyer of the clubs, rolling around in our tuxedos as people were arriving! I remember one time Terry, Gary Spiers, the late Steve Cattle and I were on a train going to Denmark. We spent most of the journey grappling. Steve was a very good judo man, Gary had done ju-jitsu and wrestling, and we rolled around in the corridors. We looked up at one stage and we were in a station, with people pointing at the 'mad English' and calling 'Politzie!' "

Terry O'Neill and Gary Spiers are practically legends in the martial arts and door work in this country. Terry is well known for his enormous skill level. He could use his techniques in the street just as easily as he used them in competition, when he became the KUGB National Champion for about seven consecutive years, as well as being captain of the All Styles British Karate Team. He would use high kicks, which everyone in self-protection will tell you shouldn't be used in the street. Terry was the exception because he was so skillful, so fast, and so powerful that he could do it. I worked with him for many years on the door and never saw it fail to do the job. He never had to kick anyone twice! I once saw it written (Combat September 1979) that Terry had fifty knockouts with head kicks on the door. Well, from personal experience I can tell you it could well be in the thousands! My old mate Tommy McNally, who started Terry on the door, put it this way: "If there was just you and Terry working, it was like working with a gang!"

Now – Gary Spiers had probably got the best fighting brain for unarmed combat of anyone I have ever met. He is enormously strong and very, very skillful. I first met him on the day he arrived in England in 1971. He turned up in the middle of the night at Terry's having travelled from Japan, via Russia, overland. We were going to London and Terry turned up with this guy who I took to be a Yank. He had a cravat, a big camelhair coat and a Hawaiian shirt on! We got on really well and he joined us on the doors. Gary's techniques were less classical than Terry's, for example he'd use head butts! He was the first guy I'd seen launch someone through the air with a back head butt! He used front kicks a lot with his enormous feet. We used to say they were like kids' drawings of feet. He used to go into the middle of a crowd fight and just scoop people into the centre and kick them with these huge (usually bare) feet! Terry had beautiful form. There are countless photos of him scoring points in World Class Karate competitions, with textbook techniques. Well, he was just the same in the street. He'd be in the middle of a crowd, kicking guys out, left, right and centre, with perfect kicks, back straight, faultless. Gary was more like an animal. Not in the nasty sense, just like a big bear who fights with utter confidence because it has no natural enemies. Gary's nickname in Japan was Kuma, which means bear. We'd be mixing it good style in some major kick off, and I'd see Gary with a big grin on his face, and bodies all around his feet. It was a great time working with these two, and I never stopped laughing!

What follows is the transcript of an interview with Gary Spiers by Terry O'Neill. It was published in Terry's magazine Fighting Arts International No.38 (Vol 7 No2)

T.O. *What sort of opponent do you find the most dangerous?*

G.S. *Well, they are all dangerous to a greater or lesser extent, but I know what you mean. It's not down to their physical size – nor their actual capabilities that is the most important factor in my book – it's who is the nastiest and most cunning – that's the worst kind. Very often it's the small guys who turn out to be the most vicious, probably compensating for their lack of size. Then there are exceptions like Eddie Palmer, who you may recall I had a major 'difference of opinion' with.*

Palmer was, as you know, a notorious hard case with twenty years of reputation preceding him. He was widely known as the 'Terror of Toxteth'.

He was around six foot usually over 18 stone (252 pounds) and he had been in his time a very able and hard heavy weight boxer, and he was quite willing to fight anybody. Very few people liked him but hardly anyone would tell him to his face – not even the other hard cases – because he had battered a large percentage of them. Some of them had several return matches with him and they had still ended up out of the game. He hadn't taken many seconds in his fighting career. We are talking about a proper determined man who made a vocation – in between prison stretches – of going round intimidating other people and, as often as not giving them a really good bashing.

Anyway, him and me had a severe 'do.'

T.O. *Let's have the full story.*

G.S. *How it got started was that he had knocked a girl unconscious on the dance floor of a club I was working in.*

T.O. *Why?*

G.S. *She had refused to dance with him – lots of these people don't need much reason to start performing, anyway, I don't exactly know what had gone on prior to that – All I was told was that Palmer had kicked off upstairs. Now by the time I got up two flights of stairs, there were two bodies stretched out on the floor – the girl had been joined by a little Indian doctor. He had been all of five foot but he was the only one in the room with the guts to go over and remonstrate with Palmer over punching the girl. He had also been treated to a right-hander, which had broken his glasses; his nose and also removed a few of his teeth. Now I did not touch Palmer at that stage, simply because I did not know then what had happened. I only found out later, I just said to him: "You have got to leave boss." Now, even though I'd been told many times about how fast this fellow was with his hands – I still got 'nailed' he caught me with a real nice 'hook' right in the jaw. I have to be honest and say that I did not see it – BOOM! It was perfect.*

T.O. *Did it put you down?*

G.S. *No, it did not put me down – probably due to a combination of my rather large bone structure, the way I'm put together and to the fact that I'm not in the habit – mentally – of being put on my arse by people. It did shake me though and I lost time – fractions of activity – but I was able to take him to the floor. He should really have followed up on his lead with another shot, but he was probably that used to 'sparking' all and sundry with just one shot, that he wasn't geared to putting a combination attack together. I ducked low, grabbed behind the knee with one hand and pulled his foot out from under him and drove my shoulder into his groin – down he went and I was right on top of him. I automatically had him in a half strangle – just a reflex action – now at that point I would have finished him there and then. I would have strangled him properly, wrenched his neck out or gouged him – or maybe all of those things, depending upon how well he stood up to a bit of 'treatment.' But he had a little crew with him, who were justly famous for their willingness to get people with their Stanley Knives – they were nicknamed 'the Stanley boys.' Obituaries have even been placed in the local newspaper for people who were alive – it was just designed to upset them, reading their own death notice in the paper – signed 'love from the Stanley boys.' Now I believe you have to show a death certificate before they will publish the notice! Now I knew that had I started to do the business on Palmer, I would probably have been cut to pieces – remember he was still conscious underneath me, and I'd not yet recovered from his punch. So I let him up, much against my wishes and he promptly challenged me to a straightener outside – just him and me.*

Rather than get involved in what possibly could have been a massacre – of me, because his mates were all around us – I agreed. I don't like going outside the premises – there is much more chance of police involvement and also of my ending up on my own in the street with him and his pack. Even though I was working with people – There were other 'bouncers' on with me, one really never knows what people will do in serious circumstances that just flare up instantly. Conditions can change even amongst trusted colleagues and if for some reason your friends – whom you are relying on to hop in – do not come to your assistance right away – you could easily be killed. Something that's gone wrong at home – even a silly argument with their wife, before they come to the club, can change a person's mind about the determination with which he'll do his job. The fear of physical reprisals and/or legal repercussions can also alter a man's commitment to 'performing.'

T.O. *Have you ever had people – other bouncers – desert you in similar situations?*

G.S. *It has happened twice in my life – I haven't had it occur much, because I take it very personally!*

(The interview sounded very menacing at this point! which suitably reinforced his sentiments)

We went outside and I agreed not to kick him – somebody had obviously informed him of my 'pedigree' – he wanted 'rules' which to me is so much bullshit, when you fight, you fight, and that's it. Anyway, his people were there with him and several of them already had their hands in their pockets obviously holding their working 'tools'.

He says. "We won't kick."

I said: "That'll do me 'lets go.' "

We started and as I charged, he punched and we ended up with my right forearm in his mouth – he bit me almost to the bone whilst I held my right fist with my left hand and started smashing his head back against the wall behind him. His teeth were hurting me a lot, but at the same time he was choking on my forearm. Well, because he was biting me, he could not let go, and as I was trying to knock the wall down with the back of his head, I instinctively put my knee into him twice – once in the stomach and once in the hip – I'd have had him in the groin properly with the next one. You see, I'd used a left and a right HIZA GERI to get a fix on his position and the third one would have crushed 'them' for him. But my knee attacks brought savage threats from his gang – who by this time had apparently pulled their knives out.

My colleagues had thankfully chosen to come out with me – for which I'm eternally grateful – because even if they hadn't, I'd have been obliged to go out anyway. I wouldn't have particularly relished the idea but neither would I have backed down from this pack of! ! !!! I'm certain that it was only my people's presence there that prevented the other team form tearing me to ribbons. Oh yes – I also gave him some elbow smashes in the gut with my left arm but because of the way our bodies were locked in, I couldn't get any real 'shots' into him from that angle.

Now I was not able to knock him out. People have told me that he had been K.O'd but I have never met one who had actually done it. As it was though, he wound up that exhausted he was unable to continue, whereas I had 'loads' left in me. Now I had great difficulty in restraining myself at this point from finishing the job off, when he was in this state. It flashed through my mind that if I did drop on his throat or his spleen with my knees – as I wanted to, or stomp him with a Fumikomi Geri, that the incident would immediately escalate – so I left it at that. But he was well F——D.

T.O. *What's this dropping of your knee on opponents – you seem quote fond of that technique.*

G.S. *Oh I am 'quite fond' of it as you put it, I think it's a very valid technique – I'll show you how I like to do it during the photo session later. If you do it properly, you have every chance of breaking something on them. At the very least you severely wind them. I'll tell you this – I have never done it to anybody and had them get up after it, at least not for a while and then not under their own steam, they have had to be carried away.*

* * *

The Cabaret Club in Duke Street which was run by Jack Murphy, was a fairly large club with a proper dining and cabaret lounge and a casino. It was popular and therefore successful.

The main man running the door was Beech Keighley. He was a large powerfully built man, with a good reputation. I remember being told that he was an able boxer who could have been British Heavyweight champ, – with the right handling. With him on the door were the massive Billy Vaughn and Billy Doherty.

In the 50's and 60's when he was running the door, clubs were very strict, there weren't that many clubs to go to, so they could afford to be fussy.

One night, or so I was told, Beech had a run-in with some Scots and it got nasty. He kept them out and they swore revenge. A short while later he was walking home one night and a Jaguar car mounted the pavement and ran Beech down. His legs were very badly injured, and it was touch and go whether he'd ever walk again.

Word went out that Eddie Palmer had been paid to drive the car.

Beech had to start the long battle to recovery. Eventually, he did regain the use of his legs, though he always walked with some difficulty after that.

I remember seeing him a couple of years later, limping along with a very upright bearing, wearing a long black overcoat and a Homburg hat on his head and carrying an umbrella. Very stylish.

There was a club in Liverpool 8 called the Peel Labour Club, which was more or less open to anybody. I was told, one night Eddie Palmer was in there and so was Beech with his wife and daughter, Palmer walked over to their table and pointed at Beech's wife and said: "I've had her" and then at his daughter: "And I've had her as well!" Thc final lying insult. He then left, I believe with two girls. They climbed into a taxi outside on the car park. Eddie was sat in the back seat with the girls, when somebody opened the taxi door, reached in, and stabbed him in the chest. He rolled out onto the ground, obviously seriously injured.

People apparently were stepping over him, saying things like: "It's only fuckin' Eddie Palmer!"

He died on the way to hospital.

Beech was charged with his murder. It was reduced to manslaughter and he got three years, in fact, somebody said that the judge implied that he'd done the local population a favour.

There was some doubt as to whether Eddie did actually drive the car that injured Beech. On the day of the funeral, bars up and down Park Road held parties of celebration. Eddie certainly wasn't popular!

On a personal level I had no problems with Eddie. Whilst I never got into an extended conversation with him, our association was, I would say amenable. He was a wild card and troublesome, but I did admire his guts

Terry O'Neill was working on the door of the Banyan Tree which was a nightclub on the lower ground floor of the Adelphi Hotel, the entrance was round the corner to the left of the Adelphi's entrance opposite the Big House pub. Tommy McNally worked with him which meant there was never a dull moment. Bob Hardy was the manager, he'd worked for

Terry Phillips as manager at the Wooky Hollow prior to this. On one particular night, just a couple of days before Xmas, everyone was festive and Father Xmas walked in with the crowd.

He was a huge man carrying his sack, he opened the door, shoving his sack full of something or other at Terry saying: "Ere fuckin' mind that", which sounded strange coming from Father Xmas.

He pulled down his beard and Terry looked at his eyes. They were covered in scar tissue, this was a real tough face, he was taller than Terry who's six foot tall, and to use Terry's words, "Would scare the shit out of any kid."

Terry was going to stop him and Tommy Mac' said: "He's alright Terry – let him go straight in". As he'd come in he'd boomed out: "Yo' Ho' Fuckin' Ho". He said to Tommy: "Alright Tom". Terry said: "Who is he?" "Oh, he owns a shop up London Road, lots of stolen property moves around there, he's a bit of a baddy – I'll watch him." Terry told me what happened next – "Within five minutes girls are screaming and a girl comes running to the door saying: "Father Xmas is drinking my ale!" And another one: "Father Xmas just put his hand up my skirt!" '

Tommy said: "Let me go and speak to him." By now he's sitting among a pile of people with his beard now off drinking ale and making them all look very uncomfortable. Tommy went over to speak to him and I think he told Tommy to Fuck off. So Tommy walked back and said: "He'll be alright" – "he'll probably make his own way out."

Terry with Arnold Schwartzenegger and Carl Wethers on the set of 'Predator'

Terry O'Neill in fighting mode

from **The Governor**

Terry O'Neill

Anyway, a girl came out complaining, then he pushed someone, and so I went over to where he's still sitting and he told me to fuck off as well. He still had his Father Xmas hat on, big white eyebrows, and his red suit. He'd decided he wouldn't leave and I'd decided he was causing trouble, Tommy was now with me, then was called to the door, the door closed after him and I was on my own – Tommy had warned me that this guy was bad news. So my first thought was "I'll stop him". I told him to leave, he wouldn't, he put his hand out and I caught hold of his arm and elbowed him in the face, a real strong shot, which spun his head round – he just shook it off and then stood up. He wasn't fazed at all. I dragged him over, stepped back over the table and roundhouse kicked him in the face – a forté of mine. In my defence I did hit a chair with my foot on the way up. I'd kicked him on the side of the cheekbone using my instep and not the ball of my foot like I used to kick – this knocked him only halfway down before he started to get back up again. I ended up putting another strong arm bar across his arm with both arms. I was trying to break it, he was reaching over to get a glass, when Tommy McNally came over, and the two of us had to drag him out, I had to kick him twice more before he was unconscious. People were yelling: "He's battering Father Xmas." By the time I threw his sack after him he was starting to come to. He got to his feet effing and blinding, and staggered up the street.

Tommy Mac' said: "Wait till I tell our kids you beat up Father Xmas, you'll 'ave no luck you!" I now had the reputation of having beat up Father Xmas. Tommy made it worse by telling everyone it was because I'd "had no toys as a kid."

Terry was introduced to Arnold Schwarzenegger by London gym owner Wag Bennett a long time friend of Arnold. They had an immediate rapport developing into a friendship. As a result of this Arnold invited Terry to get involved in the film *Conan the Destroyer.* As well as helping with fighting techniques, Terry played several characters in the fighting scenes. Terry liked the acting business and took a serious interest which has led to him having parts in many T.V. dramas including, – *Liverpool One*, *Supply and Demand II*, *Thief Takers III*, *Comics*, *Civvies*, etc. His most memorable part in my opinion, was in the Governor where he played Victor – a psychopath who insisted on being called Tarzan, Terry's physique came in handy for the Governor, both 1 and 2.

He's also been in at least a dozen films so far, including *Dragonheart*, *Red Sonja*, *Kull the Conquerer*, *Quills* with Michael Caine, *Entrapment* and *The League of Extraordinary Gentlemen* – both with Sean Connery.

His additional skills must have helped. They included: –

Firearms – Class A in Practical Pistol Shooting –
Weaponry – Sword, Knife, Staff, etc. plus horse riding.

In spite of all this Terry has a reputation of being an amenable gentleman.

* * *

Another impressive Karate man was a big good-looking guy called Joe Farley. He was six foot two and fair-haired. Joe was to become a very well known figure in Liverpool. He was something of an entrepreneur who ventured into various businesses such as bars and restaurants. He was and is obviously a very physical man, with a good build and capable of looking after himself in a dicey situation.

In one competition Joe had his little finger almost bitten off – they strapped it up and he carried on – helping to win the British Championship. Terry O'Neill told me he was impressed by Joe's commitment in that bout. Joe was in the two teams that came second and third in the National Championship.

We became friends when we met Joe twenty years ago when he joined Health & Fitness World in Liverpool city centre. It was a state of the art gym owned by Terry Phillips and I. Derek Hatton and various colleagues of his from the City Council were members as were Suzy Quattro and T.V. comedian Les Dennis.

He was to venture for a while into acting, having a leading part in a British film about Liverpool, which was written by Frank Clarke from Kirby, Liverpool. The director's grand-father directed the film *Gone With The Wind.*

Joe played the flamboyant gangster running protection in believe it or not – health clubs, saunas, etc., – and other places. It starred Robbie Coltrane and Bruce Payne becoming a cult film in America.

It was called the *Fruit Machine*, though in America they changed the name. They didn't like the word 'fruit' in the title.

In the film Robbie Coltrane owned a gay club, Bruce Payne was Joe's enforcer, and Coltrane was a target. Bruce Payne is doing well now in America.

The club scenes were filmed in the Fruit Exchange building, (pure coincidence) which is located between Victoria Street and Mathew Street. They used what used to be the Auction room on the first floor. I know it well because I rented the whole of the ground floor, which became Gatsbys, and basement, which eventually became Erics. The auction room was beautifully panelled, with tiers of seats all around. During the war (1939 to 1945) it was used as a courtroom for trials involving war crimes.

Joe however, had other fish to fry, deciding not to pursue an acting career.

He said it was too tough!

Joe Farley squaring up

~ 14 ~
Personalities

IN 1966/1967 WHEN I was working on the Pyramid, Terry Phillips used to call by to see how things were going. I told him my main problem was the number of different trades working at the same time in such a large place created a hell of a mess. Security was also a problem; things went missing all the time. Terry said: "You need my old fella down here; I got him to sweep up at the Wookie Hollow and keep the job tidy. I only paid him a couple of quid!" So, Terry took me to see Joe his dad, who mainly occupied himself with his dogs and his pigeons. Joe had had a colourful career during and after the war, he'd also been a gymnast, and actually performed gymnastics for Gustav, King of Yugoslavia in a display. He'd also been a guest of Her Majesty and was a renowned bare fist street fighter. Joe came to work for me, he was always there, watching the job and keeping it tidy. One morning when the men were having their tea break, Joe spoke out. He said: "A tin of paint went missing last night." The men looked at each other shaking their heads, Joe pointed to the electrician saying, "You took it, you were the only one here after I left. Just make sure its back here tomorrow!" It was, and not another thing was taken. Joe was not someone to fall foul of. When he was inside, I was told, that when paedophiles came in, Joe's job was to get in the cell and give them a hiding, they might as well have thrown a pit bull in there.

I weighed him up continuously, thinking I could really use someone like him on the door, he had run his own shebeens in the past, but I thought he might look a bit rough and ready on the door. I mentioned these thoughts to one of the contractors. He said: "I think Joe will be very disappointed if he doesn't get the job!" That made my mind up for me, I gave him the job and it was one of the best decisions I could have made! As always at that time, when opening a club you invited all the best people and got as up market a trade as possible. The chances always were that the place would gradually go down in time and reach a level. So it was wise to start at the top to get established. On the opening night, Joe was in charge of the door, looking extremely smart in his evening suit, and the customers took to him right away. They loved his down to earth yet polite manner, helping a lady with her fur coat saying: "Give it to me girl, I'll watch it for yeh." When Gary Spiers arrived in Liverpool, Terry O'Neill told me he wrote to a colleague in New Zealand saying, "You've got to come over, I've just seen a fella with the best right hand I've ever seen." That fellow was Joe Phillips.

One day not long before the club was completed Joe and I were busy with the many bits and pieces of last minute jobs when two youngish girls came through the door.

The Pyramid was very big for a club at that time being two warehouses knocked together. I took them around showing them the layout. It turned out they were students and extremely attractive girls. I asked them what their ambition was and one of them told me she wanted to be an actress.

She had beautiful long dark hair and a pretty face but I thought it was a girlish fantasy. They asked for a job and started working at the weekends after we opened. After about six months, they left. A year or two later I saw a play on TV and who should be in it but our pretty barmaid. After that she went from strength to strength becoming very well known, about ten years later she starred in the famous Maxwell House coffee advert. Her name was Sharon Maughan. She married Trevor Eve whose first major role was as a detective in *Shoestring*.

Over the years, Joe often used to mention Sharon wondering how she was. Whenever the Maxwell House advert came on I would point Sharon out as the first ever Pyramid barmaid! Trevor has become a very accomplished actor in fact I'd go so far as to say he is a favourite of mine having seen him play some very strong parts, usually as a detective.

Some of our local villains were speculating on doing some protection on Liverpool clubs, they had the Pyramid in mind and approached Joe to get his sanction. Joe's reply was "If you're going for Roy you've got to get past me first, nobody bothers Roy while I'm around!" They decided to give it a miss. He never told me about it, but one of the villains did years later.

There was a well-known con man I got to know in Southport called Sidney Cain, who used to introduce himself as 'Sir Sidney Patrick Rawlinson Cain' in a wonderful Oxford accent. He was in his early 70's when I met him at the Kingsway in Southport, where he became one of the most popular customers. He was in prison with the Krays and Frankie Fraser. Joe was also there at the same time. Joe never spoke of his past to me, although I knew him more than 20 years. However, Sidney told me that he was in charge of the prison library, and somehow he upset mad Frankie. He was obviously very worried because Frankie started to give him a bad time, so he went to see Joe. Joe said: "Come on, let's go see him." They went together to see Frankie Fraser and Joe said: "Hi Frankie, Sidney's a friend of mine and I'm watching his back!" Frankie looked at Joe and said: "Right – I'd like you to watch my back as well Joe!" After which, all was amicable.

* * *

The Pyramid became a very busy club and Joe made it the main focus of his life, for the next twenty years. The police had formed the VICE SQUAD in 1964 and basically gave

Roy with Uncle Sonny at Shorrocks Hill Club in the late 1970s

all the clubs a bad time, enforcing laws which were becoming increasingly outdated, making it hard to make a living in the night club business. People went to nightclubs after the cinema, the pub, or even a restaurant, although all nightclubs had to serve food. The problem was when people started to arrive at nine or ten o'clock, if they wanted to drink, they had to sit down and have a meal. Obviously if you've got more than a hundred people in, this isn't practical, so all sorts of dodges had to be thought up in case the police paid a visit. I remember in the Chequers we used to put a pile of empty plates on the bar. They were placed there instead of being taken to the kitchen after being used. The policeman would say to me on looking around "Have all these people eaten?' I'd say: "Of course Officer, there's the dirty plates!" I wouldn't mind, but very often, that policeman would be one I'd have to pay two quid a week to tip me off. Everyone with a club had a member of the VICE SQUAD on the take. They'd ring up and say two words "They're out", which meant the VICE SQUAD, were doing a few raids that night.

The so called Vice Squad seemed to concentrate all their efforts on the night clubs which, let's face it, weren't involved in vice. The nightclubs had become one of the most popular sources of entertainment; they were great places to be. As well as the social clubs which catered for varied organisations, British Legion, Dockers, Golf, Football etc. (as they still do). The nightclubs also had variety in the different clienteles which they catered for. Country & Western, jazz, cabaret, skiffle, rock 'n' roll, etc., as well as the usual drink 'n' dance nightclub. I recall being told there were over four hundred licensed clubs in Liverpool in the 1960's. It didn't surprise me – but vice! Vice in the context most people think of such as prostitution, heavy drugs, etc. No. The Police knew precisely where to go for these vices, and it wasn't to nightclubs in general, though that's where they liked to focus. It was such an easy touch; the licensing laws were so antiquated it was impossible to stay within the designated boundaries and survive.

Club owners were happy to hand over a couple of pounds a week to a friendly bobby to help them out.

At the Cavern, the Police duty jeep would slowly pass down Mathew Street with the back door open, a member of the Cavern staff would put a tray of pints of beer into the back, and on the return patrol, the empty tray and glasses would be collected in the same way. The jeep carrying on without stopping. This was all harmless stuff, the Police in the main were allies who often had to help out during trouble. The vice squad raids on the other hand could be very heavy handed; especially in view of the fact that everyone knew the laws needed updating. The only skulduggery I came across was the sale of dodgy goods between customers. The popular technique was to offer something that had 'fallen off the back of a lorry'. People would buy them because it had to be a bargain because of its origin. What the punters didn't realise was that he went straight to the wholesalers. He could sell cheaper 'cos he cut out the middleman. Jewellery was also popular for the same reasons. Of course, these activities have always gone on in pubs, social clubs, etc. A small part of nightlife.

The Pyramid became very popular on a Sunday night. We used to get a lot of villains in, as well as normal punters. We'd stay open late; sometimes it would be daylight when we walked outside, eight hundred people on a Sunday wasn't unusual. The villains were the best customers; they were always having minor wars with each other, and then making up. Consequently, they loved to ingratiate themselves with someone they'd fallen out with

Ellen with celebs ~ Shorrocks Hill Club, 1979
Kenny Lynch, John Jones, Ian Gallagher, Ellen, Jimmy Tarbuck, Keith Airey, Phil Boorsman, and other.

by buying them drinks! I was friendly with them all, why not? They were my customers. They would tell me anything; I always kept my own council! It's always a mistake to agree with a villain when he's slagging another villain off. You can be sure when they make up again, they'll repeat your criticism to the other party, making you the enemy! I realised very early in the business that you could make an enemy every night if you weren't careful. You could also make a friend every night, which was a policy I stuck to.

Norman Paterson and I went on holiday to Torremolinos in Spain. It was my first holiday abroad. At that time, there wasn't much in Torremolinos compared to now. There were two streets of shops and cafes leading down to the beach from the main road, which ran parallel to the shore. At the end of one of the streets there was a stone staircase which led on to the shore where there was an extensive open area of black bare ground where a couple of horses stood offering rides along the front. There was practically nothing else down there. However, up on the main road there were several bars and cafes. We tried a couple which had fabulous neon signs at the front with photo's of dancing girls etc. When you got inside there was practically nothing – just a bar and a small dance floor with continuous music. I was struck by the inviting sophisticated frontage compared to the interior. I realised how important presentation was.

We stood at the bar where we were immediately approached by girls offering their company, inviting us to buy drinks for them. One of them asked Norman if he'd like to share a bottle of Champagne upstairs with her. He walked up the open staircase smiling down at me. After half an hour, I decided to see where they'd gone. I climbed the staircase, which led to an open mezzanine floor, which looked down on the bar. It was a tiny area with about four little tables against the wall at the back. Norman was at one of the tables opposite the girl with the bottle of champagne between them. Not an exciting prospect!

We went to the bar and I asked for the bill, which at that time was outlandish about three thousand pesetas. I refused to pay it so the manager went through the door and came back with a policeman. He was a tiny little old boy about seventy years old wearing a crumpled old uniform.

We laughed, I handed over eight hundred pesetas and we walked out. However, those places got me thinking.

Back in Liverpool, we were paying out good money for live music every night. I got the latest state-of-the-art jukebox, which had two separate speakers as big as the jukebox itself. On weekday nights I put it centre stage with a speaker each side, only using a live band on Friday and Saturdays. Then I decided to open up a bar on the first floor. I had life size plaques of mummies placed around the walls and had the whole lot sprayed in dark red with a new type of nylon which gave a luxurious felt like finish making the mummies look like part of the walls. I then put in a large dance floor made of fibre glass with two platforms at the back the whole lot finished in red with gold dust sparkling in it. This was all in one piece taking in the two platforms. I then got two attractive girls who had been in my beauty contests and offered them a job as dancers. They wore hot pants and skimpy tops and went down a storm. I had a record deck behind a counter backstage. The girls put the records on and took turns dancing, sometimes together. There was no microphone so no talking, just continuous music. It was Liverpool's first discothèque. Cleopatra's Bar and a big success! With no DJ.

Georgia Neale, the Pyramid's first D.J. Go-Go Dancer

A very talented local artist, John Geary, did wonderful Egyptian themes on the walls and also modelling the Mummies.

In 1973 Billy Butler was the DJ and promoter at the Mardi Gras, a very successful club at Mount Pleasant not far from the Adelphi Hotel.

Billy managed to book the famous American Group the Drifters; I think it was their first booking in Britain. Billy approached me asking if I would like to share the booking as they were costing £1,000, a fair lump of money at the time. I agreed and we decided they could do their first spot at the Pyramid, their second at the Mardi gras. It was a terrific night for both clubs, both working to packed houses.

To my shame I missed it – I'd booked a long overdue holiday in Australia and couldn't cancel. However, after their gig, the Drifters had a meal in the Pyramid. Ben. E. King was so taken with the steak that on two subsequent visits to Liverpool he hotfooted it over to the Pyramid for one of Mendy's steaks, Mendy being our chef. On those occasions, I had the pleasure of meeting Ben. E. King!

On my journey to Australia, I was sat in Singapore airport waiting for a flight when a little guy sat next to me saying. 'Alright der Roy, how's it goin' are ya still at the Pyramid?" There's no escaping when you're famous! However, I walked over to the newsstand to buy a book and noticed the Rolling Stone, the famous musical paper was doing an article on Mersey beat.

I bought a copy and who's photo was in the centre pages? Mine! It was an article on the Cavern, which I had taken over. I got a kick out of that – being in the Rolling Stone!

* * *

Around about that time, Bob Wooler (who achieved fame as the Cavern DJ during the Beatles time decided to book the Walker Brothers and put them on at the New Brighton Tower. It was a complete sell out, and when Bob came on stage people were jumping up and down in anticipation.

Bob got them all to sit down eventually and announced. 'The Walker Brothers!' The crowd was screaming and yelling. Bob couldn't quieten them so he asked the boys to withdraw behind the curtain. There was stunned silence – he said: "I'm not bringing them back on unless you all settle down." So they sat down and he went to the mike and announced them, twice. Nothing happened. They didn't appear. He went back stage and said: "Didn't you hear me announce you?"

They nodded – "Well what's the problem?" he asked them.

"We were only booked for one appearance and we've made one, you took us offstage, it wasn't our idea!"

So poor old Bob had to re-negotiate their terms to get them back on the stage!

One day a pal of mine, who was in touch with most of the villainy, rang me, and said: "Roy, there's a crew coming up from London, they want to expand their protection business. There's talk of working you over, being the best-known club owner, and setting you up as an example. You see what happened to Adams, that can happen to you." (He as referring to the meeting in the Victoria Club). Well, it wasn't long after I'd had all the other aggro, where I'd relied on the law. I wasn't prepared to go through all that again. I decided I'd have to do it my own way. I had the shotgun in the office, (it was legal at that time) I thought, the first stranger to come in this office unannounced is gonna get this! I also kept it with me in the car. I had a few anxious weeks and my pal rang me again. He said: "Roy, they've been here and decided it wouldn't be worth it plus they've weighed up the Liverpool attitude and don't fancy it."

Unfortunately, my training suffered during those years. I just didn't have the time or the energy. My weight went up to almost seventeen stone, – a lot for me! One thing I'll say for the police in those days, if we had nuisances who just wouldn't go away, causing disruption when customers were arriving, so much so that phoning the police was the only option, they'd turn up in the hurry up wagon, which was a jeep, and open up the back door. At the same time pulling on their leather gloves and punching a fist into the other palm saying.

"O.K. Roy, where are they?" Whereupon they'd grab them and throw them in the back, no nonsense, and let them sleep it off in the cells and just chuck them out in the morning without charges! These days the police would be the villains for doing their job!

10th February 1981.

Mr. Brian Roberts,
Echo Crime Reporter,
Liverpool Daily Post and Echo Ltd.,
Old Hall Street,
Liverpool 2.

Dear Sir,

As a person connected with city night life for over 20 years I would like to say something in defence of city clubs.

As you are no doubt aware clubs get a bad press from all sections of the media, crimes committed in the city are usually reported as having taken place 'in the heart of city's clubland', automatically relating in some way clubs with the crime. In my experience, which is considerable, most incidents which occur outside night clubs are as a result of people being refused admission because they are considered unsuitable - this opinion being borne out by their behaviour outside. The ones who spend the evening dancing drinking and socialising are contented and only interested in going home or escorting someone home. Liverpool is historically a violent city, 50 years ago dockers carrying their wage packets home, had to watch out for muggers.

Surely your newspaper should say something in favour of city night clubs, after all when tourists come to the birth place of the Beatles (the swinging city) they do expect to find some evening entertainment, as do visiting ships etc. Most of the club owners I know have mortgaged themselves to the hilt to start their business and they are finding it very tough to survive with such overheads as high electricity charges rates, V.A.T. etc., believe me the idea of night clubs being a money making Shangri La is purely a dream, at least in this depressed city. If people cannot afford expensive restaurants, or if cultural evenings are not to their taste - what are they to do apart from sit at home and watch television.

I know that during the time that I was a proprietor of the Cavern, we used to get a couple of thousand young people in over a weekend - the reason we got so many was that nobody else wanted them and entertaining and policing them was an expensive undertaking, but at least they were off the streets , enjoying themselves and keeping out of mischief.

Surely if the police have knowledge of criminal activities they have the power in the courts to stop applications being granted.

It is unjust to make all encompassing statements which lead the public to believe that all club and pub owners are criminals. More should be said about the many goods works for charities, assisting the police when being attacked etc. which club people do, and how about applauding the enterprise and risks taken by such people as Terry Phillips at the Wookey Hollow and Alan Knipe with the Royal Court, who else would stake all they have got to entertain us. It should not be forgotten that over a thousand people are employed in the licensed trade in the city centre alone.

In the last few years this city has died in the daytime - lets not kill it off alltogether by destroying our night life.

Yours sincerely,

R. Adams

R. J. ADAMS

~ 15 ~
Chelsea Times

JOHN CHASE AND I remained friends after we finished working at the Basement and some years later John told me that his father George was looking for a new occupation. I suggested a nightclub involving the three of us might be a good idea. They looked at the Wirral across the river from Liverpool and discovered that the Old Royal Ferry Hotel was for sale. It was close to New Brighton Pier and used to be the first pub people flocked to as they poured from the Liverpool ferry. They used to have hundreds of pints of bitter lined up on the very long bar ready for the punters as they flooded into the place.

When the ferries stopped going to New Brighton and the pier went into decline, the old pub closed down. I got in touch with the brewery, we bought it for a song, and we went into business together. We did a job on the place and opened it in 1971.

I used to enjoy the odd trip to London, visiting antique markets in places like the Portobello Road and the Kings Road in Chelsea. In the evening, I'd go to the Playboy club, for a drink and the odd flutter in the casino.

I was walking down Kings Road one day and I noticed quite a few people going into a bar. I decided to have a look and was surprised when a doorman stopped me, demanding four bob entrance fee. I thought – marvellous! – Getting people to pay to go in a pub. I'd never seen that before.

Inside there was a square room with a bar along the wall to the left, and another along the wall to the right. Eight feet in front of each bar, was a wrought iron barrier, and the floor space in the middle was a dance floor with a D.J. at the end. I bought a drink and the D.J. put a record on. A pretty girl appeared from behind the D.J. stand and started dancing. She was topless – after a couple of records, another girl replaced her. The room was packed with men. I thought, this is like a club in the middle of the afternoon – but it's a pub!

John and I had been working on our place in New Brighton, and John had asked me a couple of times, whether we were going to run it as a pub – or a club.

I'd been hovering a bit with my answer, because I had this Kings Road place in the back of my mind.

I discovered that it was possible to get a late license on a pub. After all, a licensed club is only a pub with conditions on the license, such as keeping a record of everyone who attended, and limited admission to those people only, e.g.: – a club.

A pub obviously has an open license. The main reasons pubs didn't go for a late license, was the extra expense. Food had to be served after normal hours, which meant building a kitchen and employing extra staff, plus introducing emergency lighting and many other extras, not normally required. When I realised you could charge on the door of a pub, – my mind was made up.

George Chase had loaned me a book about a stretch of water in London called Chelsea Reach. I'd left the book on the coffee table and Ellen pointed to it, saying – "That would be a good name for the new place." – I'd mentioned that I wanted something with a

The Chelsea look at New Brighton

ONE of the oldest landmarks on the New Brighton riverfront, the Royal Ferry Hotel, is to be given a new lease of life as the Chelsea Reach.

The 30-bedroom premises, which have stood derelict for the past three years, have been bought from Threlfall's Brewery for an undisclosed sum, and are to be reopened early next month.

The men behind the project are **Mr. John Chase**, a Londoner who has been living in Allerton for the past ten years, and **Mr. Roy Adams**, a well-known Merseyside club owner who took over the Cavern about 12 months ago

Mr. John Chase

A RUNAWAY SUCCESS AS THE AUDIENCE STORMS STAGE

Jackie Fox of the Runaways at the concert.

A bouncer was injured and a security fence was smashed when most of a 500-strong audience rushed the stage to get a closer look at teenage American girl group, The Runaways, in Liverpool last night.

About 20 top bouncers were drafted into Eric's, in Matthew Street, to cope with the frenzied and mainly male crowd. But there was little trouble until over halfway through the act.

Then the audience surged forward, the wooden barrier was smashed and the bouncer had to be carried away by colleagues, suffering from a knee injury.

The sexily-dressed female group from California, all aged 16, played on undeterred for over an hour.

Guitarist and singer Lita Ford, said: "It was really good to play in Liverpool. The audience seemed much more receptive than some we have seen.

Many young men had queued for over an hour outside the club to get in and the doors were closed about half-an-hour before the group appeared on stage.

Lita added: "We really enjoyed the show and the guys in the audience seemed to. Although we knew we were near the Beatles' home, we didn't have time to think about it."

The girls, whose single and long player records are both said to be selling well in Merseyside, make a final appearance at Leeds tonight before flying home to Los Angeles.

"But we want to come back. All the girls enjoyed themselves. Next time we hope to do even better," Lita said.

Factory wo on the gre

WORKERS at Lucas's factory in Bowring Park Road, Liverpool, will soon be swapping their overalls for costumes and greasepaint.

They are busy rehearsing for their 13th annual Christmas pantomime—"Aladdin"—which is being staged next month

PAUL McCARTNEY at the Chelsea Reach

Chelsea Reach, situated on New Brighton's Pier, is a grand, spacious well decorated and softly lit pub. No wonder it was the personal choice of Paul McCartney for the setting of a typical pub scene for a television film by A.T.V. The film is being made to promote Paul's new group 'WINGS' and will be shown here sometime in May, before being distributed to the States.

Paul, his wife, members of his family and friends all got together to create an atmosphere that is characteristic of the typical British pub. The beer was flowing and soon the three hundred or so guests were joining in with a few old fashioned choruses followed by the most nostalgic Beatle numbers. Among a few of the more famous personalities present were Gerry Marsden and Alan Rudkin.

The filming went on for about four hours, under the huge arc lights and surrounded by numerous camera men and crew, an exhausting business to say the least, but one hopes in the end, worth every minute of it.

Most of the National press were represented and although security was tight, one can see from our front page that 'Nite Out' had a ringside seat.

Chelsea theme and that was it. There are several pubs now in London called Chelsea Reach – but I think we were the first.

John Chase and Paddy Delaney

Although it was a pub, we fitted it out like a nightclub and got a late licence. Running the door was a bit awkward for the doormen because they didn't have recourse to the old excuse for refusing people, which was, "sorry, members only," added to the fact that it could be troublesome. Birkenhead was nearby and we were well away from our familiar stomping ground, which was Liverpool. My old pal Larry Newport agreed to take the door job for us. He was the most capable doorman I knew, being very experienced. Larry did an amazing job, handling the door virtually on his own most nights. He would simply steer people back out of the door at the same time saying "sorry, not tonight." He had a real wild eye, which made people think twice about arguing with him. We promoted it well, John did a great job of running the place and it used to get packed. Larry deserved a lot of credit for its success.

There was a girl who had entered one of my beauty contests and I remembered her dancing after the competition at the Pyramid. I dug out her entry form and got her phone number. She came to work for us as a regular 'go go' dancer. She was extremely pretty and she used to dance along the full length of the room. She had a way of smiling at the men as she moved along, making each one feel important. Remarkably, she did that job for three years and remained popular the whole time. Her name was Dinah May.

There was an electrician who did work for us (Ian Harris), who was a cousin of Paul McCartney. He told John that Paul wanted to have a reunion night out with his family, but their local pub was too small and he'd suggested the Chelsea. So it was all arranged. Paul and Linda turned up with loads of relatives and the place was absolutely packed. I was there but couldn't get closer than 15 feet to Paul and Linda. I had to hold my camera above my head to get a couple of shots of them. Of course, it made the papers and gave us welcome publicity. We didn't realise until the last minute that it was for a TV spectacular to promote Paul's new group Wings – that was the main reason I couldn't get near! Coincidentally, the programme went out in May 1973, the same month that the famous Cavern closed down, the place where the Beatles found fame.

As time went on, Larry left the Chelsea and other doormen came and went. I remember one particular night a new doorman called Steve had brought his mate in to work the night. I nicknamed him 'Warman.'

A gang came to the door and were refused, their leader was a burly guy who was very aggressive to the doorman and was fronting him up. The gang were certainly moving in and the situation was dicey. 'Warman' walked into the cocktail bar, which had its entrance right by the door. He came out and sauntered past the guy causing the problems. As he walked past him, he suddenly gave him the most almighty crack on the head with a full

Meet Miss Alluring, Beautiful, Delightful, Delectable, Demure, Delicious, Charming, Chic, Enchanting, Exciting, Sexy, Shapely, Scrumptious, Vivacious Girl of 1972

You'll gather from the title that Dinah May is the girl who has everything.

A beauty contest's judges thought so too. But the title is such a mouthful that the charity organisation who arranged the contest didn't present blonde Dinah, 19, with an official sash when she won.

For they couldn't crowd all those sparkling adjectives on to it.

Dinah said yesterday at her home in Neston, Cheshire : "I just hope I can live up to it. It's certainly very flattering.

Stunning

"I'm a bit worried, though, that if I attend functions in my official capacity it's going to be a bit of a tongue-twister for the poor person introducing me."

She added: "But the thing which attracted me to the contest in the first place was the intriguing title."

A spokesman for the Liverpool-based organisation said :

"As Dinah will be working for charity we wanted an eye-catching title for her.

"It required a stunning girl and she fills the bill admirably.

"We think she has probably the longest beauty title in the world."

Extract from the Daily Mirror, early 1970s

bottle of lager, knocking him cold! It was one of the most calculated, ruthless moves I'd seen a doorman make whilst working on the door. The rest of the gang fled and the situation was resolved!

This act was a precursor to a life of many acts of ruthlessness, this guy not giving a toss for any sort of authority! He didn't stay with us for long, but we did follow a lot of his future exploits!

A couple of years later a guy came to work at the Chelsea. He was good at the job eventually becoming head doorman. His name was Eric Gillard. That was back in 1978 and he's still there after twenty-five years, that's a long time in any job – but on a club in Merseyside, it's a lifetime.

Just a year after Eric started a young guy started to work for us at the Grand also in New Brighton. His name is Gary Sandland. He was to become one of the most impressive men I've known when it comes to fighting ability, particularly when it comes to fighting in controlled situations under pressure with nowhere to hide. Of course, I'm talking about competitive fighting sports.

Gary was 18 and already possessed an imposing persona. He'd taken up Judo at the age of 14eventually becoming 1st Dan British Champion.

After a year at the Grand, he moved over to the Chelsea to work with Eric where they made a good team.

Gary took up Shotokan Karate becoming 3rd Dan and with the British team won the British title and the European title. He moved on to Goju-Ryu, which was taught by Gary Spiers. Through Gary, he reached 4th Dan. Gary Sandland and a guy called Richie Herbert were Gary Spiers highest achievers in his Goju applied Karate.

In recent times, again through Gary Spiers, Gary took up kick boxing in 1991. By the end of 1993, he'd won numerous titles in full contact kickboxing, including Welsh Heavy weight title, British Heavy weight title, European heavy weight, also the Commonwealth, and the World heavy weight titles. When he won the World Heavyweight title in Australia, Gary had to fight a formidable opponent, Stan ('the man') Longinedus. In his previous fight; he had broken the leg of Dennis Alexis, actually snapping his leg in half at the shin with a roundhouse kick.

After becoming, World Champion Gary defended his title twelve times over the following six years.

When Gary won the European Heavyweight Kick boxing championship, the National press started to take an interest. One paper likened his knockout right cross punch to a Tornado jet at full speed, – this punch has been measured at nine hundred miles per hour! Pretty imaginative!

Gary likes to finish his fights quickly – as he said: "I get in, do the job and get out. I can punch through bricks and walls because I'm very strong, yet it's the speed and velocity that does the damage." He likens his punch to a shot from a gun.

Compared to a normal heavyweight, whose punch is more like a rock thrown from the hand. Most boxers punch with a tensed muscle, which makes it slower.

"I punch with a relaxed muscle, this way I fire the punch in quickly. It strikes before you know it's coming. I learned my punching disciplines and techniques through Karate."

The high kicking in kickboxing, sometimes necessitating being six feet in the air when it is applied, requires a very high level of fitness.

Some thugs picked on him with Baseball bats on one occasion. A bat broke his nose. It was their mistake, – they landed up in hospital.

Gary also did some amateur wrestling at our gym in Liverpool.

He's a good looking man, with a passing resemblance to Sylvester Stallone, though much bigger at six foot tall and fifteen and a half stone, and probably better looking.

Gary had been fighting in Canada against the Canadian Heavy weight champion. The fight was on Canadian National TV and also on American TV. Film-makers who were watching the kickboxing and the following interview with Gary were impressed by his personality and resemblance to S.Stallone. They contacted his agent in Birmingham, England and invited him over to Los Angeles for screen tests. They sent him 1st class tickets for three people and initially offered him a stand in part for S. Stallone in a film called *The Assassin*. He followed this up with two or three other parts and they asked him to move to L.A. He declined because of business and family commitments, however he has recently had parts in some British based films including, *51st State*, with Samuel L. Jackson, – *My Kingdom*, with Richard Harris and *Rich Man Eddie*, a TV film.

Gary told me whilst on the set he was very impressed by the stunt men's multi skills such as sword fencing, horse riding, diving, etc. The only thing he had was his fighting knowledge.

The fight choreographer was telling him what to do; Gary was thinking to himself he would do it differently. Later on while having a drink with the stunt men, he mentioned it. They said he should tell the producer, he did this, explaining that punches from a 15 stone man would have a far greater effect than in the way he portrayed it.

The producer said: "Show us how you'd do it."

He did it showing how he'd flatten three men in short time. He did it in one take; they were thrilled and got him to do the choreography after that.

He enjoys the film work though it's a part time occupation for Gary.

During my recent years, Gary worked the door for me at the Kingsway in Southport; he just enjoyed the place and looked on the job as a convivial night out. He didn't need the money! Having said that, the job was not always a bed of roses, and there were some hairy situations to deal with during his time there. Although it's not my intention in this book to deal with these years, – there was one occasion which deserves a mention whilst writing about Gary Sandland.

One of my doormen at the Kingsway, Steve Core, was getting married and the doormen decided to have a stag party in Greece. I'll tell the story as related to me by Gary ……

We were all good friends and so got on really well, and on deciding to have the week away, some of us, Steve McKay, Garth Graham, and myself, stipulated that if two friends of a couple of doormen, (who were not doormen) were joining us, then, – we wouldn't go. These two guys were notorious troublemakers – and all we wanted was a good time. We eventually went on the holiday, – these two guys didn't come with us, however, three days into the holiday, these characters showed up. By this time we'd established ourselves, we

World Heavyweight Kick Boxing Champ Gary Sandland

8 PAGES OF SUNSPORT TAKE SOME BEATING

My 900mph punch lands faster than a jet

KICK BOXER GARY IN WORLD TITLE SHOT

Extract from The Sun, Tuesday, May 25, 1993

were a group of nine or ten men, all very well built – some with very good physiques, some with fantastic physiques – and everyone in the town knew of us.

We used to do acrobatics on the beach, performing stunts, not in an aggressive way, but in an entertaining fashion. On the third night we went to a club, we'd frequented, which unknown to us was the hangout of the local mafia, – for want of a better term. Lots of the local club owners from Kabos used to go there.

So – we're having a night out. The next thing, one of these particular lads, who we didn't want to be with, was arguing with the doorman. I was looking right at him, right at the start of the incident. This idiot looked around to see what support he had, and punched the doorman right in the face.

The doorman rolled over, got to his feet, and went straight out to the door. I turned round, put my drink down, thinking – oh my God what's going to happen now.

Next thing, the doormen that were available, came charging in – probably six or seven of them. There were about nine or ten of us – we'd been drinking for most of the evening and it was now two o-clock in the morning. We weren't drunk, but we'd had a considerable amount to drink. There was a head doorman, a big bulky guy who was carrying a baton – it was like a long Policeman's truncheon. They came storming in – they had C.S. gas, knives, and batons. You know the score Roy – if a doorman's been attacked, all hands grab what they can and get involved, now these guys were used to dealing with all kinds, it being a holiday resort – so they were well prepared for it. This head doorman made his way straight at me – he tried to strike me across the head with the baton – which I stopped with my forearm, and kind of took it under my arm, swept him to the floor in a typical Karate move and punched him a couple of times and tried to pull the baton off him. Un-beknownst to me he had it strapped to his wrist, so he couldn't release it. From short range, I must have hit him six or seven times, until he couldn't move. Realising then that I had to untie the baton, I turned round and there's mayhem everywhere – there's bottles gettin' smashed on peoples heads, there's two or three doormen on the floor, there's a doorman trying to slash at people with a knife – it ended up with the doormen backing off a bit. Because we'd gained the major upper hand, they stood back and let us make our way into the street.

There was now six or seven of us walking down the street, when these two hooligan's, as I call them, ran up to the nearest group of lads playing Pool, shouting at them.

"Are you Greek?" One said: "Yes" – so he smashed him in the face.

The guy falls onto the floor and he jumped right on his head, I thought, he's killed this lad here. What happened then, was we've now got that bunch of lads, after us, as well? There's a group of doormen running from door to door, saying: "Come on lads, we've got a gang of thugs here, lets get them!" I've got this baton in my hand – there's myself, Garth, Steve McKay and Frank Valerio, who all worked at the Kingsway together, as you know, Roy. We're running down the street, turned down an alley, 'cos the road ran parallel to the beach, knowing that our accommodation was a mile or so down the beach. We ran down the alley to the beach, turned round, and silhouetted against the sky in front of the town lights, were at least fifteen or twenty fella's, running after us. There's now just the four of us, the others had jumped over hedges, laid on the floor, whatever. The ones who'd instigated the whole thing had disappeared. We run down the beach while they're firing bullets at us. It's serious. They shot at us six or seven times, we turned up the alley which we recognised as our own, a very straight street with light at the far end – none at the beach end.

One group were chasing us along the beach and another group had run along the parallel road, looking down the alleyways. They spotted us and headed down the alleyway. We were now halfway up, just outside our accommodation. There were seven of them, and another seven coming up from the beach end. We were trapped!

It was like an old movie, we stood back to back, one thing that stuck in my mind, was that one of them was brandishing a car exhaust pipe, they were all tooled up.

They came at us and it was mayhem again – we were punching, kicking – whatever.

I dropped the baton and, thank God, Garth picked it up. We were all karate men.

And Garth was like myself – a Goju-Ryu; very accomplished, and very highly rated. We were all very adept, but Garth steamed in like a Ninja – he was everywhere. People's heads, legs, and arms, whatever. I was tussling with three or four; a particular guy jumped on me and bit me on the shoulder, taking a chunk out. As I forced him off, I saw a glint of something coming at me, which I thought was a baton, and ducked my head into it, only to find it was a machete, which jammed and stuck in my skull. It was one of those instances in time you remember, he looked at me and I looked back at him. I think he expected my head to fall in half. I think I did too! And I punched him. As he fell down, the machete dropped with him. I pushed another guy, Garth hit him with the baton right across the face, I turned round, Steve McKay had fallen to the floor, a fellow's got a metal pole about six feet long, T-shaped at the end, he was smashing Steve on the head with it. Steve had all these horrendous gashes on his skull. He has them to this day. I grabbed hold of this pole and swung it round, smashed his attacker across the face with it. Steve managed to get to his feet, and we carried on tussling with them. Unfortunately for us I think. We were four capable men, they were probably fifteen or sixteen men strong, not particularly fighters, just grabbed things for weapons and came after us. When they were hit once, they didn't want to fight. I'm not saying we were super heroes, but when the chips are down, everything helps. Eventually, there was a pile of bodies, with only one left fighting. He turned and ran. We got into our apartment and decided to get out before any more of them came back. I had to help Steve to get up this eight-foot wall, Garth pulled him from above, Frank got over the wall, and there's only one left, which was me. Two lads came back, but they couldn't fight, and when they rushed me, I was lucky enough to be able to sort them out. They were unconscious and I could hear the sound of feet running. I couldn't get up the wall, so I jumped into a bush, which was literally right next to me; there were two unconscious guys in front of me. The crowd ran in and helped these guys out, I heard them chunnering away as they went. I looked through the bush, between two gateposts. On a driveway, I could see a mass of six or seven bodies, motionless, shoes, weapons, and poles, all over the deck. I put my hand to my head and I could feel blood hitting it, so I had to take off my brand new shirt, which I had bought for the holiday, and wrap it round my head to suppress the blood, I must have looked like 'Bugs Bunny.' I sat there for a few minutes, and in that moment in time, I felt terrified, I thought these lads are gonna' come back, I can't get over this wall. They're gonna' find me, so much damage has been done to these people, they're gonna' slit my throat and take me out in a boat and weigh me down and dump me. I was terrified. I heard voices – thinking – here we go.

Garth Graham

Fortunately, it was two lads with two girls, who weren't with us. They came round the corner and saw the bodies everywhere. One of the lads was Paddy, a Kingsway doorman. They helped me over the wall, where there was a white marble path, which looked like someone had trailed a gallon of red paint all along it. I followed the trail to a door and knocked. Two lads answered and let me in; they'd just arrived on holiday. They'd let the other lads in and sheltered us all for the night. We had to ferry ourselves three or four at a timeout of the town, in disguise. We got someone to get our cases. The reps came in the middle of the night, – they said: – They're looking for you all over town, the last time this happened they followed them to the airport, dragged them out and shot them in the legs, you've done some horrendous damage to these people, particularly the head doorman, who's in a bad way. We had to get on the midnight ferry and hire a boat to take us to mainland Italy, from where we flew home. That was a stag do, to remember, 'tho' I think they'd rather forget it!

Gary still teaches applied Karate e.g. the use of elbows, head butts, choking, kicking, and punching. He still puts time in at the Chelsea, though now as the owner. He also owns at least one other club and several gyms. We are good pals and have been for years.

* * *

A popular place in the mid-seventies, was a Greek restaurant called Renos's Taverner in York Street, by Ugly's Club on the corner in Duke Street. The owner Renos was a popular figure with star quality. He was a Cypriot, flamboyant and good looking. We would often go to his restaurant after the club had closed at the weekend. 4am wasn't unusual, it would still be busy. He did terrific steaks, prawns and lamb dishes with rice in the traditional style. A friend told me he went with Renos on a short trip to Cyprus. He said there was a crowd waiting for him at the airport. He was their celebrity.

Renos had left Cyprus in 1957 and came to England in 1959.

He'd met up with a dancer, an Anglo Indian girl. They started a relationship, she was in a group with an American boy and doing a cabaret routine. Renos went along with her to the various gigs. One of the shows was in Bat-a-dan, the club. Renos went for a drink and met up with a guy named Raymond Nash. When the group were rehearsing in London he used to come and listen to them, he loved the accompaniment to their dance routines which was Congo drums, and bongos etc. One night when they were in Geneva, Renos bumped into him again. They had a few drinks and went to a night club, giving Renos his card when they parted, suggesting Renos look him up the next time he was in London.

The cabaret job went a bit sour and they got stranded in Paris, where they'd been doing a show. They managed to get the night train to London where they were both stranded; they contacted a couple of friends who put them up.

Renos was looking through his wallet and found the card Raymond Nash – so he called him, – he had nothing to lose. He said: "Where are you?" "I'll come and pick you up", Renos said: "It's OK – I'll find you". He was living in Earls Court, he went to se him and told him what had been happening and he very kindly gave him some money to tide him over. Renos could see he was doing well , driving a Rolls Royce, living in a nice place, so he said: "Could you give me a job – in my situation, anything will do?"

He said: "How about doing a door job in one of our clubs?" Renos said: "No problem!" He was young, twenty-two years old and up for anything He sent him to a club called Le Chelle, Renos told me, "I saw the manager who went through the door routine with me, and I had a job". "There were two or three other guys on the door so it was no great pressure". "Six months went by and they were given notice to quit, – the lease was running out". "I offered to take it over for the remainder of the lease". "I was paying them £100 per week, a quite substantial rent, equivalent to £1,000 per week now". "I made sure I missed no payments and was doing alright'. "Now the consortium who had the club didn't own it". "It belonged to Peter Rachman, – he used to come in with his girlfriend Mandy Rice Davies who always carried a little Chihuahua dog in her arms". "Sometimes Christine Keeler would also come in".

This was a couple of years before the notorious Profumo affair when the Secretary of State for War was involved with a call girl sharing her (Christine Keeler) with a Russian Intelligence agent, ending Profumo's political career in 1963.

Renos got to know Peter Rachman well, they spent a good bit of time talking and drinking together. One night he said to Renos, "This place is finished – you have a look around my properties and tell me which one you fancy".

Renos found a nice property on the corner of West Cromwell Road in Earls Court. He told Peter which property it was, telling him he really liked it.

It was a five storey building with a nice basement for a club. Rachman said: – "O. K. it's all yours" – he went away and came back with a cheque for £1,000 in 1960.

He said: "Start the work, if you need more let me know". So Renos took any useful equipment he needed from the old club, which was nearby. In no time he was in business there, calling it the same name Le Chelle. Around this time gambling was legalised, so Renos converted the ground floor into a casino. There were lots of students in the area, Arabs, Iranians, Philippinos, etc. They were all wealthy students, driving expensive sports cars and so on.

Renos was making a lot of money. Peter Rachman sent his man every week for his money and everyone was happy. The collector was called Jim Houlihan.

This went on for two years, then suddenly Renos got the news – Peter Rachman had died. It was a big shock, when Renos had taken the place he refused a lease, he didn't really want to be tied into anything at that stage. Unfortunately, the consequence was that he had no legal rights and he was left with nothing. All the other guys in his position who had taken leases, finished up with their properties. Rachman never leased in his own name, he was after all, the notorious Rachman – the property shark. This reputation was undeserved, but that's another story. Once again Renos was stranded.

He and his girlfriend split up and Renos decided to visit a pal in Liverpool. He decided to stay a while and with his catering experience, started working for the Deering restaurants becoming Head waiter at the Mariners in Lord Street.

It was now 1964, – he moved on to the Boulevard in Southport.

Renos had met a girl called Frankie in Liverpool who was a local beauty and part-time model, they moved onto London where they married and had three children. Eventually they came back to Liverpool and Renos opened Renos's Taverna in York Street in Liverpool.

* * *

Another well known Merseyside character is Robbie Davis who's prime joy in life was the noble art.

Before taking up boxing Robbie was a young tearaway, always up to mischief and always fighting. He was a real pain to doormen – in fact, Terry O'Neill told Robbie that he was thankful to him for keeping him in work! However, once he took up the sport of boxing he knew it was his destiny.

He had a busy amateur career.

He went to the Commonwealth Games in New Zealand in 1974 where he fought Lotte Mwale who finished up fighting for the World Light Heavyweight title, Robbie had knocked him down in the first round starting the count.

In the run up to the European Games in 1974 he was sparring with Pat Cowdell. They had light dumbbells in their hands and as Robbie ducked to the left, was caught on the nose by Cowdell, creating a wound down the centre of his face which required ten stitches in his nose, consequently he missed the Games. He boxed Billy Lauder of Scotland in the Olympic trial, at Crystal Palace. As he caught Lauder on the chin with his right he went back over the ropes causing the accompanying left to the midriff to go low, disqualifying Robbie.

He competed in the Montreal Olympics in 1976 and in 1977 he won the A.B.A. Middleweight title against Roger Maxwell with a first round knockout. Then on to the European Games in Halle, East Germany. Robbie went steaming in with his characteristic roundhouse punching; he was also accused of throwing a head-butt. They disqualified him for boxing like a professional.

In between these events he boxed for England many times before turning professional.

Whilst standing in line at the Olympics, another boxer nudged him, saying, – "Look who's behind you!" Robbie looked round to see Princess Anne who was competing in the three day event horse trials.

Robbie said: "Ello there girl – ows your ma?"

Princess Anne smiled and said: "Very well, Thankyou." Robbie grabbed a camera and got someone to take a picture of him with the Princess. He still treasures that photo.

Upon turning professional he derived even more enjoyment from the sport. He was obviously a very capable boxer and appeared at Liverpool Stadium on numerous occasions. He loved the atmosphere of the Stadium with it's crowds of enthusiasts, which to Robbie was an integral part of the sport.

When the tickets to the Stadium were printed with Robbie on the bill, he would call into various shops, clubs, restaurants, bookies etc., where he knew the people and flog them tickets for the night. I always bought some tickets and went to support him. The personal touch made the night more interesting and he always got a good turn out. I remember the last time he came to the office with the tickets. He said to me: "Roy, if I win this, – it will be my last fight."

Robbie Davis meets Princess Anne at the Olympic Games.

Now Robbie was a rugged looking guy, – in fact, to say he was rugged looking was an understatement. This was largely due to his nose, which was probably the most damaged nose I've seen.

When he looked straight at you, the tip of his nose looked as if it rested against his cheek just below his eye, so that from a frontal view, you looked at the side of his nose.

When he said he'd be packing it in if he won, I said: "If that's the case, you'd better go out and win and as a present, I'll get you a new nose!" We shook hands on it and after the fight I phoned a cosmetic surgeon in Liverpool's Rodney Street and arranged an appointment for him.

After turning pro, Robbie's nose starts to show for it.

Robbie went on his own to the appointment. He was a bit put out by the surgeon who laughed when he looked at Robbie's nose, saying it was the worst he'd ever seen.

I think he wanted to emphasise the fact that it was a difficult job.

After the operation Robbie came to see me – the transformation was incredible.

He had a perfectly balanced straight nose and was now ruggedly handsome. He told me he was having to fight the women off – which I'm sure was a lot less painful than the fighting he'd been used to.

Robbie's still a popular figure around town.

Left to right – back row: Kevin McGuire, Paul Chase, Finlay Buchanen; front row: Tony Adams, Manooch Gorbanion, Mahmoud, Tony Watling.

My darling daughter Diane

No. 1 son Rowland

No. 3 son Paul

MY BOYS

No. 2 son Tony

Miss Pyramid, Jenny McAdam wins the Miss Night Club of Gt. Britain, receiving a £1,000 cheque from Bob Monkhouse.

~ 16 ~
Gatsby Girls and Punk

AFTER REALISING THAT I couldn't completely replicate the Cavern, I closed it down and converted it into two clubs; Gatsby's on the ground floor and the Revolution in the basement. Gatsby's was reasonably successful, the Revolution less so, although both were great atmospheric places. To walk into the Revolution, you had to pass between the heads of Che Guevara and Fidel Castro. These heads were eight feet high and about seven feet across. Girls used to sit on Castro's cigar, waiting for their friends. Back of the stage was a terrific sculpture of Jimi Hendrix head, his hair spread out to the sides, spanning about fifteen feet, plus many other revolutionary figures.

Gatsby's was art deco and very large. When I opened I engaged a dancing troupe, which we called the Gatsby Girls. Their act was choreographed by Nora Button who did the same job for the Royal Court and other theatres. They were all attractive girls and wore turn of the century type costumes, with corseted waists, long legs and feather boas, creating a very stylish clubby atmosphere. I put on various types of cabaret, including comedians, singers and groups. Friday lunchtimes we used to get busy with local solicitors and other professionals who'd entertain their clients to lunch. I started putting two exotic dancers and a comedian on. I remember lunchtime one day, I had local comedian Jackie Hamilton, who was invariably intoxicated by lunchtime! The two girls who were on before him were particularly attractive and as the last one finished her spot, Jackie slouched on, cigarette dangling from his mouth. He said: "Did yeh see dem? Did yeh? Weren't dey gorgeous? An tink o' dem tings we've gorra go 'ome to!" This was funny and I was really tickled, but I looked across at my solicitor Peter and his friends and thought about his particularly attractive wife, Leslie, wondering what they made of it. Fortunately they were amused. The tables were arranged around the semi-circular dance floor. I remember one particular night when a group of paraplegic girls came in and we arranged their wheelchairs around the dance floor. A group of young guys came in; it was early on with not much happening. The disco was playing and one of the lads approached one of the girls and said.

"Are you getting up?" She spread her hands out appealingly.

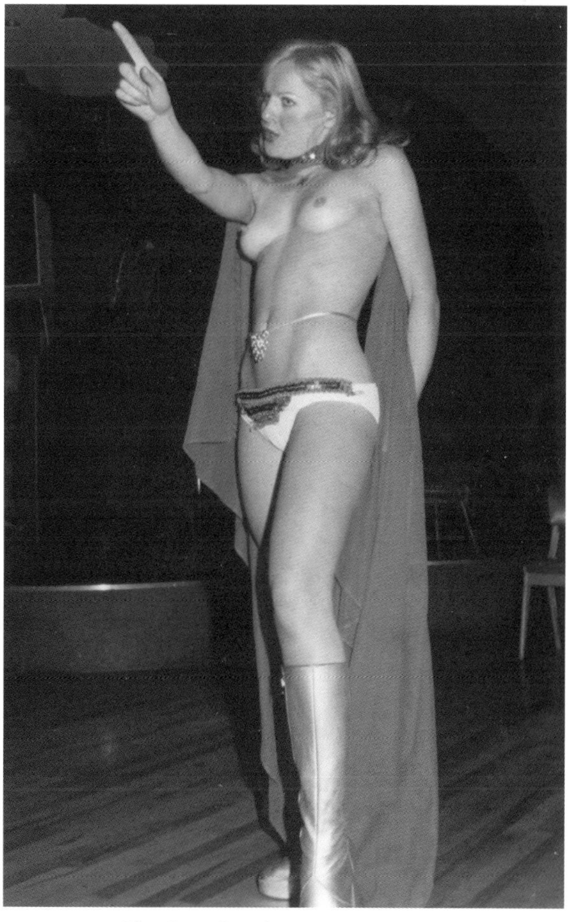

Charlie (Gatsby Exotic Dancer)

Into the Revolution

He bent forward and said: "Put your arms around my neck". She did and he lifted her out of her chair and held her up by her bottom and proceeded to dance round the floor. His pals did the same. Those lads stayed practically the whole evening, buying the girls drinks and giving them the time of their lives. It was the sort of scene you'd only see in Liverpool!

There was an odd-looking girl who used to walk up and down Matthew Street. She wore deathly-white makeup, with black lipstick; her head was shaved completely bald, black shadows painted around her eyes. Her name was Jayne. She was way ahead of the Punk revolution, which started some time later. She palled up with a lad who was as strange as she was, he also had a shaved head and scruffy clothes. They used to walk up and down Matthew Street, sometimes sitting on the step of the Revolution, looking really spaced out – this was a deliberate look.

Her full name was Jayne Casey and she helped form a punk band, which had some success – it was called Big in Japan.

His name was Holly Johnson, who eventually made it big with Frankie goes to Hollywood.

Around this time, a trio became popular round the clubs – it was headed by a pretty girl with short hair, called Etna – she played the violin beautifully. One of the lads in the trio was Paul McGann, now a well known actor – they were called Special Brew.

I booked the Sex Pistols with Johnny Rotten and Sid Vicious it was one of their first bookings being in their earliest days. They were obviously extremely vile, spitting at the audience and screaming down the mike. Soon after this, Roger Eagle, who had been working as a D.J. at the Twisted Wheel in Manchester, asked if he could rent the Revolution with a couple of friends, Pete Fulwell and Ken Teste. They called it Eric's and it became home of the punks!

Roger was a six foot three inch good-looking man. His prime interest was music, being extremely knowledgeable about trends, styles, bands and performers. He was well spoken and favoured a collar and tie and tweed jacket. In fact he was the antithesis of the Punk style which he promoted. I knew him for a couple of years before he created Erics club. He helped me find acts for Gatsbys and the New Cavern, enjoying the Mathew Street atmosphere.

There was a café in Matthew Street called Antwackys which also sold second hand clothes, where like-minded people used to meet forming a nucleus for the coming cult.

Jayne and Holly obviously walked up Matthew Street from Antwackys, and enjoyed soaking up the Cavern magic.

It turned out that Big in Japan was to become a very influential group on the punk scene.

Holly Johnson played bass for a while in the group, as did Clive Langer.

Jayne Casey was lead singer. They epitomised what Erics was all about at that time. Roger Eagle gave them their debut at Erics where they also gave their last performance, before, as it turned out, prematurely breaking up.

Roger Eagle also produced his own record label also called Erics – Big in Japan did put out a single on the label, as did Holly Johnson, with two singles as a solo artiste.

The Punk era became a worldwide phenomena. Quite a lot of the bands still exist today. Although Erics was created in my club, it was a completely foreign scene to me. I took little interest, being heavily involved in my other places at the time. Names of some of the groups I do still remember.

Deaf School comes to mind as a band with more experience and ability than most. Groups such as Siouxsie and the Banshees, the Lurkers and Wayne County and The Electric Chair played there. Wayne appeared at Erics wearing a nightdress and calling himself Jayne County.

They had a number one hit in the alternative charts with their E.P. *'Blatantly Offensive'*, – the first song on the E.P. was titled *'Fuck Off'*! – typically Punk.

The Lurkers recorded on Beggars Banquet records.

A fairly high profile figure was Pete Wylie with his band The Farm.

Tony Wilson who was an announcer on Granada TV was always there, as was Elvis Costello. Lots of future names came to Erics – it spawned places like the Hacienda in Manchester, which Tony Wilson and Roger Eagle were both involved in. Curiously, Roger Eagle's favourite record of all time was, *'Sixteen Tons'* with Tennessee Ernie Ford.

Roger went back to Manchester to become involved with Gareth Evans at the International.

Sad to say, Roger Eagle has since died – quite prematurely.

Erics was arguably as inspirational to the music scene as the Cavern.

* * *

Pete Price (who was a successful comedian and well-known character) approached me one day and suggested that we got together and raise money for a commemorative sculpture dedicated to the Beatles after the old Cavern closed. We commissioned Arthur Dooley who was a quite famous local sculptor, a controversial character who had been featured on *'This Is Your Life'* on TV. Arthur was a rumbustuous guy to say the least. When Eamonn Andrews approached him with his red book, saying, "This is your life", Arthur told him to fuck off. However, the show did go on, cutting that bit out!

Arthur had been in the Irish Guards with me and there's a bit of a story to him! When I joined the battalion in Germany, Arthur was already an old soldier, having been in since he was a boy. Arthur also had aspirations when it came to boxing. He was very enthusiastic and when the battalion was stationed at Chelsea barracks, he liked to go for a run in the mornings.

He'd run across London Bridge wearing Army denims, an old sweater and pumps on his feet, shadow boxing and frightening the lives out of office workers and others who were walking to work. He'd trot around some of them throwing punches over their shoulders and snorting and blowing theatrically as he made his way... Unfortunately, although handy with his fists, he never quite made it into the battalion boxing team.

When we joined the battalion at Dusseldorf, on visiting the NAAFI in the barracks, Arthur greeted my hoppos and myself at the door. His greeting was "Hello there mucker – lend us a ha'penny." We were flattered that a Guardsman in the battalion actually spoke to us. He caught us one at a time and we all gave him a ha'penny. He always wore denim and had plimsolls on his feet. He was excused boots and was in charge of one of the battalion dogs. He would bring the dog into the NAAFI and everyone would give it bits to eat, which meant that Arthur was able to save the dog's meat allowance. When he was due to go on leave, he stood on the table and said: "Gentlemen, I'm going on leave and I've just drawn eighty pounds to go with, thanks to your kind contributions!" Eighty pounds was a substantial amount of money in 1951!

Arthur had handled substantial money before. When he was with the Irish Guards battalion in Tripoli, he had just completed twenty-four hours guard duty when the sergeant informed him that due to a 'problem' (I don't know what), he would have to stay on guard duty for the next twenty-four hours. Arthur said something like: "Fuck this for a game of soldiers" and did a runner taking his Bren gun. He took up with a band of Arabs who made him a leader. They started holding up and stealing army trucks and selling them in the Arab markets. Arthur eventually gave himself up. He was apparently almost unrecognisable in his Arab garb, including the obligatory beard. He had a massive roll of notes too! (Currency that is!)

Arthur Dooley

This was before I met him, so I can't confirm any of it, tho' it was legend in the battalion. He was sent to Bederfelt detention barracks and after a time back to the battalion, where he befriended the battalion priest, Father Daley, and became a Catholic. When I was demobbed, I met up with Arthur and he talked me into going on a retreat with the Jesuits at Loyola Hall, just outside Liverpool. This was for four days and included a vow of silence except for religious matters. I was tearing my hair out with the boredom when one evening I heard a loud voice down the hall. Arthur was sat on his bed reading from the Bible in a very strong scouse accent: "Hiya Roy, de say readin' out loud 'elps ya talk prop'ly." As it happens, as time went on and he would appear on TV and radio, his scouse accent came in to good effect!

He called at my mum's house one day, saying: "Here y'are Roy, what d'ya think of these?" He was holding a wax figure of Christ, which he'd made, and a head and shoulder also. They were very primitive and childlike, but I did think they had something and said so. He said: "That's good, cos I'm putting in a bid to do the Stations of the Cross at the Church of Little St Bride in Catherine Street. In wood!" I asked him if he'd done any woodcarving and he hadn't. I told him to have a word with Charlie Thompson, who had been in our battalion and was a wonderful wood carver, knowing he would show him what a skilled trade it was. He didn't get the job. Arthur was undaunted and went ahead with his wax figures eventually turning them into bronzes. He put in a bid to do the Stations of the Cross at a new church in Leyland, Lancashire. Epstein, the famous sculptor who made the statue for Lewis's building, apparently also bid for it at, I believe, £8,000. Arthur got the commission because his fee was so low – £1,000 for the twelve sculptings! He offered me a daytime job taking him to the foundry in my little Morris van. I was doing the door job at nights. I also helped him in his workshop finishing off the figures etc. The commission was a success. A lot of people visit the Leyland church just to see his sculptings.

Sometimes on the way to the foundry, he'd stop and go into the bank. I went with him one day and he came gleefully out of the manager's office saying "He's let me have another fiver on my overdraft." He went to the counter with a cheque for five pounds. The teller said: "How would you like it Mr Dooley?" He said: "Give it to me in gold." We went to the cigarette shop next door where he bought 5 woodbines for two and three pence, asking the girl if she'd take a cheque! He also started preaching at lunchtimes to groups of young people, mainly schoolgirls, who were fascinated by the amount of swearing he indulged in! He also famously had an iron sculpting stolen from the Jacaranda in Slater Street, which was to be a hang out for the Beatles – this brought him publicity.

During the time he did the Leyland Church, he lived from hand to mouth, his bid had been far too low. He was living in an empty shop in the front room on the ground floor next door to the Jacaranda. The front door was permanently open. I'd go in and knock on the door on the left of the passageway. Arthur had fitted a metal sheet over this door. When I banged on it he'd shout "Fuck off!" When I'd done this three times, I'd say "Okay Arthur, get yourself to the foundry – I'm off!" He'd then shout "OK" and throw back the bolt, dashing back into bed. It was an old iron bedstead with all the bedposts leaning inwards. He'd be rolled up in an old Mexican patterned blanket. It was freezing cold, the windows were all broken and he'd wedged pieces of polystyrene in the broken panes to try and keep the weather out. There was a trestle table and a dustbin in the centre of the floor, which was bare board. There was yellow wax everywhere. The blanket was wrapped round his head and he'd try to look appealing without his teeth in. He'd say "Go and get us a bacon butty and a cup of tea from the Jac. Oh, and a bottle of Lysol!" which was a very strong disinfectant. I remember on this particular day bringing his tea and butty, after wolfing them down he jumped out of bed and poured the hot water from the kettle into a plastic hand basin. He then poured in the whole bottle of Lysol and threw off his blanket. No wonder he was cold – he wasn't wearing a stitch, although he was (luckily) covered in hair. He then started to cup the water in his hands and splash it all over his body, at the same time saying "That'll sort you out, you German bastards!" As he grabbed his trousers, some money fell on the floor. He picked it up, throwing some ha'pennies in the bin saying: "I hate fuckin' ha'pennies, don't you?"

If, on the way to the foundry, we passed someone pushing a handcart or sweeping in the street, he'd tell me to stop so that he could give them a couple of bob, in spite of the fact that he really couldn't afford it!

Dooley expects Beatles' statue to shock

By Edna Ellis

LIVERPOOL sculptor Arthur Dooley, put the finishing touches to his monument to the Beatles last night and said: "A lot of people will dislike it but nobody will be indifferent."

Beatle fans from all over the country are expected to travel to Liverpool today for the unveiling of the Beatles "shrine" which will be placed high on the wall of the famous Cavern club in Mathew Street.

But those who are expecting to find a statue in the image of the famous four are in for a shock.

Arthur's gold coloured sculpture is of a woman, representing Mother Liverpool, with three babies. The fourth, which is holding a trumpet, will be placed on the wall nearby.

Said Arthur: "The only thing that I will say to people who don't like it is that this is my interpretation and that has got to be accepted. I think it would have been rather staid if I had just done four statues of the Beatles.

Arthur Dooley has also made a street sign for Mathew Street. It will be placed near the plaque and Arthur is hoping that the famous home of the Cavern officially beome Beatle Street.

Left to right: George Pateman, Roy Adams, Pete Price, The Spinners, Alan Rudkin (centre front) and Tom O'Connor (rear) at the unveiling of Arthur Dooley's 'Four Who Shook The World'

Pete Price and I set about raising money for the Beatles sculpting. I put a do on at Gatsby's and Pete raised money at various gigs. When Arthur came to do the job, I went along to see how he was getting on. He'd made a figure of the Virgin Mary in fibreglass which I presumed that he was going to use as some sort of base for the final sculpting. However, when he put it together on the wall outside the Cavern he had placed three babies in the arms of the figure of Mary, the fourth baby was attached to the wall, it was flying and represented Wings. Underneath was written 'The Four Who Changed the World'. We met up to view the finished article, which was unveiled by local folk group The Spinners. Arthur gave an explanation – something about Byzantine figures representing the Beatles with Wings with their mother figure representing the city of Liverpool! This seemed to satisfy everyone, although I was quietly disappointed. Arthur's works were no strangers to controversy. Back in 1969, he had made a statue, which was placed on the wall of the ultra modern Princess Park Methodist Church. It was an impressive piece of work in as much as it was the figure of the crucified Christ. There was no cross just the figure which was leaning out from the wall at an angle of thirty degrees the feet against the wall and the arms extended upwards in a V shape.

When it was unveiled, it sparked off a rash of threatening phone calls to the chairman of the Liverpool Methodist area Reverend Reginald Kissack over the erection of a dynamic but black statue of Christ. There were threats to burn down the church and Liverpool C.I.D. launched a full-scale investigation and set up various precautions. One theory was that the fuss was not because the statue was black – which it wasn't anyway but that the prostitutes of the area felt that the figure of Christ was damaging their trade. A leaflet was circulated pointing out that the figure was not intended to be black and is in fact multi coloured although it looks dark, its made up of brown orange black yellow pink red and green combined by Mr Dooley to contrast against the light brick wall of the church. His idea being to produce his own interpretation of a multi racial Christ. It certainly raised public interest and gave Arthur more publicity.

Arthur carried on, getting himself a studio in Seel Street. He was popular and had visitors from as far away as Sweden and America, plus many friends from TV.

Arthur introduced me to a man who he thought could help me with promotions when

I opened the Gatsbys club. He was a tall good looking man in his fifties: – his name was George Sheppard. His speciality was raising money for the Blind as a result of which he knew a lot of celebrities. Some of these celebs had a particular interest either because family members, or they themselves had sight problems.

One person who worked a lot with him in the North West, was Anne Kirkbride. (*Coronation Street's* Deidre.) He told me she was always willing to put herself out if it was for the Blind. I'm pleased that her career is still successful, as a caring person, she deserves it.

However, for my purposes he said he could arrange for the world's top performer to do a night for me. He said if the venue could hold a thousand people, he would do a concert for the Blind.

This was in the mid nineteen seventies and Elton John was the world's highest paid performer, – in spite of this he'd said he would do it. His conditions were that we charged five pounds per head so that we'd raise five thousand pounds for the Blind. David said that John Lennon would come in towards the end of the show, as a surprise guest. He said Elton wanted the tickets to go to ordinary working class kids, – he didn't want the rich kids with the E Type Jaguars. David said my responsibility was to bring the police in – they would have to close the nearby streets to traffic as John Lennon was hyper about security – he said he was convinced someone would try to kill him.

It was obviously a great opportunity – but I decided not to go for it. For one thing I wasn't sure I could get a thousand working class kids to cough up five pounds each – a lot of money then. I'd be expected to pay any shortfall. I'd also have to pay the policing costs, which would be considerable.

I didn't mind paying out so much as I minded maybe having a poor turnout. Having said that I did regret not biting the bullet later on – it wasn't like me not to have a go at it. I think the fact that it was a really bad economic time just then, had a lot to do with it.

When John Lennon got shot in New York I realised that his fears had been justified. Fears, which I had thought, were just showbiz hype.

Arthur Dooley sadly died in 1994, aged sixty-five. A requiem mass was held for him at St Joseph's in Kirkby, with a commendation by Canon Frayling. Six priests were on the altar, including a bishop and two canons – they were a mixture of denominations, Catholic and Protestant. He was certainly highly respected for his good works!

Legendary figure Serge Nubret, Roy and John Brown after his Mr. Universe win

Roy aged 53 with Sheilagh in Majorca

Norman and Roy, (Majorca, 1998)

Tony Buck, 2003

Spencer Churchill at 74 years.

Terry O'Neill and Roy, Liverpool, 2002

With Robbie Davis, 2003

Below: Roy with Norman Paterson, Tony Buck and Pat McMullen, 2001

And finally…

ERIC ARMITAGE, who owned Leighton Court on the Wirral, purchased Sir Richard Formby's family house in Formby, which was called Shorrocks Hill. He converted it into a very nice country club with a restaurant, outdoors pool etc. He ran it for a couple of years and eventually sold it to Jim Simpson (a business friend) and myself.

I did a conversion job on it and introduced various artefacts. The main one being a mounted elephant head, which came from Eden Hall in Chester, this thing weighed close on a ton, the skull and jawbones weighed 4cwt! It became very popular and people like Bruce Forsyth, Kenny Lynch, Jimmy Tarbuck and all the top footballers at the time, mainly Liverpool and Everton players, used to be regulars. Ellen basically managed the place, I mainly worked the door usually with one doorman, sometimes two – names I can think of were Richie Harper, Tony Buck, and the impressive Tierney brothers, Bill and Jim, these fellows also worked other doors for me. After a couple of years Ellen brought in an assistant called Keith Airey who took over the management doing a great job for seven years.

Paul Chase while still quite young, came to work at Shorrocks Hill Country Club for me. Paul still retained the family ability to speak English in beautifully moderated tones. I remember one occasion at Shorrocks Hill; a mixed crowd from Kirkby was refused at the door. (Kirkby in those days had a bad reputation. Families had been uprooted from Liverpool city after the war and shipped to Kirkby about five miles out of town. The mix of people from different areas of Liverpool didn't always work out). One of the women started shouting abuse at the doormen. She screamed:

"You lot 'ave 'ad it. Arf a Kirkby'll be 'ere tomorra. Take it from me, you'll 'ave 'arf a Kirkby to deal with!"

Paul heard all the yelling and came out of the cocktail bar with a glass of brandy in his hand, saying in his posh voice "Who is this Arthur Kirkby?"

Paul nowadays has a business running courses for licensees and door staff, so that they can obtain the required certificates and door badges needed these days. He's also involved in the licensed trade.

Shorrocks was extremely popular one of it's main features being what I described as a 'Gastronomic Round the World Tour', each Wednesday night.

We had a great chef called Ronnie Malpas who created a magnificent buffet, each week featuring food from a different country. Starting with Merrie England – a really special one which launched the promotion. In the summer we had barbeques and swimming in the outdoor pool. I had Shorrocks Hill for ten years, actually selling it in 1981.

* * *

This was the last place I owned within the first twenty years which I've set myself. Ellen and I finally went our separate ways back in 1982. Things hadn't worked out for us for some time – so we called it a day, getting a divorce. Our children Rowland, Tony, Diane and Paul are now grown up with kids of their own and happily we have all remained very close. I'm immensely proud of them all – Ellen is still a close friend

Showing off the elephant head at Shorrocks Hill Country Club, 1971.

I finished with my last business venture in the year 2000.

Now that I've finally finished with the nightlife, I have the chance to look around me at people with normal lives. Forty-two years I worked in the nightlife, dancehalls, night-clubs and restaurants. All of it was stressful, but equally – it was exciting.

It was all about creating enjoyment for other people and getting the enjoyment from that occupation. I'm definitely a people person – I loved all the greeting, smiling, joking and socialising, in general. I'm always bumping into people I've met over the years and it's always a pleasure.

I seldom venture out to nightclubs anymore; to me they seem an exaggeration of how they used to be.

In most cases the individual touch is no more – most clubs used to reflect the personality of the owner, which meant they were all different. These days the owner is most likely to be a faceless organisation or company. Doormen in many cases wear protective vests and police are on horseback, violence is so commonplace.

Nightlife has become of major importance in many cities and features heavily in planning.

Liverpool is an example of a city being regenerated by it's nightlife. Large amounts of money from clubs has been ploughed into the economy, through property acquisition and development etc., obviously a good outcome.

Where we had lots of able individuals, some quite physically large, manning the doors – now they are monstrous, mainly working for security groups. Doormen now have to cope with the drug and gun culture, not forgetting knives – it's an unenviable task.

There aren't many places where you can walk in totally relaxing at the bar, chatting to the barmaid, without looking over your shoulder. Gone are the days when you could go out to a club in your car. Meet up with friends have a good drink and a dance, get in your car a little worse for wear and drive home happily without worrying about seatbelts and speed cameras. Ah! – the good old days!

* * *

When we look at physical culture now, it's difficult for myself and my peers to accept the way the sport of bodybuilding has changed.

Gone are the days when a pair of broad shoulders were something to be admired, something to aspire to. To get a pair of them would mean lots of hard work and dedication. Unfortunately when you see a well developed body now – you immediately think of substances. It's the same when athletes beat a long standing record, you can't help wondering what that athlete has used for fuel in order to take that hard won record from the past. It's a shame for the genuine athletes still doing things the hard way. Unfortunately, it applies to most physical sports these days.

Bodybuilding nowadays means just that! – Body Building. That's OK – as long as it's understood that a good building needs strong foundations.

The whole object of this radically changed occupation is to massively increase the size of the muscles. It is extremely competitive and one can understand why it has such appeal.

Any young man nowadays can become a real superman in a very short time (at least in appearance.) We resent these massive physiques because we don't consider them to be real, they weren't possible in our day – but that was then.

We know that these physiques in many cases have been achieved at great cost to the inner health because of some of the methods used. The way I think now is that if they're enjoying it and I know they are because they look how they want to look, then why not? I suppose they could be doing a lot worse to their bodies, which could be more harmful.

Unfortunately, it's gone so far down the road now with contestants pumping materials into the muscle to make it larger for just the time of the contest. That can't be physical culture – it's actually a negation of that term.

The parallel sport of physical culture continues. To each his own.

The fact is it's not necessary to take substances to develop a good physique. With the foods that are available now, the terrific range of supplements and the advanced equipment, a good long-lasting physique is within everybody's reach. On more than one occasion, I've had guys in the gym say to me: "These days, you've got to go on the gear to compete, otherwise you've got no chance!" I agree that is the case, but isn't it saying the reason for training is to win physique contests? What happened to training simply to develop health and strength and improve your body at the same time?

* * *

I know that an autobiography is intended to feature the life of the individual writing it. This can't be done without talking about the influence, in many directions, of other people in one's life. I know in my case, other people are heavily involved in my story probably more than is normally the case. I suppose this has to do with the fact that I'm concentrating on a particular couple of slices of my life which contain these personalities.

Sheilagh and I have been together for the past twenty years, although I've known her a lot longer. She is a beautiful person in every way and very unselfish. We're looking at the future together. She went to Art School and also worked in nightclubs, actually managing three of them eventually.

There's a thought! Maybe we could pool our experience and think of something to do with it … Only Kidding!